A F R I C.

The Ethiopian
Red Terror
Trials

AFRICAN ISSUES

The Ethiopian Red Terror Trials
KJETIL TRONVOLL, CHARLES SCHAEFER & GIRMACHEW ALEMU ANEME (EDS)

Diamonds, Dispossession & Democracy in Botswana
KENNETH GOOD

Published in the US & Canada by Indiana University Press
Gender & Genocide in Burundi The Search for Spaces of Peace in the Great Lakes Region
PATRICIA O. DALEY

Guns & Governance in the Rift Valley Pastoralist Conflict & Small Arms
KENNEDY AGADE MKUTU

Becoming Somaliland
MARK BRADBURY

Undermining Development The Absence of Power Among Local NGOs in Africa
SARAH MICHAEL

'Letting them Die' Why HIV/AIDS Prevention Programmes Fail
CATHERINE CAMPBELL

Somalia Economy without State
PETER D. LITTLE

The Root Causes of Sudan's Civil Wars
DOUGLAS H. JOHNSON

Asbestos Blues Labour, Capital, Physicians & the State in South Africa
JOCK McCULLOCH

Killing for Conservation Wildlife Policy in Zimbabwe
ROSALEEN DUFFY

Angola: Anatomy of an Oil State
TONY HODGES

Congo-Paris Transnational Traders on the Margins of the Law
JANET MACGAFFEY & REMY BAZENGUISSA-GANGA

Africa Works Disorder as Political Instrument
PATRICK CHABAL & JEAN-PASCAL DALOZ

The Criminalization of the State in Africa
JEAN-FRANÇOIS BAYART, STEPHEN ELLIS & BEATRICE HIBOU

Famine Crimes Politics & the Disaster Relief Industry in Africa
ALEX DE WAAL

Published in the US & Canada by Heinemann (N.H.)
Peace without Profit How the IMF Blocks Rebuilding in Mozambique
JOSEPH HANLON

The Lie of the Land Challenging the Received Wisdom on the African Environment
MELISSA LEACH & ROBIN MEARNS (EDS)

Fighting for the Rainforest War, Youth & Resources in Sierra Leone
PAUL RICHARDS

AFRICAN ISSUES

The Ethiopian Red Terror Trials

Transitional Justice Challenged

Edited by
**KJETIL TRONVOLL
CHARLES SCHAEFER
& GIRMACHEW ALEMU ANEME**

JAMES CURREY

James Currey
www.jamescurrey.co.uk

is an imprint of
Boydell & Brewer Ltd
PO Box 9
Woodbridge
Suffolk IP12 3DF
www.boydell.co.uk
and of
Boydell & Brewer Inc.
668 Mt Hope Avenue
Rochester NY 14620, USA
www.boydellandbrewer.com

British Library Cataloguing in Publication Data
The Ethiopian red terror trials : transitional justice
challenged. - (African issues)
1. Trials (Crimes against humanity) - Ethiopia 2. Political
persecution - Ethiopia 3. Ethiopia - Politics and
government - 1974-1991 4. Ethiopia - Politics and
government - 1991-
I. Tronvoll, Kjetil II. Schaefer, Charles III. Aneme,
Girmachew Alemu
345.6'3'025

ISBN 978-1-84701-320-0 (James Currey paper)

Typeset by
Long House Publishing Services, Cumbria, UK
in 9/11 Melior with Optima display

Printed and bound in ???

DEDICATION

Dedicated to the memory of the Ethiopian victims of human rights

CONTENTS

vii

Girmachew Alemu Aneme (PhD and M.A., Faculty of Law, University of Oslo, and LL.B from Faculty of Law, Addis Ababa University) is Lecturer at the Faculty of Law, Addis Ababa University, and a research fellow at the Norwegian Centre for Human Rights, University of Oslo. His PhD thesis analysed the African Union's right of intervention against genocide. He has been following the Red Terror trials from the beginning and has published research on different aspects of the trials.

Frode Elgesem is a lawyer practising in Oslo. He holds a Law Degree (Cand. jur) from the University of Oslo and an LL.M degree (with merits) from King's College, University of London. He was admitted to the Bar of the Supreme Court in 1995. He has extensive experience from the Office of the Attorney General – Civil Affairs, where he had a leading role in the Norwegian Government's international litigation, including human rights cases. He is currently partner in the law firm Hjort DA. He has published several studies and articles on human rights, including the 1998 study *The Derg Trials in Context: A study of some aspects of the Ethiopian judiciary*, Norwegian Institute of Human Rights, Oslo.

Elsa van Huyssteen conducted research, published, and taught in the areas of the sociology of law, human rights and democratization, and transitional justice in the Department of Sociology at the University of the Witwatersrand, and as a member of the International Human Rights Exchange. Her PhD in Sociology focused on the South African constitution-making process and Constitutional Court, and included an analysis of the role of the South African Truth and Reconciliation Commission in the constitutionalist project. More recently, she completed a postgraduate degree in law. She has now joined the Bar in Cape Town, and practises as an advocate of the High Court of South Africa.

Charles Schaefer is Associate Professor of History at Valparaiso University (Indiana, USA) and Chair of the International Service Program. He taught at Addis Ababa University from 1992 through 1994 as a Fulbright Lecturer. Beyond articles on economic history, election monitoring and human rights, his new research initiative has necessitated a rereading of the hagiographic literature and imperial chronicles of

Ethiopia to ascertain pre-twentieth-century indigenous methods of peace, reconciliation and restorative justice in Ethiopia. Some article titles include 'Scriptures, *qenē* and traditions of restorative justice in nineteenth century Ethiopia: Forgiveness with consequences' and 'Re-examining the Ethiopian Historical Record on the Continuum between Vengeance and Forgiveness.' Since January 2006, he has accepted the volunteer position as Country Specialist for Ethiopia for Amnesty International, USA.

Kjetil Tronvoll is Professor at the Norwegian Centre for Human Rights, University of Oslo. As a political anthropologist he has a PhD from the London School of Economics and an M.Phil from the University of Oslo. He has researched political development, elections, human rights, and war and identities in Eritrea and Ethiopia since 1990. More recently, he has done extensive fieldwork in Zanzibar on political reconciliation and the formation of identities. His books include: *Mai Weini: A Highland Village in Eritrea* (Red Sea Press, 1998); *Brothers at War: Making Sense of the Eritrean-Ethiopian War* (co-author, James Currey/Ohio UP, 2000); *Ethiopia Since the Derg: A Decade of Democratic Pretension and Performance* (co-editor, Zed Books, 2002); *The Culture of Power in Contemporary Ethiopian Political Life* (co-author, Sida, 2003); and *War and the Politics of Identity in Ethiopia: The Making Enemies and Allies in the Horn of Africa* (James Currey, 2009).

Sarah Vaughan is Honorary Fellow of the School of Social and Political Studies, at the University of Edinburgh, Scotland. Initially trained in languages and philosophy, she completed a PhD in politics and social theory at the University of Edinburgh in 2003. Her academic work theorises issues of identity – particularly the politicisation of ethnicity – using ideas drawn from the sociology of knowledge. Dr Vaughan has taught African and Ethiopian politics and social theory at graduate and undergraduate level in Scotland and in Ethiopia. She has recently returned to a new position in Edinburgh after four years seconded into the Ethiopian government, where she researched and advised on the analysis of conflict.

Bahru Zewde is currently Emeritus Professor of History at Addis Ababa University and Executive Director of the Forum for Social Studies. He got his BA from Haile Selassie I University (1970) and his PhD from the School of Oriental and African Studies of the University of London (1976). He has authored a number of books and articles, including *A History of Modern Ethiopia 1855–91* (James Currey/Ohio UP, 2001, 2nd edn and with an Amharic version) and *Pioneers of Change in Ethiopia: The Reformist Intellectuals of the Early Twentieth Century* (Addis Ababa UP/James Currey/Ohio UP, 2002).

Ethiopia's troubled past makes poignant inroads into the everyday life of its citizens. Experiences of state violence create torpidity long after the physical pain has disappeared; and the memories of lost ones linger for decades. Each individual confronts and tackles these occurrences differently, based on personal capacities and convictions. Coming to grips with the experience of massive human rights violation is not only an individual concern, but a collective endeavour. It is also a process fraught with political ambiguity. As such, the role of the state and its institutions is vital in accommodating both individual and collective claims within accountable procedures and frameworks.

The Derg military junta run by Col. Mengistu Hailemariam ruled Ethiopia from 1974 until 1991. It was, at that time, one of Africa's most brutal and authoritarian regimes. During what has been called the Red Terror from 1976 to 1978, tens of thousands of Ethiopian intellectuals, opposition party members and sympathizers were imprisoned, tortured and killed. The current Ethiopian government, the Ethiopian Peoples' Revolutionary Democratic Front (EPRDF), managed to topple the Derg by arms in May 1991, and in the process detained hundreds of officials from the Derg regime in order to make them accountable for the human rights atrocities conducted in the 1970s and 1980s.

In 1992 a Special Prosecutor's Office (SPO) was established and vested with the authority to investigate and institute proceedings against any person responsible for the commission of an offence by abusing his/her position under the Derg regime. Moreover, the broader intention of the SPO was, according to its enabling proclamation, to be working

in the interest of a just historical obligation to record for posterity the brutal offences committed and the embezzlement of property perpetrated against the people of Ethiopia and to educate the people and make them aware of those offences in order to prevent the recurrence of such a system of government.

In short, the EPRDF wanted to establish a societal consensus on the Derg period, apparently in order to draw a line and start afresh with a new mode of governance in the country.

The Norwegian Centre for Human Rights at the University of Oslo has been actively researching the political development of Ethiopia since the coming to power of the EPRDF. We have, *inter alia*, researched the conduct of elections, the situation of minority and human rights, and the impact of war on Ethiopian society. The aim of the Centre's research activity in the Horn of Africa is to understand how contemporary political processes are impinging on everyday life, and how individuals perceive and relate to these events.

In addition to our scholarly activities, the Norwegian Centre for Human Rights, through its programme Norwegian Resource Bank for Democracy and Human Rights (NORDEM), has dispatched election observers to all elections except one since the coming to power of the EPRDF. In the initial phase, the Centre through the NORDEM programme also provided capacity-building support to the Ethiopian authorities in organizing the Red Terror trials, as well as dispatching trial observers to the first rounds of court hearings under the trials. Thus, when the Derg trials commenced, there was also an institutional interest to engage in research into the conduct and understandings of the trials.

A multi-disciplinary research programme was designed, analysing different aspects of the trials from a juridical, historical, anthropological and political perspective. The main objective of the research programme was to assess the conduct of the trials in relation to international standards of human rights, as well as to analyse the impact and understanding of the trials within the broader Ethiopian context. An important secondary objective was to document the process in order to gather comparative insights into transitional justice mechanisms in Africa. This is particularly important, since the Ethiopian Red Terror trials have received hardly any attention by international researchers on transitional justice.

The prolongation of the trials has also affected our research programme. Initially, the trials were scheduled to be finalized by 1998. As this is being written, a decade later, the trials against Col. Mengistu Hailemariam and his top accomplices have just been completed, although other Red Terror trials of lesser stature are still ongoing in Ethiopia. Instead of finalizing the research in 1998 as initially planned, we maintained the project on a slow fuse with the aim of incorporating the analysis of the final verdict and sentencing of the top-level individuals responsible, as this provides a coherent conclusion to the study.

Kjetil Tronvoll
Charles Schaefer
& Girachew Alemu Aneme

ACKNOWLEDGEMENTS

The Norwegian Centre for Human Rights is grateful for the financial support from the Norwegian Ministry of Foreign Affairs to carry out this study, and for their patience in awaiting the final result. It must be stressed that the analysis and conclusions reached in this volume are the sole responsibility of the respective author(s), and do not necessarily reflect the views of the Ministry.

Data gathering and assistance in the field have throughout the project period been provided by Ato Abebe Hailu, attorney at law, to whom the Centre is extremely indebted. We are also grateful to the many Ethiopian lawyers and colleagues who have provided valuable information and documents pertaining to the trials. In the final phase of the project, the project leader Kjetil Tronvoll was offered invaluable scholarly input and assistance from Chuck Schaefer and Girmachew Alemu Aneme, in order to secure a truly inter-disciplinary approach and ensure the quality of the edited volume.

We would also like to thank the late Prof. Makonen Bishaw, Prof. Andargachew Tiruneh, Ato Tafesse Olika and Dr Bård Anders Andreassen for participating in the original research group.

All royalties from the sale of this book will be donated to a cause working to enhance the implementation of Ethiopia's human rights obligations.

ABBREVIATIONS

ANC	African National Congress
AZAPO	Azanian Peoples' Organization
CSP	Chief Special Prosecutor
EC	Ethiopian Calendar
EHRCO	Ethiopian Human Rights Council
EPLF	Eritrean Peoples' Liberation Front
EPRA	Ethiopian Peoples' Revolutionary Army
EPRDF	Ethiopian Peoples' Revolutionary Democratic Front
EPRP	Ethiopian Peoples' Revolutionary Party
EWLA	Ethiopian Women Lawyers Association
FDRE	Federal Democratic Republic of Ethiopia
ICCPR	International Covenant on Civil and Political Rights
ICESCR	International Covenant on Economic, Social and Cultural Rights
Ma'ison/ Meison	Amharic acronym for the 'All-Ethiopian Socialist Movement' party
OLF	Oromo Liberation Front
PDO	Public Defender's Office
PGE	Provisional Government of Ethiopia (June 1991)
PM	Prime Minister
PMAC	Provisional Military Administration Committee (the Derg)
POMOA	Provisional Office for Mass Organizational Affairs
PPG	Provisional Popular Government
PSC	Peace and Stability Committees
SPO	Special Prosecutor's Office
TGE	Transitional Government of Ethiopia (June 1991–May 1995)
TPLF	Tigray People's Liberation Front
TRC	Truth and Reconciliation Commission (in South Africa)
WPE	Workers' Party of Ethiopia (the party that was established by Derg members)
UDHR	Universal Declaration of Human Rights

xiv

Abuna	Head of the Ethiopian Orthodox Tewahedo Church
Anja	Faction
Abyotawi Saddad	Revolutionary Fire
Askari	Indigenous troops in the service of Europeans (orig. Swahili term)
Derg	'Committee', popular term for the military junta
Fukara	Traditional war chant
Kebele	The lowest administrative level of the state (similar to ward)
Kebra Nagast	The book of the Glory of Kings (Ge'ez)
Ma'ikal	Centre
Ma'ison/Meison	Amharic acronym for the 'All-Ethiopian Socialist Movement' party
Makwanent	Nobility
Natsa Ermeja	Summary execution
Negus	Emperor
Qay Fana	Red Flame
Shamma	Traditional cloth
Shengo	Ethiopian parliament under the Derg
Tabot	A sacred replica of the Ark of the Covenant
Taraba Buden	Killing squad
Woneda	Administrative district
Zamana mesafint	Era of the princes

1

The 'Red Terror' Trials

The Context of Transitional Justice in Ethiopia

KJETIL TRONVOLL
CHARLES SCHAEFER &
GIRMACHEW ALEMU ANEME

Introduction

Three decades after the appalling bloodshed and killings of tens of thousands of Ethiopians in a counter-revolutionary campaign called the 'Red Terror', the main officials who orchestrated the violence and gross human rights violations – Col. Mengistu Hailemariam and the key political leaders of his military junta – were found guilty of genocide and crimes against humanity on 12 December 2006, twelve years after the trial began. The Ethiopian Federal High Court sentenced Mengistu and his accomplices to life imprisonment. The verdict and sentencing were supposed to close one chapter in Ethiopia's horrendous and turbulent past. By evading capital punishment, however, the court's decision sparked angry reactions since others accused who were of lower political stature had previously been handed the death penalty. 'Today's sentence makes a mockery of justice,' exclaimed Ethiopians,[1] and what was supposed to be the last chapter of the Red Terror trials seems sure to continue into a second phase, as both the prosecutor and the defence appeal to the supreme court.[2] Moreover, after the verdict was read, increasing demand is being put on Zimbabwe to extradite former Derg leader Col. Mengistu Hailemariam from exile in order for him to serve his punishment in Ethiopia.

The issue of how to deal with human rights violations of former regimes – commonly termed as transitional justice – has developed into a broad field of study, involving scholars from different academic disciplines as well as advocates, human rights practitioners and government policy advisors. With the growing importance of human rights in international politics after the cold war and the establishment of the International Criminal Court in 2003, the quest for transitional justice has become more prevalent and perhaps more frequently demanded by social

---

[1] Reuters, 'Life sentence for Ethiopia dictator', 11 January 2007.
[2] BBC News, 'Appeal for Mengistu death penalty', 8 February 2007.

forces in times of political transition. Academic studies are reflecting this trend and the study of transitional justice has emerged as an important interdisciplinary field of human rights studies. This has also led to the emergence of different approaches and modalities on how governments and people ought to handle the historical legacy of political terror and grievances, in order to achieve justice, reconciliation and lasting political stability. Hence, to deal with the past, societies that emerge from systematic and state-sponsored human rights violations have taken one or a combination of the following approaches: criminal prosecution, lustration, amnesty, truth commissions, compensation and restitution. Every society has its own reasons and political contexts for selecting a particular approach to administer the process of transitional justice.

The different contributions in this anthology analyse the approach taken by the current government of Ethiopia led by the Ethiopian Peoples' Revolutionary Democratic Front (EPRDF) to deal with the massive human rights violations that took place from 1974 up to 1991, during the administration of Col. Mengistu Hailemariam's Derg[3] regime. Covered in this volume are the range of procedures and various levels of trials prosecuted in different courts throughout the country that are collectively known as the 'Red Terror trials'. These include the prosecution of top officials, cadres, security people and operatives of the defunct regime responsible for massive human rights violations. The unique approach of *The Ethiopian Red Terror Trials: Transitional Justice Challenged* is the multi-disciplinary framework that goes beyond juridical analysis of the conduct of the trials in order to embed the trials in the appropriate historical and political context. This facilitates an understanding of the trials' broader social and political impact. Thus, the following chapters are written by specialists on Ethiopia from the disciplines of law, history, political science, sociology and social anthropology. Moreover, this volume is the first comprehensive analysis of the trials, thus filling a glaring void for studies on Ethiopia and transitional justice.

Terror in the Context of Regime Change in Ethiopia

'Transitional justice' was a new concept in Ethiopia's understanding of regime change (although, as Charles Schaefer discusses in this volume, there has been a historical tradition of restorative justice in Ethiopia), and as such the EPRDF should be praised for its efforts to introduce juridical accountability in political transitions. In recent history, Ethiopia has experienced the rule of three radically different governments: an imperial monarchy with its roots in Abyssinian feudalism, a communist military dictatorship that possessed a nationalist agenda, and a one-party-dominated democracy based on the notion of ethnic federalism. Recent

[3] Derg is Amharic for Committee, a popular term used for the military junta.

history has also witnessed two violent regime changes: the *coup d'etat* against the imperial reign of Emperor Haile Selassie I in 1974 and the defeat of the Marxist-Leninist military junta of Col. Mengistu Hailemariam by the EPRDF, headed by Prime Minister Meles Zenawi in 1991. In the first case, the political violence took place after the change of regimes had occurred, as the military leadership used terror and purges to consolidate its power after the demise of Emperor Haile Selassie. In the latter case, the use of military force and political violence was necessary for the EPRDF to wrest power from the Derg in order to achieve a change of regime.

The Red Terror occurred in connection with the 1974 revolution that toppled the regime of Emperor Haile Selassie. That year a popular movement primarily carried out by students, peasants, and workers led to the breakdown of the monarchy that ruled Ethiopia for over 40 years. In the revolutionary disarray, a military junta seized power, overthrew and jailed the Emperor, suspended the constitution, dissolved the parliament and established a provisional military government. While the military takeover abolished the quasi-feudal government structure of Emperor Haile Selassie, neither a juridical tribunal nor a political reconciliation process was carried out to hold the imperial regime accountable for its political and humanitarian failings. Rather, the military regime made wide-sweeping arrests of those associated with Haile Selassie's reign. In order to define a new start for the Ethiopian people 60 generals, ministers and high-ranking officials were executed, thus marking the beginning of seventeen years of state sponsored human rights violations. By the end of 1974, Emperor Haile Selassie was secretly killed and buried under the floor of the royal palace without any public trial or even a secret hearing.

Following the summary executions, the period from 1975 to 1988 was characterized by massive, systematic and atrocious human rights violations. In the days before May Day 1977, the youth committees of the Ethiopian Peoples' Revolutionary Party (EPRP, a leftist political party opposed to the military junta) were planning a nationwide demonstration demanding the establishment of a civil government in the country. The Derg, however, managed to thwart their plan in what was later known as 'the May Day Massacre,' where hundreds of young people planning to participate in the demonstration were killed. The killing continued in the following days and over one thousand students and intellectuals were slaughtered, their bodies left in the streets to be ravaged by hyenas at night (see Bahru in this volume). Some families who were fortunate enough to identify the bodies of their murdered youths were required to pay for the bullets that were used to kill their sons and daughters before they could take the corpses for a proper funeral.

The Red Terror massacre was launched in 1976 and lasted until 1978.[4] In July 1977 the 'ferreting-out' campaign was directed and conducted by

---

[4] Some scholars claim that the Red Terror lasted until 1980. See G.A. Aneme (2006: 65).

the Derg against what it called anti-revolutionary and reactionary elements. The action resulted in the death of over one thousand people and the arbitrary detention of even more persons accused of belonging to one or another political party (Engelschion 1996: 43). This event marked the intensification of the notorious urban *Red Terror* campaign; a term borrowed from the Russian revolutionary lexicon meaning the liquidation of counter-revolutionaries (Yacob Hailemariam 1999: 677). The Red Terror in Ethiopia was the most systematic and infamous campaign of human rights violations perpetrated by the Derg. Throughout the campaign, the Derg killed a generation of mostly young intellectuals without any resort to the rule of law. The conduct of the campaign has been described in the following terms by a survivor:

> Feed a man his own flesh, pull out his nails, boil him in oil, stuff his mouth with a cloth soaked in urine and human excrement, use pincers to rip off his nose, smash a bottle in a woman's vagina, cut her nipples and breasts, brutalise loved ones in front of him or her and then, only then, cut his/her throat or strangle them with piano wire. This is no 'simple' murder. This was the 'Red Terror' (Babile Tola 1989[1997]: vi).

There is no definite number of the persons killed during the Red Terror. The estimate ranges from 150,000 to 500,000[5] of persons killed all over the country during the Red Terror (see Bahru in this volume; see also Yacob Hailemariam 1999: 678, note 49; Andrew and Mitrokhin 2005: 457). The entire era of the Derg was characterized by massive human rights violations, which constituted state-sponsored terror in the form of sexual abuse, summary execution, torture, arbitrary arrest and detention, disappearance, unlawful dispossession of property, the use of food aid as a political tool, and forced settlement.

The armed revolutionary resistance to the centralist policies of the successive authoritarian Ethiopian regimes originally began in the 1960s under Eritrean political movements struggling for self-determination and independence (Iyob 1995). Armed resistance in mainland Ethiopia, on the other hand, originated in the beginning of the 1970s. The Tigrayan People's Liberation Front (TPLF) was established in 1975, one year after the coming to power of the Derg. In the beginning, the TPLF defined its struggle as a war of liberation with the objective of liberating the northern Ethiopian province of Tigray. However, after internal differences within the central committee in 1976/77 were resolved, the objective of the struggle was redefined to achieve cultural and political autonomy for Tigray within a democratic Ethiopian entity (Young 1997). After the military defeat of the EPRP was accomplished by unleashing the Red Terror, the Eritrean Peoples' Liberation Front (EPLF) and the TPLF, together with the Oromo Liberation Front (OLF), were the main military

---

[5] The BBC put the figure at half a million. See BBC News, 'US admits helping Mengistu escape', 12 December, 1999. Available at http://news.bbc.co.uk/2/hi/africa/575405.stm , accessed 31 March 2008.

opponents of the Derg regime, in addition to a number of other minor ethnic resistance movements. The TPLF gained military control over the Tigray region in the late 1980s, and subsequently redefined its military objective in order to continue its armed struggle beyond Tigray. This was based on the belief that Ethiopia could not become democratic until the Derg had been toppled. Once this occurred, the issue of self-determination for nationalities could be secured for all the suppressed groups in the country.

In order to continue the armed struggle beyond Tigray, the TPLF was in need of other representative ethnic resistance movements, since their ideological platform defined ethnicity as the core political, mobilizing factor. Therefore, in 1989 the TPLF organized the establishment of the coalition movement called the EPRDF, including first an Amhara party, subsequently an Oromo component, and finally a party to represent the multi-ethnic southern region of the country (Vaughan and Tronvoll 2003).

In the early spring of 1991 it became clear that the Derg military forces were collapsing and that the EPRDF forces and the EPLF in Eritrea soon would capture the two capitals Addis Ababa and Asmara (in Eritrea). The head of state, Col. Mengistu Hailemariam, fled Ethiopia for Zimbabwe on 21 May 1991 when the EPRDF forces advanced on Addis Ababa. General Tesfaye Gebrekidan formed a new government and tried to negotiate an agreed transition, but his government survived only one week (Teferra Haile-Selassie 1997). On the morning of 28 May 1991, EPRDF tanks entered the city and after a few hours, sites of military and political importance were captured, without any notable resistance by a demoralized Derg army. Bloody urban warfare was avoided and, after a week, most government offices and private shops were once again open for service. The Provisional Government of Ethiopia (PGE) was established on 1 June 1991, and Meles Zenawi, the chairman of TPLF and EPRDF, was appointed as the executive head of state. In a radio announcement the following day, Meles Zenawi promised the Ethiopian people a new broad-based democratic government composed of representatives from all opposition movements and other distinguished Ethiopian individuals without any connections to the former regime. The old parliament (*Shengo*) was dissolved and leading civil servants and military officials started to surrender to the new government, together with tens of thousands of Derg soldiers who flocked into Addis Ababa.

During the unstable period in the aftermath of the EPRDF take-over, there were very few incidents in which people took the law into their own hands in order to punish the collaborators of the Derg regime. The PGE carried out mass arrests of key officials of the former Derg regime and its Workers' Party of Ethiopia (WPE) – a party which was established by Derg members and their collaborators in 1987.[6] Simultaneously 'Peace

---

[6] On the tenth anniversary of the revolution in 1984, a communist party called Workers' Party of Ethiopia was established, and Col. Mengistu Hailemariam became its chairman. This also signalled that Ethiopia had formally become a Marxist-Leninist single-party state and a 'civilian'

and Stability Committees' (PSC) were established throughout Addis Ababa with a broad mandate to investigate, arrest and detain suspected human rights perpetrators of the Derg regime (US State Department 1992: 118). Many of those arrested were brought to the attention of the PSC and the police by former victims or their families who had recognized the perpetrators in public. During the first few months of EPRDF government, over 2,000 central military and civilian officials were arrested, and later several thousands more would follow. Following preliminary investigations, however, several hundred were released after a comparatively short period in detention.

In July 1991 a national, transitional conference was convened where more or less all Ethiopian opposition movements were represented (Vaughan 1994). The conference formally endorsed and established the Transitional Government of Ethiopia (TGE). The conference also endorsed a National Charter that worked as an interim constitution and a governmental framework for political priorities, until a new permanent constitution was ratified by the newly elected federal parliament in 1995. Since then, Ethiopia has carried out regular (although controversial) multiparty elections (2000 and 2005), which the EPRDF has won. The former resistance leader, Meles Zenawi, has thus maintained his position as the executive throughout the post-Derg period (after 1995 as prime minister).

Transitional Justice Mechanisms Adopted in Ethiopia

The EPRDF government had a range of options available on how to deal with the perpetrators of the gross human rights violations during the Derg regime when it assumed power in 1991. Prime Minister Meles Zenawi acknowledged that the strategy of criminal prosecution was already decided upon by the TPLF during their resistance war before they assumed official governmental authority.[7] But criminal prosecution was not the sole strategy pursued, as the process also incorporated the lustration of members of the Derg regime and their collaborators. Some of the victims of widespread human rights abuses also received restitution. Furthermore, an element of reconciliation most often associated with restorative justice was incorporated into the mandate of the Special Prosecutor's Office (SPO) as a corollary objective of the trial, focusing on a record to be compiled for posterity of the brutal offences perpetrated against the people of Ethiopia. The rationale for this record was to unveil and make public the horrendous acts committed, in order for the truth about the Red Terror to become public knowledge in Ethiopia. This was

---

[6] (cont.) government was appointed. The charges against the Derg regime thus also include the officials and cadres of the WPE.

[7] Cf. Kjetil Tronvoll's interview with Prime Minister Meles Zenawi, Addis Ababa, 16 January 2002.

intended to serve as a reconciliatory device to educate Ethiopians to prevent the recurrence of such a harsh system of government in the future.

Criminal Prosecution of Derg officials

The mechanism of prosecution as a response to past human rights violations is not an easy path to take. The lack of skilled manpower needed to effectively investigate and prosecute the violations in a reasonable time period is a huge problem for countries in transition, which usually are ravaged by war or corrupted by political ineptness. The problem is particularly notable when large-scale human rights violations are committed under a systematic government structure that persists for a long period of time. This is particularly the case as criminal prosecution presupposes a well-established judiciary. The judicial system needs not only to be well equipped and independent, but also to be run by qualified judges and prosecutors with knowledge of human rights norms and the ability to incorporate up-to-date developments in law. This is particularly a problem in an economically poor country transitioning from dictatorship to democracy. Furthermore, in a transition to a new political system, new governments attempt to reform the judicial system. This in itself requires qualified persons with legal education and courtroom experience lest any reshuffling of the old judges and prosecutors leaves the court empty.

The other major problem in prosecuting massive human rights violations is the lack of laws in existence to prohibit these crimes when they occur. The issue of retroactivity has been criticized since the Nuremberg trials (Minow 1998: 30–2). Furthermore, the existing domestic laws of the state may be silent on many human rights violations. What is worse, some violations may have been barred by statutes of limitations under the existing domestic laws. Nevertheless, in these situations, Nuremberg precedents and human rights treaties allowing prosecution for violations of general principles of law have given courts the tools to side-step the *ex post facto* problem (Roht-Arriaza 1995: 288). In addition, the silence of domestic laws may not bar the prosecution of international crimes such as genocide and crimes against humanity. The elements of these crimes are also recognized under customary international law and are obliged to be punished wherever they occur (Czaplinski 2001: 177).

From the beginning, the TGE rejected the option of amnesty as a mechanism to deal with the violations of the Derg regime. In a letter to the UN assistant secretary-general for human rights, the TGE explained that the decision was grounded in the international society's fight against impunity, as stated in the Vienna declaration adopted by the World Conference on Human Rights.[8] The declaration emphasized that states should abrogate legislation leading to impunity for those responsible for

[8] Vienna Declaration and Program of Action, World Conference on Human Rights, Vienna, 14–25 June 1993, A/CONF.157/23, paragraph 62.

grave violations of human rights and rather seek prosecution of such violations. Furthermore, the Declaration reaffirms that it is the duty of all states, under any circumstances, to undertake investigations whenever there is reason to believe that an enforced disappearance has taken place on a territory under their jurisdiction. If allegations are confirmed, it must also prosecute its perpetrators. According to these principles, the TGE explained its duty in a letter to the UN:

> To bring to justice those persons with respect to whom there are serious reasons for considering that they are responsible for serious violations both of international law and domestic law that can be assimilated in some cases to crimes against humanity. [...] The crimes committed under the former regime were not only crimes against the victims and the Ethiopian people; in many cases they were crimes against humanity – crimes that the international community has a particular interest to prevent, to investigate and to punish. The Transitional Government of Ethiopia is aware of its obligations concerning the duty to prosecute the systematic violations of human rights and the grave breaches of humanitarian law.[9]

After rejecting amnesty as a mechanism, the TGE decided to use the national court system and Ethiopia's Penal Code to prosecute members of the Derg-WPE and their collaborators for the massive human rights violations from 1974 through 1991. To this end, the TGE established the Special Prosecutor's Office (SPO) with a mandate to investigate and prosecute the detained members of the Derg regime and their collaborators in 1992. The investigation resulted in the 1994 opening of what are collectively known as the Red Terror trials, which were heard in various courts all over the country. Mechanisms of transitional justice other than criminal prosecution were also pursued by the Ethiopian government in order to redress Red Terror violations.

Lustration of Derg officials
Lustration is the legal mechanism that disqualifies and removes the officials of a former regime and their collaborators found guilty of massive human rights violations from public office. It also curtails their civil and political rights, i.e. to vote and be elected to office (Huyse 1995: 337). In spite of the fact that lustration is criticized for being a collective punishment, the TGE decided to use it to disqualify all former officials of the Derg regime and members of the WPE at different ranks from continuing in their positions after the EPRDF takeover. Those people were formerly employed in the different ministries, courts, mass organizations and security forces. All security institutions, including the army and police, were completely dismantled and their personnel discharged. The civil

---

[9] UN doc. E/CN.4/1994/103, 'Question of the Violation of Human Rights and Fundamental Freedoms in any part of the world, with particular reference to colonial and other dependent countries and territories'.

and political rights of the former officials and members of the WPE and their collaborators – such as the right to political assembly and the right to vote – were also restricted.[10]

Restitution for Derg victims
The TGE also attempted to restore the legal rights of the victims who experienced massive human rights violations under the Derg regime during which many people were arbitrarily evicted from their private properties.[11] Laws and procedures that would allow victims to reclaim their properties were thus promulgated in 1995.[12] Some victims were able to recover their properties as a result of investigations by the government. The properties returned to their owners include dwelling houses, buildings, manufacturing firms, coffee processing plants, service enterprises, dairy farms, and vehicles.[13] However, thousands of claims for restitution by victims are still being investigated by the government, and their outcome is thus pending at the time of writing.

The Contribution of the Red Terror Trials to Transitional Justice Studies

The Red Terror trials took place within a global context that stresses the importance of identifying mechanisms which secure smooth and accountable transitions of power from authoritarian or semi-democratic regimes. This volume demonstrates how the Red Terror trials contribute to the scholarship on transitional justice.

After its establishment in 1992, the SPO immediately commenced investigation and submitted its first charges in October 1994, marking the beginning of the Red Terror trials. The trials were initially welcomed by large segments of the Ethiopian population and the international community. The objectives of the SPO were ambitious: (a) to prosecute

[10] See, for instance, Proclamation 3/91, Peaceful demonstration and public meeting procedure proclamation, Article 8 (2): 'As long as the council of representatives has not decided otherwise, no WPE or security members may participate in any political activity, the organization being anti-democratic and criminal has been disbanded'; Proclamation 23/92, A Proclamation to provide for the independence of Judicial Administration, Article (7) 'Persons prohibited from being judges': 'No person who (1) was a WPE member (2) was engaged in security activities in the Derg-WPE/regime (3) had high position in the police and the armed forces of the Derg-WPE regime' can be a judge in the central government.
[11] See reports from observations made in 1996, 1997, 1998 and 1999 by the Trial Observation and Information Project, Addis Ababa.
[12] Proclamation No.110/95, The proclamation for the review of properties taken in violation of the relevant proclamations; Directive No. 001(1996), A Directive that established the procedure of restitution of properties as per proclamation 110/95, the Ethiopian Privatization Agency Executive Board.
[13] *Privatization Review* (2001), Published by the Public Relations Department of the Ethiopian Privatization Agency, vol. 1, no.1: 4.

the officials of the Derg regime responsible for killing thousands of students, intelligentsia and urban elites, and (b) to leave a permanent record of the atrocities by compiling all the written evidence and by soliciting literally hundreds of oral testimonies from victims and victims' families – similar to the atonement aspect of South Africa's Truth and Reconciliation Commission (TRC).

The Ethiopian Red Terror trials thus appear as evidence of Africa's retributive justice; just as the TRC was Africa's laudable contribution to restorative justice. However, in a secondary manner the twofold mandate, noted above, essentially split the difference between trials (retributive justice) and truth commissions (restorative justice) and as such should offer much to the burgeoning study of transitional justice. Furthermore, by establishing a trial process, the EPRDF made an effective breach with the violent practices of the past where new power-holders summarily executed, imprisoned or exiled members of the defunct regime, which in itself can be interpreted as a reconciliatory move. The decision to conduct the trials in the society where the atrocities took place and to have Ethiopian nationals, not foreign experts, preside over trial hearings which were open to the general public, may also be interpreted as a strategy to 'cleanse old wounds' in order to create collective healing of the societal trauma inflicted by the Red Terror.

Yet the literature on Ethiopia's Red Terror trials is paltry, to the extent that even when authors cite modern examples of transitional justice, Ethiopia is rarely mentioned. Reasons for this abound but certainly the duration of the trials (1993–2007) and the fact that they were prosecuted in Ethiopia, by Ethiopians under Ethiopian statutory law with very little assistance – except right at the beginning – from jurists from the international community meant that they were 'out of sight, out of mind'. It is a pity that the Red Terror trials have been either neglected or forgotten, for the literature on transitional justice appears to be arriving at the conclusion that a path between trials and truth commissions would optimize prospects for closure and bring about reconciliation. Yet scholars appear to be foraging in untilled meadows; in contrast, the Red Terror trials offer a test case that shows the gridiron of a ploughed field, with all its contours, associated simultaneously with pursuing retributive and secondarily exemplifying aspects of restorative justice. A brief review of the existing literature on the Red Terror trials will be followed by an attempt to place this volume into an evolving field of transitional justice.

Existing literature on the Red Terror trials
One would assume that one of the first indigenous African trials that brought to justice the whole leadership of a defunct regime would attract a variety of international scholars from the broad field of transitional justice studies. But this is not the case. There is no comprehensive study on the Red Terror trials in Ethiopia to date. Various scholars have,

however, written piecemeal on different aspects of the trials. As early as 1995 Julie Mayfield wrote an article that assessed the Red Terror trials in terms of international human rights standards such as, the issue of detention without charges, the right to speedy trial, and the issue of adequate facilities for the defence. Mayfield concluded that it was not clear if there was a violation of the International Covenant on Civil and Political Rights (ICCPR) in the long detention of the accused without appearance in court and the delay in the trials. In 1996, a Norwegian jurist who assisted Ethiopian lawyers and prosecutors in juridical training wrote a descriptive article on the trials based on his experiences (Engelschion 1996). The most critical writing on the trials was presented by Frode Elgesem in a 1998 report commissioned by University of Oslo's Norwegian Centre for Human Rights. Elgesem concluded that there were already violations of the right of the accused to fair and speedy trial. The report also took note that the judiciary was not able to carry out its historical responsibility of trying the former officials and their collaborators (Elgesem 1998).

In 1999, the Ethiopian jurist Yacob Hailemariam wrote an article that compared the Ethiopian Red Terror trials in the Federal High Court with the International Tribunal for Rwanda. Yacob observed that the Ethiopian Red Terror trials violated the right to be brought before the court of law as well as the right to speedy trial of the accused. Nevertheless, Yacob concluded that, when compared to the Rwandan international trial conducted far away from the Rwandan community, the Ethiopian Red Terror trials were better suited to delivering justice to victims as they were national trials carried out in communities where the victims of the massive human rights violations lived. The same year, Jeremy Sarkin published a short descriptive article on the trials and criticized the incurred delays (1999).

In 2000, Todd Howland wrote an article that analysed the involvement of the Carter Center in the early activities of the SPO in order to show how international organizations can best perform what he called 'proactive human rights intervention' to positively influence the adherence to international human rights standards in the prosecution of past human rights violations. Howland concluded in his article that the Carter Center had failed in its attempts to ensure the respect of human rights of the accused, as the SPO was not able to meet its human rights objectives because of arbitrary arrests and long detentions without charge. In the same year Dadimos Haile (2000) published a book that provided extensive background on the massive human rights violations during the Derg regime as well as the possible reasons behind the EPRDF's policy decision to prosecute former officials. Dadimos raised the long detention of the accused without the sanction from the courts and the lack of adequate provision of legal counsel to defendants as serious problems of the Red Terror trials. Dadimos's book also reflected upon the possible application of international laws such as the Convention against

Genocide and the four Geneva Conventions in the Red Terror trials. Mehari Redae (2000), furthermore, argued that taking into consideration the various shortcomings of the Red Terror trials, the prosecution of a large number of officials and operatives of the former regime was unrealistic. Thus, Mehari suggested that prosecution should be focused only on the selected former officials who are well known for their involvement in massive human rights violations.

In 2006, Edward Kissi published a book that compared the revolutions in Cambodia and Ethiopia in relation to one of the thorny issues of the Red Terror trials, i.e.. the issue of the commission of genocide. Kissi concluded that unlike in Cambodia the killings of the Derg regime in Ethiopia do not qualify as genocide, as the Derg's actions were not aimed at destroying a specific group of people as per the definition provided under the Genocide Convention. Kissi thus rejects the main argument of the SPO and the juridical basis on which the court has passed its verdicts. In a 2006 article, Girmachew A. Aneme argued that a recent request from the top officials of the Derg regime under trial to apologize to the Ethiopian people should be taken seriously as it is not contradictory to the ongoing trials, but rather an important step for the publicity of facts concerning the violations and reconciliation in Ethiopian society. In 2007, Firew K. Tiba briefly analysed the sentencing judgement in *Special Prosecutor vs. Col. Mengistu Hailemariam et al.*, the main Red Terror trial. In his remarks, Firew pointed out that while the sentencing of Col. Mengistu and his colleagues was a landmark in holding African leaders accountable for their decisions, the trial was marred by long delays and logistical problems.

The Red Terror trials within the literature on transitional justice
To an extent, the decision by the leadership of the EPRDF to try high ranking Derg officials accused of committing genocide and crimes against humanity followed the accepted international impetus after the fall of the Berlin Wall. For a rebel force struggling to gain legitimacy, it may be presumptuous to expect the EPRDF to have defied the Nuremburg precedent of retributive justice. This is what Prime Minister Meles Zenawi alluded to when he stated , 'We [EPRDF] didn't think of a truth and reconciliation commission. In any case there was no such experience at that time.'[14] Evidently he was unaware of the low-profile truth commissions being conducted in Latin America. Yet, as Sarah Vaughan describes in her chapter in this volume on the Special Prosecutor's Office, the Ethiopians were determined to record past events to educate future generations about the offences, thus presaging South Africa's TRC. The TRC model, however, introduced conceptions of restorative justice to public discourse and legitimized the idea of forgiveness being a pre-

[14] Quoted from Kjetil Tronvoll's interview with Prime Minister Meles Zenawi, Addis Ababa, 16 January 2002.

requisite to reconciliation. This initiated the academic debate between proponents of retributive justice (vengeance) and restorative justice (forgiveness).

Without going into depth with this argument, various authors such as Desmond Tutu (1999), Martha Minow (1998), Gary Bass (2001) and Pumla Gobodo-Madikizela (2003) argue that retributive justice is victors' justice that ignores the needs of the victims and alienates the population in the process. Yet the TRC model itself gave rise to a forceful rebuttal stating that restorative justice merely sweeps societal wounds under the carpet by making the assumption that faked contriteness equals true forgiveness and, pushing further, that if amnesty is granted as a result of being forgiven then the process leaves victims feeling dissatisfied (Krag, 2000; Hayner, 2002). Others, notably Eric Posner and Adrian Vermeule (2004) and Jeffrie Murphy (2003), made stronger cases for trials and punishment as the best alternative in cases where society is in transition from autocracy to democracy. While the discourse revolved around justifying one or the other opposing view, some scholars began to assess the virtues of both. Perhaps first relayed in Robert Rotberg and Dennis Thompson's edited volume (2000) was the notion that transitional justice should be a system endogenously conscribed to time, place and particulars of each case. This idea has almost become the mantra of the transitional justice field today. Raquel Aldana (2006) argues that 'a victim-centered approach to transitional justice should consider, whenever possible, the co-existence of truth commissions and prosecutions, because each can provide distinctive and superior benefits to victims.' To an extent, recent works on transitional justice, rather than making recommendations or even championing a particular form of justice, are content to document case studies (De Brito *et al.*, 2001; Elster, 2004). Along these lines, Lyn Graybill and Kimberly Lanegran (2004) examine South Africa, Rwanda and Sierra Leone to determine the 'ideal balances between trials and truth commissions'. Unfortunately, with the exception of South Africa, the other two are incomplete; moreover, South Africa established the precedent by which all truth commissions are judged and never sought to pursue both restorative and retributive justice. Herein lies the usefulness of Ethiopia's Red Terror trials.

The main phase of the trials has been concluded with a verdict and sentencing of Col. Mengistu Hailemariam and the top leadership of the Derg by the Federal High Court. The Federal Supreme Court has also passed its decision on the appeal filed by both parties (see conclusion in this volume). However, a point has been reached where some overarching conclusions can be drawn about their conduct and wider social implications. The SPO started out with a dual mandate that incorporated significant aspects of both transitional justice systems, although the trials themselves were purely retributive. In this regard, the Ethiopian case illustrates a myriad of problems in carrying out a two-fold mandate: prosecution and documenting the atrocities. Finally, as concluded in this book, the SPO and the trials themselves have not managed to reach their objective of bringing about national healing, since they have not allowed Ethiopian society to forget and reconcile itself with the past. Thus, rather than speculate about the virtues of combining or splitting the two camps within transitional justice, Ethiopia offers the world a concrete example of lessons learnt from pursuing aspects of both retributive and restorative justice, albeit with the emphasis on the first.

The Contributions in this Volume

In Chapter 2, Bahru Zewde provides a nuanced history of the Ethiopian Revolution, showing the complexity of ideological alliances and betrayals in which the Red Terror took place in the late 1970s. He weaves through a contentious history highlighting three distinct phases of repression that ultimately led to systematic, state-sponsored human rights violations comparable to the genocide in Cambodia. In Chapter 3, Frode Elgesem and Girmachew Alemu Aneme critically assess the Red Terror trials from the perspective of the rights of the accused and the efficiency of the institutions involved in the process. In this ambitious chapter, they apply national and international laws to find that the rights of the accused were not respected. In Chapter 4, Sarah Vaughan investigates the mandate and performance of the SPO, an institution established for the specific purpose of prosecuting the suspects in the Red Terror trials. She describes the rationale for creating the SPO, its early development including obstacles it had to overcome, the agenda it was tasked with, and finally the relationships between: (a) the SPO and the Ethiopian judiciary; (b) the executive and general public; and (c) Ethiopia and the international community.

Departing from the trial itself, Charles Schaefer asks in Chapter 5 whether a trial format was the best way to bring about national reconciliation. He argues that incorporation of historically validated forms of restorative justice employed as late as the early twentieth century and accepted by the Ethiopian public were overlooked by the EPRDF. In Chapter 6, Kjetil Tronvoll contextualizes the decision-making behind the selection of a trial format and the popular perceptions of the trials within the existing political environment. Tronvoll provides the broadest appraisal of the consequences of the prosecution and trials, particularly focusing on institutional and personality conflicts within the EPRDF and Ethiopia at large over the role the trial played in creating political legitimacy for the incumbent.

In Chapter 7, Elsa van Huyssteen brings in a comparative perspective, contrasting the model chosen by Ethiopia with the TRC in South Africa, and debates the effectiveness of these two different systems of transitional justice. Elsa van Huyssteen's intent is to compare notions of justice and reconciliation to respectfully address a painful, abusive past in order to build new democratic states and civil societies. In Chapter 8,

Girmachew Alemu Aneme analyses the Red Terror trials within the framework of normative and institutional guarantees of non-repetition, as part of the response to past human rights violations. He offers pragmatic suggestions concerning how the Ethiopian government and civil society institutions could nurture mechanisms to guarantee the non-repetition of massive atrocities similar to the Red terror.

In the conclusion, the editors Kjetil Tronvoll, Charles Schaefer and Girmachew Alemu Aneme provide an analysis of the verdict and sentencing handed down on the main group of accused, the appeal process, and based on the experiences from the Red Terror trials, draw some general observations on transitional justice theory.

References

Aldana, Raquel. 2006. 'A Victim-centered Reflection on Truth Commissions and Prosecutions as a Response to Mass Atrocities,' *Journal of Human Rights* 5: 07–126.

Andrew, Christopher and Vasili Mitrokhin. 2005. *The World was Going Our Way: The KGB and the Battle for the Third World.* New York: Basic Books.

Babile Tola.1989 [1997]. *To Kill a Generation: The Red Terror in Ethiopia.* Washington, DC: Free Ethiopia Press.

Bass, Gary Jonathan. 2001. *Stay the Hand of Vengeance: The Politics of War Crimes Tribunals.* Princeton, NJ: Princeton University Press.

Czaplinski, Wladyslaw. 2001. 'State Responsibility for Violations of Human Rights,' in *International Law in the Post-Cold War World-Essays in Memory of Li Haopei.* Sienho Yee and Wang Tieya (eds). London: Routledge Studies in International Law.

Dadimos Haile. 2000. *Accountability for crimes of the past and the challenges of criminal prosecution: The case of Ethiopia.* Leuven: Leuven University Press.

De Brito, Alexandra Barahona, Carmen Gonzales-Enriques, and Paloma Aquilar (eds) 2001. *The Politics of Memory: Transitional justice in democratizing societies.* Oxford: Oxford University Press.

Elgesem, Frode. 1998. *The Derg Trials in Context: A study of some aspects of the Ethiopian judiciary,* Human Rights Report No.1, Norwegian Institute of Human Rights, University of Oslo.

Elster, Jon. 2004. *Closing the Books: Transitional Justice in Historical Perspective.* New York: Cambridge University Press.

Engelschion, Tore Sverdrup. 1996. 'Prosecutions of war crimes and violations of human rights in Ethiopia,' *Year Book of African Law.* Vol. 8. Köln: Rüdiger Hopper Verlag.

Firew Kebede Tiba. 2007. 'The Mengistu genocide trial in Ethiopia,' *Journal of International Criminal Justice,* vol. 5: 513–28.

Girmachew Alemu Aneme. 2006. 'Apology and trials: The case of the Red Terror trials in Ethiopia,' *African Human Rights Law Journal,* vol. 6, no.1.

Gobodo-Madikizela, Pumla. 2003. *A Human Being Died that Night: A South African woman confronts the legacy of Apartheid.* Boston, MA: Mariner Books.

Graybill, Lyn and Kimberly Lanegran. 2004. 'Truth, Justice, and Reconciliation in Africa: Issues and Cases,' *African Studies Quarterly,* vol. 8, no. 1 (Fall).

Hayner, Priscilla B. 2002. *Unspeakable Truths: Facing the Challenge of Truth Commissions.* London: Routledge.

Howland, Todd. 2000. 'Learning to make proactive human rights interventions effective: The Carter Center and Ethiopia's Office of the Special Prosecutor,' *Wisconsin International Law Journal,* 18: 407.

Human Rights Watch/Africa. 1994. *Reckoning under the Law,* New York: Human Rights Watch.

Huyse, Luc. 1995. 'Justice After Transition: On the choices successor elites make in dealing with the past,' *Law and Social Inquiry*, vol. 20, no.1.

Iyob, Ruth. 1995. *The Eritrean Struggle for Independence: Domination, resistance, nationalism 1941–1993*, Cambridge: Cambridge University Press.

Kissi, Edward. 2006. *Revolution and Genocide in Ethiopia and Cambodia*. Lexington, MA: Lexington Books.

Krag, Antjie. 2000. *Country of My Skull: Guilt, Sorrow, and the Limits of Forgiveness in the New South Africa*. New York: Three Rivers Press.

Mayfield, Julie. 1995. 'The Prosecution of War Crimes and Respect for Human Rights: Ethiopia's balancing act,' *Emory International Law Review*.

Mehari Redae. 2000. 'The Ethiopian Genocide Trial,' *Ethiopian Law Review* 1: 7.

Minow, Martha. 1998. *Between Vengeance and Forgiveness: Facing history after genocide and mass violence*. Boston, MA: Beacon Press.

Murphy, Jeffrie. 2003. *Getting Even: Forgiveness and Its Limits*. Cambridge: Cambridge University Press.

Posner, Eric A. and Adrian Vermeule. 2004. 'Transitional Justice as Ordinary Justice,' *Harvard Law Review* 117 (Jan.): 761–825.

Roht-Arriaza, Naomi, ed. 1995. *Impunity and Human Rights in International Law and Practice*. New York: Oxford University Press.

Rotberg, Robert and Dennis Thompson (eds) 2000. *Truth v. Justice: The morality of truth commissions*. Princeton, NJ: Princeton University Press.

Sarkin, Jeremy. 1999. 'Transitional justice and the prosecution model: The experience of Ethiopia,' *Law, Democracy & Development*, vol.3: 253–66.

Teferra Haile-Selassie. 1997. *The Ethiopian Revolution, 1974–91: From a monarchical autocracy to a military oligarchy*, London and New York: Kegan Paul International.

Trial Observation and Information Project. 2000. *Consolidated summary and reports from observations made in 1996, 1997, 1998, 1999*, Addis Ababa.

Tutu, Desmond. 1999. *No Future without Forgiveness*. New York: Doubleday.

US State Department. 1992. *Country Report on Human Rights Practices for 1991*. Washington, DC.

Vaughan, Sarah. 1994. *The Addis Ababa Transitional Conference of July 1991: Its origin, history and significance*. Occasional Paper no. 51, Centre of African Studies, Edinburgh University.

Vaughan, Sarah and Kjetil Tronvoll. 2003. *The Culture of Power in Contemporary Ethiopian Political Life*. Stockholm: Sidastudies.

Yacob Hailemariam. 1999. 'The Quest for Justice and Reconciliation: The International Criminal Tribunal for Rwanda and the Ethiopian High Court,' *Hastings International and Comparative Law Review*, vol. 22, no.4.

Young, John. 1997. *Peasant Revolution in Ethiopia. The Tigray's People's Liberation Front, 1975–1991*. Cambridge: Cambridge University Press.

2

The History of the Red Terror | Contexts & Consequences

BAHRU ZEWDE

Revolutionary Reigns of Terror occur within the post-revolutionary period or crisis when revolutionary regimes seek to hang on to political power in the face of opposing forces contending for that power. (O'Kane 1991: 9)

... revolution presents two contrasting faces: the one glorious and appealing; the other violent and terrifying. (Mayer 2000: 3)

Introduction

The contrasting faces of the Ethiopian Revolution are all too apparent. As in other classical revolutions, notably the French and the Russian, the euphoria that attended the initial outbreak was followed by anguish and remorse. Indeed, seen retrospectively, the latter sentiment clearly overshadows the former. Nothing illustrates this more graphically than the fact that the protagonists of the Ethiopian Revolution were imprisoned, facing charges of genocide and mass murder. The best and the brightest perished in that process, particularly in the two fateful years between 1976 and 1978. The gap left behind by this calamity is akin to the generation gap that attended the Graziani Massacre of February 1937 during fascist Italy's occupation of Ethiopia, when some of the most agile and promising minds were targeted for liquidation. But neither moral indignation nor legal prosecution can adequately resolve this national disaster. There is a need to put what looked like a monstrous aberration in perspective, to contextualize it both globally and nationally. This chapter attempts to do that. Needless to say, explanation should in no way be construed as justification.

It appears that there is no revolution without terror. Arno J. Mayer (2000: 4) opens his perceptive analysis of the 'furies' of the two classical revolutions cited above with the following categorical statement:

There is no revolution without violence and terror; without civil and foreign war; without iconoclasm and religious conflict; and without collision between city and country. The Furies of revolution are fuelled primarily by the inevitable and unexceptional resistance of the forces and ideas opposed to it, at home and abroad.

Both revolutions – the French and the Russian – bear out this characterization. The Ethiopian revolution also closely followed their pattern. In all cases, terror was the inevitable recourse for a regime beleaguered by opposition, both internal and external, from the left as well as from the right. The threat of foreign invasion played an important role in deepening and justifying terror. The aphorism of revolution devouring its children was borne out eloquently in all three cases. They had similar agencies for the execution of terror: the Committee of Public Safety in France, the Cheka (later the KGB) in Russia and the Revolutionary Defence Committees in Ethiopia. The executors of terror dispatched the real or imagined enemies of the revolution unceremoniously. The French Revolution produced the eternal symbol of terror – the guillotine. All three terrors proved fertile seedbeds from which sprouted dictators with varying hues and shades of ruthlessness. The Russian experience perhaps surpassed all by having two editions of terror: the first in the immediate post-revolution years and the second in the form of Stalin's notorious purges. In a caricature of Stalin's famous ideological departure from proletarian internationalism ('Socialism in One Country'), Mayer dubs this phase 'Terror in One Country' (2000: 13).

However, there were in history revolutions that did not have such excesses, or perhaps more accurately 'excessive excesses' (Mayer 2000: 93). Rosemary O'Kane draws an instructive lesson from the experience of countries where a revolutionary government was installed subsequent to a civil war or through protracted guerrilla warfare. The terror in those situations was mild (as in Cuba) or practically non-existent, as in Nicaragua (O'Kane 1991: 6, 196). This circumstance seems also to explain why the English could have a 'Glorious Revolution' in 1688, as all the blood-letting, including the beheading of the king, had been accomplished in the course of the Civil War in the 1640s.

Where this correlation of protracted civil war and mild terror flounders is of course in the case of the Kampuchean revolution, where the Khmer Rouge, subsequent to their seizure of power through guerrilla warfare, unleashed a reign of terror of unparalleled proportions. What makes the Kampuchean genocide puzzling is that the Khmer Rouge faced little perceptible threat to their power. The terror arose essentially out of the fanatical determination of 'a small group of intellectuals [...] to force their ideas about a better world upon the masses' (Burgler 1990: 171). Chinese experience also seems to invalidate the above dichotomy since, notwithstanding the protracted civil war – and resistance to Japanese occupation – that preceded the Communist seizure of power, there was a reign of terror in the years 1950-53 directed against the Kuomintang and other 'counter-revolutionaries' (O'Kane 1991: 196). But this was not on the scale witnessed in its Russian predecessor, let alone its Kampuchean successor. Although the Cultural Revolution of the late 1960s did terrorize large elements of the population, the damage was more psychological than physical. This last aspect is shared by the Iranian revolution, which was neither preceded by civil war nor followed by terror in the classical sense. Yet, the entire population, particularly the female population, was subjected to the rigorous canons of Islamic orthodoxy.

The causal explanation of terror is one of the greatest challenges that a historian faces. 'Unlike the lawyer, who pleads a case, and the judge, who holds the scales, the critical historian asks "why", and realizes that the answer will not be simple' (Mayer 2000: 17), because the explanation for terror seems to lie in the realm as much of psychology as contingency. There are undoubtedly objective circumstances, mainly domestic as well as external opposition, that give rise to terror. One can also try to place terror within the specific historical context. At the same time, however, terror appears to be the outlet for pent-up feelings and emotions, the settling of scores that pertain more to the world of the sub-conscious. Thus, in Ethiopia, only a psychiatrist could fathom the mind-set of a Girma Kebede, the bohemian party boy turned into the blood-thirsty *kebele* (local administration) official. His gruesome excesses, including the murdering of a woman eight months pregnant, were so embarrassing to the regime that he had to be publicly executed by the Derg; he was subsequently disowned by *Ma'ison* (All-Ethiopian Socialist Movement), the political organization to which he purportedly belonged.

What makes revolutionary terror particularly terrifying and its impact on the psyche of the people so enduring is that it eschews the normal procedure of verification. In a total reversal of due process of law, one is presumed guilty before proven innocent. 'The *suspect*, both as a concept and a representation, was the cornerstone of the Terror. Indeed, the Terror was a system of power threatening and punishing people for what they were, not what they did' (Baczko 1994: 26). The French Revolution, so replete with the symbolism of revolutionary terror, enshrined this fact in its famous 'Law of Suspects'. The Ethiopian edition of the same phenomenon has been immortalized in the popular rendering of the edict that came out on the eve of the launching of the terror: '*yasaba wayem yasasaba*' ('whoever dared to think or pushed others to think' i.e. counter-revolutionary ideas). The ultimate effect of such extra-judicial indictment and execution was to induce the cowed submission of the population. Just as it united the perpetrators in blood, terror incapacitated its targets, either eliminating them physically or rendering them politically passive.

The Ethiopian Historical Context

The enormity of the so-called Red Terror in Ethiopia inevitably forces one to ponder whether there was anything in the country's past that could prepare one for that event. Babile Tola, who wrote the first long account of the event from an EPRP standpoint, has no doubts about this. 'Violence,' he asserts, 'has almost always been the media of government-people relations in Ethiopia' (Babile 1997: 3). The history of violence and warfare reportedly reached its peak in the reign of Menelik as he subjugated the southern peoples. As a result, 'murder or violence has been inculcated into the system, into the national psyche and socio-cultural heritage' (ibid.: 4).

This is a rather simplistic rendering of the Ethiopian past. Nonetheless, it has a good deal of truth. The history of the country is replete with wars and acts of violence. Moreover, contrary to the common portrayal of the country as having to defend itself constantly against external aggression, the overwhelming proportions of the wars were internal in their genesis and impact. These internal wars have been attended by considerable loss of life and fairly often by massive dislocation. Not only have wars been fought, but they have also been celebrated. The *fukara*, the traditional war chant that preceded and concluded military campaigns (the first to goad the fighters on, the second to boast about the triumphs), has remained to this day an ingrained element in highland Ethiopian culture. Indeed, it has become modernized. Until recently, musical performances would be deemed incomplete without a performance of the *fukara*, the saxophone being the universally preferred instrument to accompany it (Bahru 1998). During the protracted war in northern Ethiopia under the Derg, it was common to see a pop star like Tilahun Gessese, eyes menacing and wearing a *shamma* with a symbolically crimson red lining, chanting blood-curdling lyrics haranguing the soldiers to finish off the 'bandits'. Even the EPRDF, which after 1991 was presumed to stand for a negation of this warrior culture, had to dip into this time-proven repertoire in the course of the recent war with Eritrea (cf. Tronvoll 2003).

The peasant, though not always directly involved in military combats, has been on the receiving end of the soldiers' fury and caprice, either by being forced to feed and host him or by being subjected to torture and persecution for failing to deliver or giving refuge to the enemy or the rebel. Nothing expresses this pillage of the peasantry more dramatically than Emperor Yohannes' words of remorse at the end of one of his devastating campaigns in Gojjam: 'I do not know whether it is through my sin or that of the peasant, but I went on devastating the country' (Quoted in Bahru 2001: 45). Yet, these words of remorse are indicative of the moral restraint that permeated the actions of even the most ruthless rulers. Alas, one would seek in vain for even a faint echo of such remorse in the recent 'memoirs' of Lt. Colonel Mengistu Hailemariam.[1] However, although war was common, it was often resorted to only after negotiation and mediation had failed. The intercession of priests averted many an imminent clash of arms. *Feqer eska Maqaber,* Haddis Alemayehu's classical portrayal of feudal Ethiopia, has that memorable passage where the *tabot* (the tablet, the most sacred item in an Orthodox church) comes in between drawn swords and prevents the bloody clash of two feudal lords. The *tabots* came out in force in 1878 and managed to ward off a devastating civil war between Emperor Yohannes and *Negus* Menilek. By contrast, the *tabots* were nowhere to be seen as the corpses of young Ethiopians littered the streets during the Red Terror. In fact, the priests themselves were hiding to save their lives.

Nor was it common to aim for total elimination of the enemy. One could of course argue that there were two standards of morality, one for the commoner and the marginal peoples, which was marked by ruthlessness, and another for the political and social peer, which was characterized by a certain degree of magnanimity (see Schaefer in this volume). Thus, castration of the fallen enemy (nay, even the parading of the gruesome trophy) was a common enough occurrence. Nor was Menelik particularly merciful in the face of the stubborn resistance of the Walayta and the Kafa. Yet, he is reported to have tenderly washed and nursed the wounded feet of *Negus* Takla-Haymanot of Gojjam after he had defeated him at the Battle of Embabo in 1882 (Gabra-Sellase 1959 EC: 107). Nor could one underestimate the role of the jester in Menilek's court, as indeed in imperial courts in general; the jester was tolerated and even enjoyed as a salutary reminder of the human foibles of the sovereign. The jester's jives provided a safety valve for pent-up frustrations and resentments.

The long reign of Emperor Haile Selassie (*de jure* 1930–74 but *de facto* 1916–74) witnessed varied acts of political opposition, including a couple of assassination attempts (in 1925 and in 1969). But only a handful of his opponents were executed. Other than the mysterious disappearance of his arch-enemy, Iyyasu, in the wake of the Italian invasion in 1935, the major cases of physical elimination were that of the patriotic leader Balay Zallaqa (who was hanged in 1943) and of the leaders of the abortive coup of 1960. The emperor's preferred mode of punishment was imprisonment, marginalization or banishment. Appointing those suspected of harbouring dangerous thoughts to ambassadorial posts or to governorships of frontier provinces was a favourite tactic of the emperor. Co-option was yet another modality of neutralization. The supreme example of this, even if it failed dismally, is provided in the long saga of Blatta Takkala Walda-Hawaryat's implacable opposition. All possible inducements were explored, from ministerial appointment to

[1] See Genet Ayele Anbesse (2001).

offer of the emperor's eldest daughter in marriage, to pacify this spirited opponent. But it proved to no avail. His attempt to assassinate the emperor foiled, Takkala finally died in his house in the course of a shootout with the police in late 1969.

Where this imperial culture of accommodation and containment crumbled was in situations of religious conflict, which, like all ideological conflicts, brokered no compromise and forced its protagonists to see things in the starkest of terms, as either black or white. In the fifteenth century, Emperor Zara Ya'eqob, determined to enforce his ruling on the veneration of Mary, went around branding heretics with hot iron. The Wars of Ahmad Grañ wrought havoc and have thus assumed apocalyptic proportions in historical imagination. The religious civil war that attended the Jesuit attempt to convert the country to Catholicism was so bloody and costly that it moved the pro-Catholic emperor, Susenyos, to abdicate. The doctrinal controversies that followed, when Orthodox Christians were engaged in hair-splitting arguments on the divine and human nature of Christ, were also characterized by a good deal of merciless blood-letting. Even when this doctrinal split was finally resolved at the Council of Boru Meda in 1878, Emperor Yohannes, who was the decidedly partisan chairman of the proceedings, bequeathed a gruesome souvenir for posterity by ordering the tongue of one of the recalcitrant priests to be cut out. He followed this up with a ruthless campaign to convert the Muslims of Wollo forcibly to Christianity.

Many of post-revolution Ethiopia's political antecedents are to be sought, perhaps more than anywhere else, in these religious and doctrinal conflicts. As in Soviet Russia, religious orthodoxy proved a fertile ground for ideological orthodoxy. The interpretation of the Marxist-Leninist principle on the national question became the litmus test of that orthodoxy. Political positions came to be adhered to with a dogmatism that would have been the envy of a Gonderine prelate. Politics, the art of compromise, was reduced to a zero-sum game. You destroy or you are destroyed. The verbal violence that characterized the student debates of the early 1970s prepared the way for the physical violence of the late 1970s. One need only compare the gentle satire of 'That Will be the Day' (a popular column of *News and Views*, the major student paper of the 1960s) with the merciless invective of Tilahun Takele's *The National Question* (written in 1971) to appreciate the new culture of verbal violence.

To sum up, while tolerance and accommodation were not entirely alien to the Ethiopian political culture, there were two tendencies that militated against this culture. The first was a deeply ingrained militarist tradition that made virtue out of killing. Second, in cases of doctrinal (and later ideological) differences, opposition tended to assume a total character. As the imperial regime collapsed, the two forces that vied to fill the power vacuum reflected these two negative traditions. The soldiers were accustomed to resort to their gun at the slightest sign of obstruction.

The students or the leftist groups that emerged out of them, particularly those that were active abroad, had come to be rent by acrimonious divisions. Minor differences that could have been resolved easily if the groups had genuinely applied themselves to the problem had assumed Manichean dimensions. Starting with the interpretation of the national question, the differences had ranged over organizational matters, the presence or otherwise of a revolutionary situation, and the necessity or otherwise of armed struggle. In retrospect, however, at the root of the problem was the rivalry between two clandestine organizations, the EPRP and *Ma'ison*, who were engaged in a relentless struggle for power.

The Build-up to Red Terror

In a way, the scenario for armed confrontation was set on the very day that saw the demise of the *ancien regime*; 12 September 1974 had a strongly ambivalent resonance about it. On the one hand, it proclaimed the change of regime that so many had struggled for, particularly after the eruption of the revolution in February 1974. On the other hand, it ushered in a military regime that threatened to be no less authoritarian than its predecessor. The Provisional Military Administrative Committee (PMAC), as the Derg had restyled itself on assuming full state power following the deposition of Emperor Haile Selassie, began its tenure with a proclamation that banned all assemblies, demonstrations and strikes, thereby negating the very revolutionary process that had engendered it. From then on, the battle lines were drawn between the Derg, which brooked no opposition to its self-assigned mandate, and its civilian and military opponents, who campaigned for the establishment of a 'provisional popular government' (PPG).

Interestingly enough, the first armed clash to resolve this contradiction took place within the ranks of the military itself. In early October, the Derg cracked down on military units that had embraced the call for PPG – the Engineers Corps, Military Aviation, and the Imperial Bodyguard. The storming of the compound of the Engineers was attended by the first bloodletting of a movement that had vowed to change Ethiopia without any bloodshed. On 24 November 1974, incompatibility between the Derg-appointed head of state, Lt. General Aman Andom, and the Derg's first vice-chairman, Major Mengistu Hailemariam, precipitated not only the death of the general, but also the summary execution of over fifty former government officials and dignitaries as well as dissidents from within the military. The execution of 'the sixty', as it has come to be known in popular parlance, initiated a culture of massive killing with impunity. Once it had started bathing in blood, the Derg developed a habit of arrogant defiance towards public opinion, be it national or international. The seeds of the Red Terror could thus be said to have been sown there and then.

The two leftist groups that came to be locked in mortal combat in the first rounds of the Red Terror, the EPRP and *Ma'ison,* found themselves ranged against the Derg in these early months of Derg rule. Both advanced the slogan of the PPG. The parting of the ways came in early 1975 as a result of two inter-related developments. First, the arrival of the *Ma'ison* leadership from abroad was followed by a shift of strategy from opposition to the Derg to critical support. Secondly, the Derg's radical land reform of March 1975 drove a wedge between the two leftist groups, as *Ma'ison* saw it as yet another reason to give the Derg qualified support while the EPRP saw it essentially as a device by the Derg to perpetuate its rule. Crucial to the decision of *Ma'ison* to pursue a policy of rapprochement with the Derg was not only its appreciation of the revolutionary measures it was taking but also an awareness of its own relative organizational weakness. To compete with the growing strength of its rival the EPRP, particularly among workers and the youth, it found it politically expedient to ally with the Derg. Through such an alliance, *Ma'ison* primarily expected to use the state machinery to reinforce its organizational setup. This expectation became particularly pronounced after *Ma'ison* came to dominate the Provisional Office for Mass Organizational Affairs (POMOA) in early 1976. Rather naively, it also hoped to eventually supplant the Derg and to assume state power through its own version of a creeping coup.

The famous debates of early 1976, between the EPRP on the one hand and *Ma'ison* and its allies on the other, were in effect a verbal dress rehearsal for the final armed clash. This is not to deny their historical importance as one of the rare instances in Ethiopia when ideas were discussed and debated openly in government media. They are comparable in this regard to the fascination of the *Berhanena Salam* newspaper published weekly in the late 1920s. They also helped to revive the enthusiasm and eagerness with which newspapers were purchased and read in the first months after the eruption of the Ethiopian revolution in February 1974. Further, they could be said to have anticipated the almost un-inhibited discussion of issues in the private media witnessed since 1991. But the debates of early 1976, interesting as they are from many angles, were not intended to convince one side or the other. They were essentially an exercise in scoring points by purportedly showing the ideological or political bankruptcy of the opponent. Once the debate was over, both sides withdrew to sharpen their tools for the armed clash, EPRP preparing its squads and *Ma'ison* drawing on the military sinews of the state.

The Phases of Red Terror

There is far from unanimity as to when the Terror started, just as the issue of who started it is contentious. In this respect, history has become as much of a battleground as the political contest and armed clash itself. The retrospective account by one of the leaders of *Ma'ison* is unequivocal in asserting that 'the armed combat [*tenenq* is the Amharic word used] of 1976 was inaugurated by the EPRP leadership' (Andargachew 2000: 366). To drive his point home, he draws both on the strident declarations of the EPRP in early September and the intimidating tactics (*taraba buden*) it had begun to use even earlier. This sentiment is echoed in some of the works on the Ethiopian revolution (Keller 1988: 199; Teferra 1997: 184). Halliday and Molyneux (1981: 120) even go to the extent of asserting that 'however prone to such actions (i.e. violence) the PMAC may have been, it was the EPRP's terrorist policies that encouraged the new phase of PMAC repression.'

EPRP historians, on the other hand, are at pains to argue that the EPRP only reacted to the preparations being made by the Derg and its POMOA allies in late August 1976 for a war of annihilation against the EPRP. The campaign was officially launched on 11 September, when the EPRP was accused in the media of various acts of counter-revolution and economic sabotage (Babile 1997: 28, 67; Kiflu 1998: 129). Ultimately, however, the question of who started the Terror is as fruitless an exercise as the all-too-familiar one of who fired the first shot in a war. The build-up described in the previous section had made the urban warfare so inexorable that the issue of who first pulled the trigger strikes one as an academic exercise.

Nor is there agreement as to when the Terror started. For EPRP partisans, it started in September 1976 when the Derg officially launched its campaign of annihilation against the EPRP. This movement was characterized by massive detention of its members and sympathizers and the execution of some of its members held in detention. In most of the standard works on the revolution, on the other hand, 3 February, when Mengistu consolidated his power following the execution of his rivals within the Derg, marks the beginning of the Red Terror. *Ma'ison*, which itself became the victim of the Terror only after its 'defection from the revolutionary camp' in the summer of 1977, tends to focus on the atrocities committed in late 1977 and early 1978. It is of some interest, however, that what could be described as the official history of the organization (Andargachew Assegid 2000) sees 3 February with marked ambivalence. It marked, it argues, not only the ascendancy of the Derg and its leftist allies over the EPRP, of revolution over counter-revolution, but also heralded the ultimate reversal of the revolution and the consecration of one-man rule.

The labels 'White Terror' and 'Red Terror' are clearly subjective. They are intended to condemn one form of terror and justify another. Rhetoric aside, however, it is clear that the period from September 1976 to at least May 1978 was marked by a scale of political violence unprecedented in the first two years of the revolutionary period. It was marked by massive and sometimes indiscriminate detentions, assassinations, extra-judicial killings and summary executions. It is possible to divide this period into three phases: September 1976 to 3 February 1977; February to November 1977; and November 1977 to May 1978. We shall now turn to highlighting the salient features and major landmarks of each phase.

First phase: the EPRP ascendant

The first phase could be said to have begun in September 1976 when the Derg and its leftist allies launched a massive campaign against the EPRP characterized by denunciation of its alleged counter-revolutionary activities and detention of its members and sympathizers. In less than a month, hundreds of people already targeted for their pro-EPRP stance in labour unions, discussion forums and the student movement were incarcerated in various prisons in the capital. The EPRP, which appears to have been waiting for just such an occasion, retaliated by what it described as acts of self-defence, that is, the assassination of leaders and cadres of the opposite camp.

The most significant, if abortive, act in this regard was the assassination attempt on Mengistu Hailemariam on 23 September. Mengistu not only survived the attempt but also used the incident to whip up public solidarity for himself and for the denunciation of EPRP tactics. On October 1, the EPRP gunned down one of the *Ma'ison* members of POMOA, Dr. Fikre Merid. This act provoked the famous 'exchange rate' statement by the Derg, when the life of one 'revolutionary' was deemed to be equivalent to the lives of one thousand 'anti-people elements'. But the actual transaction did not take place until about a month later, when the Derg executed twenty-three EPRP members, a number of whom were members of the EPRA (the rural armed wing of the EPRP) captured in Wallo and kept in detention long before the escalation of hostilities in September.

This did not deter the EPRP from continuing with its assassinations. As a matter of fact, the day after these executions, Getnet Zewde, Permanent Secretary in the Ministry of Labour and Social Affairs, was murdered. The government press continued to record faithfully the fall of one 'revolutionary' after another to EPRP guns. The *Ma'ison* version of events in this period is one of total helplessness and confusion, with its members feverishly trying to arm themselves with whatever was available (Andargachew Assegid 2000: 367ff). Mengistu, after he had established his ascendancy, also reminisced ruefully on how the hands of 'genuine revolutionaries' were tied by alleged EPRP elements within the Derg so that they had to watch helplessly as their supporters were gunned down on the streets, thrown down from buildings or mutilated.

This period of relative EPRP ascendancy took a toll on the internal health of the organization when the policy of assassinations provoked a split within its leadership. As it turned out, the policy was opposed by one of the luminaries of the organization, Berhane Meskel Redda, and another leading member of the Political Bureau, Getachew Maru. They argued that it was ultimately self-destructive. What was fateful for the future course of the organization was not so much that the opposition emerged as the way that it was handled. Getachew Maru was detained and eventually killed when the EPRP leadership, harried by the intensification of the terror launched against it, did not know what to do with him. Berhane Meskel escaped to form his own armed unit and fought until he was captured and executed by the Derg. But his followers, labelled *anja* (faction) by the EPRP leadership, joined the Derg and played a pivotal role in the ultimate destruction of the EPRP in the cities. Nor were the Derg and its leftist allies exactly sitting idle. They were busy laying the groundwork that would enable them to hit back. An important element of this preparation was the control of the *kebeles* through a new round of elections in October 1976. In view of the crucial role that the *kebeles* were to play in the execution of the 'Red Terror' campaign, this was a highly significant development. In early December, on the occasion of the anniversary of the establishment of peasant associations in Hadiya and Kambatta *awraja*, the first call was sounded for the establishment of revolutionary defence committees (*Addis Zaman*, 24.3.69 EC). As is common knowledge, these committees played an even more crucial role in the Red Terror campaign. Much more significantly, Mengistu and his hatchet man, Colonel Daniel Asfaw, were girding themselves for the final reckoning as his opponents within the Derg, allegedly EPRP members or sympathizers, were savouring their successes in stripping Mengistu of power through the restructuring of the Derg. On 3 February 1977, the balance of power shifted decisively towards Mengistu and his leftist allies.

Second phase: 'Our revolution has moved from defence to offence'
Mengistu's coup of 3 February 1977 was a turning point not only in his own political fortunes but also in the intensification of violence. Already, in reaction to the conciliatory speech on 29 January of the Derg chairman, Lt. General Teferi Bante, supporters of *Ma'ison* and kindred organizations had come out in full force, chanting slogans such as: 'Let us meet the white terror of reactionaries with the red terror of the oppressed' (*Addis Zaman*, 24.5.69 EC). Four days later, after the lightning coup that had so dramatically altered the balance of forces, the same crowd came out asserting confidently: 'Terror has passed from the revolutionary camp to the anti-revolutionary camp' (*Addis Zaman*, 28.5.69). In that very same rally, Mengistu performed his theatrical smashing of bottles filled with red ink, thereby legitimizing the merciless shedding of blood, as long as it was that of 'anti-revolutionary elements'.

Exactly one month after this rally, the Derg began arming its supporters in the *kebeles* and factories. Two weeks later, the first search and destroy campaign was launched. No sooner was the campaign in progress than the Derg and its allies boasted their major trophy, the body of a prominent EPRP politbureau member, Dr Tesfaye Debessay, who had hurled himself from an apartment building as his pursuers closed in on him. This was followed by the death in a shootout of the powerful labour leader, Marqos Hagos. At the time unbeknownst to the Derg, the campaign had also claimed the lives of three prominent members of the EPRP, Malaku

Marqos, Yohannes Berhane, and Nega Ayele, who were all killed in the outskirts of Addis Ababa as they tried to flee from the tightening noose in the city. During the second search and destroy campaign, which was launched in early May, the EPRP lost another stalwart member, Captain Amha Abebe, who had served as the organization's vital linkman with the Derg before 3 February.

This is not to say that the EPRP was entirely on the run in this second phase. On the contrary, it was stepping up its own assassination campaign. As a matter of fact, the announcement of assassinations of pro-Derg people and the posting of their obituaries became an even more common feature of the government press now than during the first phase. But the tide had certainly turned against it. Not only had it lost some of its most prominent members, but the relentless government terror had come to sap the enthusiasm of its actual and potential supporters. Furthermore, the disarmament that had accompanied the search and destroy campaigns had rendered the civilian population completely powerless, and the denunciations and self-denunciations that were taking place in factories, schools and *kebeles* had added to the sense of impotence.

And then came the climax on May Day of 1977 (or more strictly the eve of it). Amazingly, oblivious to the fact that the days of demonstrations and rallies were long gone, the youth wing of the EPRP organized a series of demonstrations by youth in different parts of the city. If earlier May Day celebrations (particularly those of 1976) were demonstrative of EPRP prowess, then those of 1977 marked the low point of its organizational strength. Benefiting from a tip-off from the faction that had defected from the organization, government forces unleashed one of the most brutal repressions of the revolutionary period. The carnage, for it was nothing less than that, continued in subsequent days and claimed the lives of some one thousand young Ethiopians. The event has also entered the history books for the cynical charge by the authorities of about 1 US$ each (at the rate then prevailing) for the bullets used to kill the youth if their families wanted to take the corpses.

Third phase: 'Let Red Terror be Accelerated' ('Qay Sheber Yefafam')
The carnage of May Day 1977 was the dress rehearsal for the massive killings that characterized the third phase of government terror. If the EPRP was relatively ascendant during the first phase and was still hitting back in the second, it was in total disarray in the third. If the second phase of government terror was measured and centrally directed, the third was one where every 'revolutionary' became a law unto himself. This was the period of the *natsa ermejja* (which could be translated in broad terms as an unrestricted license to kill). Terror had become democratized! The Addis Ababa City Council at the top and the *kebeles* with their indispensable revolutionary defence squads at the bottom were entrusted with full authority to kill any suspect. The terror targeted not

only the EPRP but also its former archrival, *Ma'ison*. Refusing to concert in life, the two organizations were united in death.

A number of factors appear to have contributed to the acceleration of 'Red Terror.' The war with Somalia gave the Derg and its agents what they interpreted as a mandate to liquidate all internal opposition mercilessly. The execution of the Derg's vice-chairman, Lt. Colonel Atnafu Abate, in November 1977 removed the last restraining influence against the vicious spiral of murder. Moreover, the splits within both the EPRP and *Ma'ison* (the group that defected to the Derg from the latter giving itself the more respectable label of *Qay Fana* or 'Red Flame') gave to the terror campaign elements with a particular zeal born of the instinct of self-preservation. Dr Alemu Abebe, the Mayor of Addis Ababa who, with Captain Legesse Asfaw, is believed to have presided over this worst phase of the terror, was a member of *Qay Fana*.

Some observers, notably René Lefort (1983: 202), have tried to give the 'Red Terror' a social dimension, characterizing it as a form of class struggle of the underprivileged members of the revolutionary defence squads settling scores with the privileged petty bourgeoisie and their children, of the old against the young, and of the soldiers against the intellectuals. This is hardly tenable. Many children of the poor perished in the government-led terror. Intellectuals were as much perpetrators as they were victims, particularly in the earlier phases. Nor, as is sometimes suggested (Clapham 1988: 55), was the lumpenproletariat exclusively the preserve of the state agents of terror. It is worth noting that the EPRP itself was successful in harnessing quite a few members of this class to serve in its assassination squads.

What distinguished the third phase from the first two phases was that the government felt no obligation to explain or justify its actions. Executions of EPRP elements in the first phase were announced by the media and given elaborate justifications. The search and destroy campaigns of the second phase were reported in the media and executed by readily identifiable agents of the state. In the third phase, by contrast, there were no public announcements. Victims were executed mostly under cover of darkness and their bodies left in the open to serve as a deterrent to all those who were harbouring similar thoughts of 'counter-revolution.' Inevitably, the process attained a level of chaos that proved embarrassing to even the most ruthless members of the Derg. As Clapham writes, 'In the final phase of the red terror, culminating in December 1977 to January 1978, it was often hard to tell who was being killed by whom' (1988: 57).

The Consequences of Red Terror

The most obvious result of the campaign of government terror was the loss of thousands of lives. There is no agreement about the number. Nor can there be, given the decentralized nature of the killing, particularly in the last phase, not to mention the partisanship that would induce an inflation or deflation of the figures. Estimates range from 5000 (Bereket cited in Babile 1997: 160) to what is dubbed a 'conservative' one of 150,000 (ibid.: 163). Amnesty International (cited in ibid.: 160) and Kiflu (1998: 269), citing EPRDF sources, give the median figures of 10,000 and 55,000, respectively, the latter for Addis Ababa alone. The figures that are sometimes thrown around also fail to distinguish between those killed and those imprisoned as part of the terror campaign. While imprisonment was understandably attended by its own trauma and anguish, at least many of the imprisoned managed to come out alive and to start leading a new life. In this respect, Babile's figure, which was computed on the assumption that only 'a fraction' of the imprisoned were released, is highly suspect.

It is also worth noting here the way society came to regard detention as a safe refuge from the horrors of 'freedom'. A common exchange between mothers at the time ran like this: 'Is your child still in detention?' 'Yes, thank God!' And then the mothers would embrace to express their satisfaction! After the madness of the Red Terror had subsided, the Derg began to examine the cases of the thousands of detainees it had kept in various prisons. A common enough retort of the police inspectors who handled the cases, to the amazement that some detainees expressed at their long detention without trial was: 'You should consider yourself lucky you were inside!'

In the end, it is not so much the quantity as the quality of those who perished in the terror campaign that is most significant. The main targets of the terror, the EPRP and *Ma'ison*, had managed to recruit between them some of the best minds of the time. A number of these perished, depriving the country of irreplaceable talent and skill. Even those who managed to survive were either forced into exile (and hence rendered irrelevant to national life) or, if they chose to stay in the country, had often lost their former drive and élan. The ramifications of this loss were felt not only in the political but also in the cultural and academic spheres. This author observed the anguish with which a mathematics professor at Addis Ababa University recalled his futile efforts to persuade an exceptionally gifted junior colleague to leave the perilous ground of political struggle and concentrate on his ultimately more rewarding academic occupation, only one day to see his body thrown at the gate of the university campus.

The end result of such unremitting terror was to produce what Clapham has called 'political *demobilisation*' (1988: 63), or what one may even characterize as political emasculation. A cowed population, stripped of its arms, reduced to seeing its loved ones lying dead on the streets, forbidden to mourn and in extreme cases even forced to celebrate, was ready to accept anything. As Babile Tola puts it, 'The aim was to crush the living by showing the cost of dissent' (1997: 158). Once it had shown the ruthless levels to which it could go, the regime could impose anything. It could force civil servants to wear uniforms or parade in grotesque military drill on Revolution Day. It could uproot peasants from their ancestral homesteads and relocate them in an ill-conceived programme of villagization. It could snatch away the youth to serve as cannon fodder in its interminable wars. Conversely, it was able to acquire the blind loyalty of a number of supporters whose hands were tainted with blood, often of their former friends and colleagues.

Ultimately, there was only one winner – Mengistu Hailemariam. The crushing of all meaningful opposition – within and outside the Derg – coupled with the military victories on the eastern and southern fronts, consolidated his grip on power. The obscure major from Harar was catapulted to a pinnacle of political might that no previous Ethiopian ruler had ever attained. He came to exercise *total* control over society and polity. After eliminating all the leftist groupings except his own, *Abyotawi Saddad* ('Revolutionary Fire'), he declared himself to be the *ma'ikal* (centre) around whom the genuine vanguard party was to be formed. That was finally accomplished in September 1984 after an elaborate recruitment process of loyal adherents. In truth, he became the *ma'ikal* not only of the party but also of national life in general.

The destruction of the EPRP and *Ma'ison* in the course of the terror spelt the end of multi-ethnic opposition and ensured the ascendancy of ethno-nationalist movements. *Ma'ison* vanished as a viable political force with the liquidation or incarceration of its leadership in the wake of the ill-prepared retreat into the underground in the summer of 1977. The EPRP opted for the rural insurrection that it had hitherto given only secondary importance. But by then, it was too late. The Tigray People's Liberation Front (TPLF), which had in the meantime grown into a credible guerrilla force, had come to resent the operations of the Ethiopian Peoples' Revolutionary Army or EPRA (as the rural armed wing of the EPRP was known) in what it considered its legitimate preserve. By 1978, the EPRA had been driven out of Tigray and forced to relocate to Gondar, where it also fizzled out before very long.

Thus, outside Eritrea, which had become a battleground between the Derg and the Eritrean People's Liberation Front (EPLF), the TPLF had come to replace the EPRP as the main opposition force to the Derg. Likewise *Ich'at*, a kindred organization of *Ma'ison*, had been superseded by the Oromo Liberation Front (OLF). This new array of ethno-nationalist opposition not only brought about the final demise of the Derg in 1991 but also determined the political culture of post-1991 Ethiopia. That culture has been long dominated by the TPLF, a product of the same intellectual climate that had produced the EPRP and *Ma'ison*, but with a decidedly different strategy for revolutionary struggle. Convinced that TPLF hegemony could only be maintained through the fostering of kindred but not independent ethno-nationalist organizations, TPLF/EPRDF has been adamantly opposed to the entry into the political process of multi-ethnic political organizations like the EPRP and *Ma'ison*. That partly explains why it has to date not faced any credible opposition – a situation that,

curiously enough, has been lamented on more than one occasion by
TPLF/EPRDF leaders themselves.[2]

[2] Eds' comment: This paper was completed before the 2005 Ethiopian elections.

References

Addis Zaman. Various issues.

Andargachew Assegid. 2000. *Ba'acher Yataqacha Rajem Guzo. Ma'ison Ba'Ityopya Hezboch Tegel West* ('A Long Journey Cut Short: *Ma'ison* in the Struggle of the Ethiopian Peoples'). Addis Ababa.

Andargachew Tiruneh. 1993. *The Ethiopian Revolution 1974–1987: A transformation from an aristocratic to a totalitarian autocracy.* Cambridge: Cambridge University Press.

Babile Tola. 1997. *To Kill a Generation: The Red Terror in Ethiopia.* 2nd edn. Washington, DC: Free Ethiopia Press.

Baczko, Bronislaw. 1994. 'The Terror before the Terror? Conditions of possibility, logic of realization,' in Keith Michael Baker (ed.). *The French Revolution and the Creation of Modern Political Culture. Volume 4. The Terror.* Oxford: Pergamon.

Bahru Zewde. 1998. 'The Military and Militarism in Africa: The Case of Ethiopia,' in Eboe Hutchful and Abdoulaye Bathily, *The Military and Militarism in Africa.* Dakar: CODESRIA.

———. 1999. 'Reflections on the changing role of intellectuals in Ethiopian politics,' in *Networking with a view to Promoting Peace. Conflict in the Horn of Africa: What can civil society do to bring about solidarity and cooperation in the region.* Addis Ababa: Heinrich Böll.

———. 2001. *A History of Modern Ethiopia 1855–1991.* 2nd edn. London/Addis Ababa/Athens: James Currey, Addis Ababa University Press, Ohio University Press.

Burgler, R.A. 1990. *The Eyes of the Pineapple. Revolutionary intellectuals and terror in democratic Kampuchea.* Saarbrücken: Verlag Breitenbach.

Clapham, Christopher. 1988. *Transformation and Continuity in Revolutionary Ethiopia.* Cambridge: Cambridge University Press.

Gabra-Sellase, *Tsahafe Te'ezaz.* 1959 EC. *Tarika Zaman zaDagmawi Menilek Negusa Nagast zaItyopya.* Addis Ababa.

Genet Ayele Anbesse. 2001. *Yeletena Colonel Mengistu Hailemariam Tizitawoch ('Memoirs of Col. Mengistu Hailemariam').* Addis Ababa: Mega Publishing Agency.

Halliday, Fred, and Maxine Molyneux. 1981. *The Ethiopian Revolution.* London: Verso.

Harbeson, John. 1988. *The Ethiopian Transformation. The Quest for the Post-Imperial State.* Boulder, CO & London: Westview Press.

Keller, Edmond J. 1988. *Revolutionary Ethiopia: From Empire to People's Republic.* Bloomington and Indianapolis, IN: Indiana University Press.

Kiflu Tadesse. 1998. *The Generation Part II. Ethiopia Transformation and Conflict: The History of the Ethiopian People's Revolutionary Party.* Lanham, MD, New York and Oxford: University Press of America.

Lefort, René. 1983. *Ethiopia: an heretical revolution?* London: Zed Books.

Mayer, Arno J. 2000. *The Furies: Violence and Terror in the French and Russian Revolutions.* Princeton, NJ: Princeton University Press.

O'Kane, Rosemary H. T. 1991. *The Revolutionary Reign of Terror: The Role of Violence in Political Change.* Aldershot and Brookfield: Edward Elgar.

Teferra Haile-Selassie. 1997. *The Ethiopian Revolution 1974-1991. From a Monarchical Autocracy to a Military Oligarchy.* London and New York: Kegan Paul International.

Tronvoll, Kjetil. 2003. 'Identities in Conflict. An ethnography of war and the politics of identity in Ethiopia, 1998–2000'. PhD dissertation, Department of Anthropology, London School of Economics and Political Science.

3

The Rights of the Accused ▨ A Human Rights Appraisal

FRODE ELGESEM &
GIRMACHEW ALEMU ANEME

Introduction

Ethiopia experienced gross and widespread human rights violations during the years 1974 to 1991. The military regime of Col. Mengistu Hailemariam – the Derg and its Worker's Party of Ethiopia (WPE) – is well-known for its brutality, especially because of the summary executions of a large number of Emperor Haile Selassie's political officials, including the Emperor himself, and the atrocious Red Terror campaign against so called anti-revolutionaries and reactionary elements. The well organized campaign of systematic violations of human rights resulted in thousands of summary executions, disappearances and cases of torture. The Derg's violent campaigns to strike down insurgencies amounted to gross violations of human rights and humanitarian laws, both under national and international law.

Following the downfall of the Derg regime in May 1991, a Transitional Government of Ethiopia (TGE) was established and assumed its responsibility under international law to exercise the state's criminal jurisdiction over those responsible for the atrocities committed by the Derg regime. In the initial phase, a large number of suspects were rounded up and detained. People were ordered to report to their *kebele*[1] about suspected perpetrators. There was a widespread practice of presenting suspects to general meetings at the *kebeles* where their cases were discussed on the basis of information gathered from witnesses. Approximately 2,000 suspects were detained by EPRDF forces in the first years after the downfall of the Derg regime, the majority of whom were detained shortly after May 1991.[2]

The Special Prosecutor's Office (SPO) was established by Proclamation 22/1992 under the TGE. In the preamble of Proclamation 22/1992, it is,

---

[1] *Kebele* is the lowest administrative level of the state, similar to ward.
[2] See the Report of the Office of the Special Prosecutor, February 1994 and Compiled Reports of EHRCO, Ethiopian Human Rights Council, December 1999, pp. 6–7, pp. 12–13 and pp. 28–9.

inter alia, underscored that the purpose of establishing the SPO was to bring to trial those responsible for the massive human rights violations during the Derg-WPE era. In addition, the preamble states that the objective was also to record for posterity the brutal offences perpetrated against the people of Ethiopia and to educate the people and make them aware of those offences in order to prevent the recurrence of such a system of government.

All the officials of the SPO were not, however, named until the end of 1992. Most of the Special Prosecutors were appointed by January 1993.[3] The TGE opted to use Ethiopia's Penal Code as the basis for the criminal charges against the perpetrators. Further, the TGE opted to use solely the domestic judiciary for the trials. No international jurisdiction was introduced in the process. The new Ethiopian Government thus undertook a tremendous task by bringing a large number of suspected perpetrators from the Derg regime to justice in domestic proceedings commonly known as the Red Terror trials.

The objective of this chapter is to assess the Red Terror trials in terms of the rights of the accused. The main issues include the right of a detainee to be brought promptly before a court of law, the right to be tried without undue delay, and the right to a hearing before the adjudicating court. Since several of the charges are punishable by death, the right to life was also an issue, including the requirement to commute a death sentence in cases of unfair trial. The section below gives an overview of Ethiopia's human rights obligations, while the following two sections identify the defendants and the charges respectively. The last section examines the rights of the accused in the Red Terror trials based on Ethiopia's national and international obligations.

Ethiopia's Human Rights Framework

After the EPRDF came to power in 1991, it convened an all-party transitional conference which endorsed a Transitional Period Charter that was used as a legal basis for the establishment and duration of the Transitional Government composed of representatives of the EPRDF and other political/ethnic organizations. The Charter adopted the Universal Declaration of Human Rights as the basis of the human rights framework of the transitional period,[4] and it pledged its commitment to the protection of human rights and the rule of law in the country. The Transitional Government of Ethiopia ratified the International Covenant on Civil and Political Rights (ICCPR),[5] the International Covenant on Economic, Social

---

[3] The Report of the Office of the Special Prosecutor (February 1994). See also Sarah Vaughan, in this volume.

[4] Transitional Period Charter of Ethiopia , Peaceful and Democratic Transitional Conference of Ethiopia, *Negarit Gazetta*, July 22, 1991.

[5] Date of Accession 11/06/93; entry into force 11/09/93.

and Cultural Rights,[6] the Convention against Torture and other Cruel, Inhuman or Degrading Treatment or Punishment[7] and the African Charter on Human and Peoples' Rights.[8]

In December 1994, the popularly elected constituent assembly adopted the draft constitution, which was passed by the Council of Representatives of the Transitional Government. On August 21, 1995, the Transitional Period Charter was replaced by a permanent constitution establishing the Federal Democratic Republic of Ethiopia (FDRE) based on ethnic federalism.[9] The FDRE Constitution proclaims that all international treaties ratified by Ethiopia are part of the law of the land.[10] In addition, Article 9, paragraph 4 of the Constitution incorporates international treaties into domestic Ethiopian law. As far as international undertakings in the field of human rights are concerned, this is strengthened by Article 10, paragraph 2 of the FDRE Constitution which requires – as a general and fundamental principle of the Constitution – that '(h)uman and democratic rights of citizens and peoples shall be respected'. In legal terms this amounts to a constitutional obligation upon all organs of the state to respect human rights as they are spelled out in the Constitution and international agreements ratified by Ethiopia. This must also be a binding guideline for the courts. Accordingly, the courts are under a constitutional duty to enforce human rights that are protected by the Constitution and secured through Ethiopia's international agreements.

The 1995 FDRE Constitution contains a comprehensive Bill of Rights.[11] Article 13 of the FDRE Constitution stipulates that the rights and freedoms of the constitution shall be interpreted in a manner conforming to the principles of the Universal Declaration of Human Rights (UDHR), International Covenants on Human Rights and international instruments adopted by Ethiopia.[12] It is not, however, clear from the Constitution what will happen in case of contradiction between the terms of the Constitution and the international agreements ratified by the country. The wording of Article 13 (2) of the FDRE Constitution appears to support the view that international human right treaties prevail in cases of conflicts with domestic laws.[13]

In addition to the FDRE Constitution and the international human

---

[6] Date of Accession 11/06/93; entry into force 11/09/93.

[7] Date of Accession 13/03/94; entry into force 13/04/94.

[8] Date of Ratification 15 June 1998.

[9] Proclamation No.1/ 1995, Proclamation of the Constitution of the Federal Democratic Republic of Ethiopia.

[10] Proclamation No.1/ 1995, Article 9.

[11] Proclamation No. 1/1995, Articles 14 – 44.

[12] Proclamation No. 1/1995.

[13] Proclamation No. 1/1995, Article 13(2) reads 'The Fundamental rights and freedoms specified in this Chapter shall be interpreted in a manner conforming to the principles of the Universal Declaration of Human Rights, International Covenants on Human Rights and international instruments adopted by Ethiopia.'

rights treaties ratified and incorporated into the domestic law of the country, the 1957 Penal Code of Ethiopia also incorporates principal human rights norms of international customary law. Genocide and crimes against humanity are expressly prohibited by Article 281 of the 1957 Penal Code.[14] Inhumane and degrading acts like torture, rape and forced disappearance are also prohibited by the 1957 Penal Code.[15] Moreover, the 1961 Criminal Procedure Code provides the accused with many rights corresponding to international human rights guarantees.[16]

In 2004, the 1957 Penal Code was repealed and replaced by the Criminal Code of the Federal Democratic Republic of Ethiopia.[17] The new Criminal Code of 2004 also contains provisions similar to the 1957 Penal Code against the crime of genocide, crimes against humanity and war crimes.[18] However, the Red Terror trials are based on the provisions of the 1957 Penal Code unless the provisions of the 2004 Criminal Code are more favourable to the defendants.[19] Thus, all references to the Ethiopian Penal Code in the body of this chapter refer to the 1957 Penal Code of imperial Ethiopia. In addition to the penal law, Ethiopia has also ratified the 1948 convention on the Prevention and Punishment of the Crime of Genocide on 1 July 1949.[20]

The Defendants

The SPO charged three groups of alleged perpetrators in the Red Terror trials.[21] The first group of defendants were policymakers and senior government and military officials of the Derg regime. *Special Prosecutor v. Colonel Mengistu Hailemariam et al.* is the prosecution of the first group of defendants with an initial list of 106 high-ranking officials of the Derg government including Colonel Mengistu Hailemariam (former

---

[14] The Penal Code of the Empire of Ethiopia 1957, Article 281.

[15] The Penal Code of the Empire of Ethiopia 1957, Article 281(a) and (c).

[16] See, for example, Article 29 of the Criminal Procedure Code which requires that detainees shall be brought before a court within 48 hours after their arrest.

[17] Proclamation No.414/2004, The Criminal Code of the Federal Democratic Republic of Ethiopia, Preface.

[18] Proclamation No.414/2004, The Criminal Code of the Federal Democratic Republic of Ethiopia Articles 269 and 270.

[19] Proclamation No.414/2004, The Criminal Code of the Federal Democratic Republic of Ethiopia, Article 5-Non-retrospective Effect of Criminal Law (1) If an act, declared to be a crime both under the repealed legislation and this Code, was committed prior to the coming into force of this Code, it shall be tried in accordance with the repealed law, Article 6-Exception: Application of more favorable Law. Where the criminal is tried for an earlier crime after the coming into force of this Code, its provisions shall apply if they are more favorable to him than those in force at the time of the commission of the crime. (See also the Conclusion in this volume where it is shown that the court used the 2004 Criminal Code during the sentence in the main Red Terror trial).

[20] See http://www.unhchr.ch/html-United Nations, Treaty series, vol. 78, p. 277.

[21] See Sarah Vaughan in this volume on the SPO.

President), Captain Fikreselassie Wegederesse (former Prime Minister), and Colonel Fiseha Desta (former Vice President). Their trial (the 'main trial') was the one that was heard by the First Criminal Bench of the Federal High Court in Addis Ababa.[22] The defendants in *Special Prosecutor v. Colonel Mengistu Hailemariam et al.* were first brought before the Central High Court of the Transitional Government of Ethiopia in October 1994. The trial was later moved to the First Criminal Bench of the Federal High Court in Addis Ababa after the establishment of the Federal Democratic Republic of Ethiopia in 1995. The two other groups were military and civilian field commanders who carried out orders as well as passed orders down, and the individuals who actually carried out many of the brutal and deadly orders. Their cases were heard by regional supreme courts throughout the country. In Addis Ababa the cases of the last two groups were heard by the Sixth Criminal Bench of the Federal High Court.

The charges follow both the formal and informal types of administrative structure within the Derg regime. Thus, both government officials involved at the formal administrative levels of the provinces, districts and sub-districts as well those involved in the various committees and sub-committees such as the Revolutionary Guards, the offices of the different mass organisations, *kebele* and the Revolutionary Campaign Coordinating Committees were charged.

Initially, the SPO charged 5,198 military and public officials of the Derg regime. About 2,258 of the defendants were charged in the regional supreme courts by delegation from the federal high court. Thus, 202 defendants were charged in Tigray region, 508 defendants in Amhara region, 421 in Southern peoples' region, 198 defendants in Harari region and 174 defendants in Somali region. Unidentified numbers of defendants were also brought before the Oromia Supreme Court. All the Red Terror cases in the regional supreme courts began in 1998 at the capital city of each region.[23]

The Charges

The SPO brought multifaceted charges against the defendants individually and collectively. All the charges were based on the national laws of the country. The following paragraphs outline the charges in *Special Prosecutor v. Colonel Mengistu Hailemariam et al.*, the leading case of the Red Terror trials.

Public Provocation and Preparation
The first charge filed by the SPO was public provocation and preparation to

---

[22] See the Conclusion in this volume.
[23] Data on the Red Terror trials in the regional states is not as clear as the cases in federal courts.

commit genocide in violation of Articles 32(1) (a)[24] and 286(a)[25] of the 1957 Penal Code. In this charge, all the defendants were accused of causing the deaths of thousands of members of different political groups in Addis Ababa and throughout the country, which they labeled as 'anti-people' and 'reactionary', by arming and organizing leaders of *kebeles*, Revolutionary Guards, Cadres and 'revolutionary comrades' as well as by inciting and openly calling for the destruction of members of political groups through public speech, pictures and writings in the public media and in various public meetings on different dates and months from 1975 to 1983.[26]

Genocide
The second charge brought by the SPO against the defendants was the commission of genocide in violation of Article 281 of the 1957 Penal Code. Article 281 of the 1957 Penal Code in its English version reads:

> Whosoever, with intent to destroy, in whole or in part, a national, ethnic, racial, religious or political group, organizes, orders or engages in, be it in time of war or in time of peace:
> (a) Killings, bodily harm or serious injury to the physical or mental health of members of the group, in any way whatsoever; or
> (b) Measures to prevent the propagation or continued survival of its members or their progeny; or
> (c) The compulsory movement or dispersion of peoples or children, or their placing under living conditions calculated to result in their death or disappearance, is punishable with rigorous imprisonment from five years to life, or, in cases of exceptional gravity, with death.[27]

The defendants were charged with planning and executing acts aimed at the extermination of political groups opposed to the Derg government in violation of Articles 32(1) (b)[28] and 281 (a) and (c) of the 1957 Penal Code. The genocide charge reads as follows:

---

[24] Article 32 of the 1957 Penal Code is entitled 'Principal Act: Offender and Co-offenders'. Article 32 (1) (a) reads '(1) A person shall be regarded as having committed an offence and punished as such if: (a) he actually commits the offence either directly or indirectly, for example by means of an animal or a natural force'.

[25] Article 286 of the 1957 Penal Code is entitled 'Provocation and preparation'. Article 286(a) reads 'Whosoever, with the object of continuing, permitting or supporting any of the acts provided for in the preceding articles [Articles 281-285]: (a) publicly encourages them, by word of mouth, images or writings-is punishable with rigorous imprisonment not exceeding five years.'

[26] *SPO v. Colonel Mengistu Hailemariam et al.*, Charge as amended on November 28, 1995 and December 2, 2002.

[27] *SPO v. Colonel Mengistu Hailemariam et al.*, Charge as amended on November 28, 1995 and December 2, 2002.

[28] Article 32 (1) (b) of the 1957 Penal Code reads '(1) A person shall be regarded as having committed an offence and punished as such if: (b) he without performing the criminal act itself fully associates himself with the commission of the offence and the intended result'.

All the defendants established the Provisional Military Administration Council or Government as of September 2, 1974 and organized themselves into a General Assembly, Standing Committee and SubCommittees and while administrating the country solely and collectively, committed or caused to be committed killings, bodily harm or serious injury to the physical and mental health of members of political groups as well as displacement calculated to result in death and disappearance of members of political groups with intent to destroy in whole or in part political groups in violation of the provisions of Articles 32 (1) (b) and 281(a) and (c) of the Penal Code by making plans and passing decisions, by establishing various institutions as well as hit squads and the 'Nebelbal' militia for investigating, torturing and killing members of political groups, and by organizing and carrying out ferreting-out campaigns, summary executions and the Red terror against members of political groups.

The SPO presented the details of the second charge in three sections. Additionally, the SPO filed alternative charges to the second charge. The following sections (A–D) explain the details of the second charge and the alternative charges.

(A) Section I –Murder

In the first section of the second charge, the SPO presented 17 counts of murder where all the defendants were accused of making plans and passing decisions for the murder of 240 individuals by labelling them as 'reactionary, anti-people, anti-revolution, oppressive members of the nobility, anarchist, EPRP members, EDU members and agents of the CIA and members of separatist groups' in violation of Articles 32(1) (b) and 281 (a) of the 1957 Penal Code. The defendants were accused of ordering the Derg operations command, the military police and the special investigation bureau to carry out their decision on the killings of the 240 individuals. The former Emperor Haile Selasse and 59 former top civil and military officials of his government are among the 240 murdered individuals listed under this section of the charge.

In the same section of the second charge, the SPO presented 153 counts of murder where the first 12 defendants (members of the Permanent Committee of the Derg) were accused of passing decisions for the murder of 1,593 individuals by labelling them as 'reactionary, antipeople, anti-revolution' and 'members of the EPRP, EDU, ELF, Shabia, OLF, Woyane and EPDM' in violation of Articles 32(1) (b) and 281 (a) of the 1957 Penal Code. The defendants were accused of ordering the military police, the National Operations Command, the administration of the province of Shewa, the administration of the province of Wollo, the administration of the province of Gojjam and the Derg investigation bureau to carry out their decision on the killings of the 1, 593 individuals listed in the 153 counts. The individuals listed as murdered according to the decision passed by the defendants under this part of the charge include Haile Fida, former leader of MEISON (Amharic acronym for All-Ethiopian Socialist Movement), and former Orthodox Church Archbishop Tewflos Geberemariam.

(B) Section II – Bodily harm, serious injury to physical and mental health
In the second section of the second charge, the first 12 defendants were accused of causing bodily harm and serious injury to physical and mental health in violation of Articles 32(1) (b) and 281 (a) of the 1957 Penal Code. According to the charges, the 12 defendants have inhumanely and systematically tortured and inflicted serious physical and mental injury on 99 individuals under three counts after illegally detaining them in various places such as the special investigation bureaus of the military police and the Derg investigation bureau after labelling them 'members of EPRP, EDU, ELF, Shabia, OLF, Woyane and EPDM'.

(C) Section III – Placement under living conditions calculated to result in death or disappearance
Under the third section of the second charge, all defendants were accused of placing 179 individuals (specified in 134 counts) who were members of different political groups under inhuman living conditions without food and medicine, endangering their lives and ultimately causing their disappearance in violation of Articles 32(1) (b) and 281 (c) of the 1957 Penal Code.

(D) Alternative charges – Aggravated homicide and grave and wilful injury
Alternatively,[29] the defendants were charged with aggravated homicide in violation of Article 522 (1) (a)[30] of the 1957 Penal Code and grave and wilful injury against the physical and mental well being of the person in violation of Article 538[31] of the 1957 Penal Code for the same acts used as the basis for the genocide charge.

---

[29] This was done according to Article 113 of the Criminal Procedure Code.
[30] Article 522 of the 1957 Penal Code is entitled 'Aggravated Homicide-Homicide in the First Degree'. Article 522(1) reads '(1) Whosoever intentionally commits homicide: (a) with such premeditation, motives or means, in such conditions of commission, or in any other aggravating circumstance, whether general (Art.81), or particular duly established (Art.83), as to betoken that he is exceptionally cruel or dangerous; or (b) as a member of a band or gang organised for carrying out homicide or armed robbery; or (c) to further or to conceal another crime; is punishable with rigorous imprisonment for life, or death.'
[31] Article 538 of the 1957 Penal Code is entitled 'Grave Wilful Injury' and reads 'Whosoever intentionally: (a) wounds a person so as to endanger his life or permanently to jeopardise his physical or mental health; or (b) maims his body or one of his essential limbs or organs, or disables them, or gravely and conspicuously disfigures him; or (c) in any other way inflicts upon another an injury or disease of a serious nature, is punishable, according to the circumstances and to the gravity of the injury, with rigorous imprisonment not exceeding ten years, or with simple imprisonment for not less than one year.'.

Unlawful Detention

The third charge against all the defendants was unlawful detention in violation of Articles 32(1) (b) and 416[32] of the 1957 Penal Code. In this charge, the SPO provided a list of 2,394 individuals illegally detained in specified places of detention described by the SPO as places without food, air, beds and medicine. All the defendants were accused of causing illegal detention by labelling the 2,394 individuals as counter-revolutionaries and members of opposition forces.[33]

Abuse of Power

The fourth charge was abuse of power in violation of Articles 32(1) (b) and 414[34] of the 1957 Penal Code. In this charge, all the defendants were accused of causing the illegal appropriation of Birr 11,521,206.15 (birr eleven million, five hundred and twenty-one thousand, two hundred and six and fifteen cents) and private cars of individuals whom they labelled as counter-revolutionaries and members of opposition forces.[35]

Analysis of Specific Rights of the Accused

A review of the Red Terror trials gives rise to a range of issues in connection with the rights of the accused. In the subsequent sub-sections, we will assess these most important issues pertaining to the accused in the Red Terror trials. The problems and issues of the rights of the accused in the Red Terror trials reflect on the general problems in the Ethiopian criminal justice system. Examples of such problems include the lack of capacity of the judiciary and the unnecessarily restrictive rules governing the defence's access to the case file.

The right of the detainees to be brought promptly before a court and to trial within reasonable time or to release

Article 9, paragraph 3 of the ICCPR reads: 'Anyone arrested or detained

---

[32] Article 416 of the 1957 Penal Code is entitled 'Unlawful Arrest or Detention' and reads 'Any public servant who arrests or detains another except in accordance with the law, or who disregards the forms and safeguards prescribed by law, is punishable with rigorous imprisonment not exceeding five years, and fine.'

[33] *SPO v. Colonel Mengistu Hailemariam et al.*, Charge as amended on November 28, 1995 and December 2, 2002.

[34] Article 414 of the 1957 Penal Code is entitled 'Abuse of Power'. Article 414(1) reads 'Public servants who with intent to procure for themselves or another an unlawful advantage or to do injury to another: (a) apart from the cases especially provided below, misuse their official position or the powers proper to their office, whether by a positive act or by a culpable omission; or (b) exceed the powers with which they are officially invested; or (c) perform official acts when they are not, or are no longer, qualified to do so, especially in the case or in consequence of incompetency, suspension, removal from office or its cessation, are punishable with simple imprisonment or fine, except where a specific provision prescribes a more severe penalty.'

[35] *SPO v. Colonel Mengistu Hailemariam et al*, Charge as amended on November 28, 1995 and December 2, 2002.

on a criminal charge shall be brought promptly before a judge [...] and shall be entitled to trial within reasonable time or to release.' According to the UN Human Rights Committee's General Comment No. 8,[36] an arrest may in any event not last longer than a few days before the detainee is brought before a judge. Article 19 (3) of the FDRE Constitution proclaims that, as a rule, an arrested person should be brought before a court of law within 48 hours. Similarly, according to Article 29 of the Ethiopian Criminal Procedure Code of 1961, the detainees are supposed to be brought before a court within 48 hours after their arrest 'or so soon thereafter as local circumstances and communications permit'.[37] A large number of suspects in connection with the atrocities during the reign of the Derg were detained shortly after May 1991 (see Sarah Vaughan in this volume). The detainees in the Red Terror trials were not brought before a court of law following their arrest.

Moreover, the rights of the detained falling within the competence of the SPO were severely curtailed by Special Public Prosecutor's Establishment Proclamation 22/92. Section 3 of Article 7 (Applicability of Existing Laws) of Proclamation 22/92 reads:

> The provisions of habeas corpus under Article 117[38] of the Civil Procedure Code shall not apply to persons detained prior to the coming into force of this proclamation for a period of six months starting from the effective date of this proclamation in matters under the jurisdiction of the Special Prosecutor as indicated in Article 6 hereof.

This part of the SPO Establishment Proclamation 22/92 restricts the rights under Article 177 of the Civil Procedure Code of 1965, according to which the detained could have applied for *habeas corpus*. Such an application lies within the jurisdiction of the High Court. The High Court may examine the lawfulness of the detention and, in cases of unlawful detention, order the immediate release of the detainee.[39] As regards the abovementioned limitation of the right to apply for *habeas corpus*, most of the suspects had been detained for more than two years when the six months limitation period expired. During these years the detainees had not been brought before a court of law.

In late 1992 and 1993, a huge number of applications for *habeas corpus* were submitted by the detainees to the Central High Court in Addis Ababa. Since the detainees had not been brought before a court – and consequently there was no court warrant for their detention – the High Court had no problem in finding that the detentions were unlawful. The High Court thus ordered the release of detainees in individual cases.

At this time, the SPO started to bring detainees before district (*woreda*)

---

[36] General Comment No. 8 regarding Liberty and Security of Person adopted on July 27, 1982.

[37] See also Proclamation 1/1995, Article 19.

[38] This is an obvious error. The correct reference is Article 177.

[39] See Article 179 (2) of the Civil Procedure Code of 1965.

courts in order to get arrest warrants. In cases where a warrant was issued, the *habeas corpus* case was closed. However, at least 900 of those originally detained were released. In addition, approximately 200 were released on bail.[40] These suspects had been detained for two years before they were brought before a court. No charges were ever brought against them.

Even after a possible initial appearance before the court of law, the rights of the defendants in the Red Terror trials were curtailed because of further restriction in their procedural rights. The Special Public Prosecutor's Proclamation 22/92 section 2 of Article 7 (Applicability of Existing Laws) reads:

> Notwithstanding the provision of sub-article (1)[41] of this Article, the provisions concerning ... the time limit concerning the submission of charges, evidence and pleadings to charges shall not be applicable to proceedings instituted by the Office.

Section 2 of Article 7 of the SPO Proclamation 22/92 seems to have allowed for indefinite detention of persons who were suspected of having participated in the Red Terror and other crimes falling under the jurisdiction of the SPO. The Central Supreme Court in the case *Special Prosecutor v. Colonel Debela Dinssa et al.* applied Article 7(2) of the Proclamation. In a decision of 22 December 2001 the Supreme Court held:

> Article 7(2) of the Special Public Prosecutor Establishment Proclamation No. 22/92 had provided that the 15 days limitation for filing a charge provided in Art. 109(1) of the Criminal Procedure Code will not apply to cases which fall within the jurisdiction of the Office of the Special Public Prosecutor. A person who will be charged by the Office of the Special Public Prosecutor cannot complain and argue that he should be released from detention unless he is charged within fifteen days.[42]

Accordingly, no time limit was prescribed within which the SPO had to file its charges. The Proclamation 22/92 thus seems to have allowed for indefinite detentions, not only during the investigation, but also after the investigation was completed.[43] The practice of the authorities and the legislative restrictions described above underscore that the right of the accused in the Red Terror trials to be brought promptly before a judge and to trial within reasonable time or to release guaranteed under Article 19 (3) of the FDRE Constitution and Article 9 of the ICCPR were not respected.

The right to be tried without undue delay

Article 14, paragraph 3 (c) of the ICCPR establishes that in the determina-

---

[40] See the Report of the Office of the Special Prosecutor (February 1994).
[41] This section confirms that in general existing laws concerning criminal procedure shall apply.
[42] Compiled Reports of EHRCO, Ethiopian Human Rights Council, December 1999, p. 177.
[43] See the conclusion in this volume on the issue of period of limitation.

tion of any criminal charge against an accused, everyone shall be entitled to the 'minimum rights' of being 'tried without undue delay'. Similarly Article 20(1) of the Ethiopian Constitution provides that the accused has the right to fair trial without undue delay.[44] Since the defendants were detained also at the pre-trial stage, this guarantee overlaps with the above-mentioned right to be tried within reasonable time; once they actually were charged they were entitled to judgment 'without undue delay' (Nowak 1993: 257). It depends on the special circumstances of each case whether final judgment has been rendered 'without undue delay'. In the Red Terror cases, however, several general features of the criminal proceedings support the conclusion that there was undue delay. The delays can be attributed to both the general handling by the SPO of the Red Terror trials, the lack of capacity of the Ethiopian judiciary and the inefficiency of the criminal procedure.

The Special Prosecutor's Office

The failure of the SPO to expeditiously investigate and prosecute the cases was one major cause of undue delay. For instance, in the first phase of the main Red Terror trial in Addis Ababa, the court allocated two days each week for the trial. However, the SPO did not manage to bring witnesses to the trial, and the court thus had to slow down the pace of the proceedings by allocating just one day a week (Thursdays) for the trial.

The failure of the SPO to efficiently investigate and prosecute the defendants was caused by multiple factors.[45] Initially, the SPO suffered from a shortage of financial resources and lack of skilled manpower commensurate with the amount of cases to be investigated and prosecuted. The Office failed to attract highly experienced lawyers because of its unattractive working conditions (Mehari Redae 2000:4). The fact that the defendants and witnesses were moved all over the country also added to the problem. The disappearance of many suspects and the ensuing procedural requirements to try them *in absentia* also contributed to the slow pace of the trials.

There was also little or no support from investigative institutions such as the police, for the SPO had exclusive power over the investigation. The investigations were more or less completed after three years, i.e. by late 1995; theoretically all cases were then ready for trial (Elgesem 1998: 7). Nevertheless, the actual criminal charges were delayed for several years in most Red Terror cases throughout the regions. The aim of the SPO to expose and record the historical damage perpetrated by the Derg regime also contributed to the long delay in the proceedings. The objective of the SPO (as noted in the preamble to the SPO Proclamation) to establish, for public knowledge and for posterity, a historical record of the abuses of the Mengistu regime guided its preparation of the trial

---

[44] Proclamation 17/1995.
[45] See Sara Vaughan in this volume.

against the top officials. Accordingly, the greater proportion of the witnesses prepared for that trial would not be required in order to obtain a guilty verdict.

The Judiciary

Following the downfall of the Derg regime, the TGE found it necessary to restructure the judiciary. At the outset, judges who had been officials or members of the WPE under the Derg were not allowed to continue as judges. However, a large number of former judges who were not WPE members continued to serve in the judiciary. Furthermore, the Transitional Government appointed new judges. As a second move, many judges were purged when the new FDRE Constitution came into effect.[46] The Federal Government vetted the judges and re-appointed only those who were deemed fit for judgeship. For the rest, their tenure was terminated. Judges were purged at all levels of the judiciary, from the Supreme Court down to the *woreda* courts. The Government describes this as a necessary 'clearing of the deck'. It must be recalled that the Transitional Government had guaranteed that the tenure of judges could only be terminated when the judge reached retirement age, or in cases of illness, insanity, breach of discipline, conviction of criminal offence or manifest inability or inefficiency.[47] In relation to several of the ousted judges, it could *not* be argued that the conditions of dismissal were fulfilled. Many of the judges who previously served in the judiciary were experienced lawyers with legal training on a high level.

The purging of a large number of Ethiopian judges diminished the capacity of the judiciary and added to the problems of an overloaded system. In Addis Ababa alone, the number of High Court benches was reduced from 20 to 6 (Elgesem 1998: 16). It seems to be common ground that one of the acute problems of the Ethiopian judiciary is the enormous backlog of cases. In 1998 there were approximately 71,000 pending cases in Addis Ababa, yet only 53 judges were given the task of working down that caseload (Elgesem 1998: 16). In Region 3, approximately 140,000 cases were pending at the beginning of 1998. The number of cases seemed to be increasing rather than decreasing. The Supreme Court in Region 3 was overloaded with cases, and only the most urgent cases were dealt with. Other cases were not entertained at all (ibid.: 21).

It is also often the case that criminal trials in Ethiopia are not conducted consecutively. Even when the case is ready for trial, the court will not allocate time for a complete, consecutive hearing from the start. The trial will proceed with several adjournments, and each hearing will only cover a limited part of the trial, e.g. the reading out of the charges, hearing of a few witnesses etc., before a new adjournment is given. Often there are long periods between hearings. The hearings often last for just a few

---

[46] For a critical assessment, see Elgesem 1998, pp. 14–16.
[47] See Article 17 of the Independence of the Administration of Justice Proclamation No. 23/1992. See also G.A.Aneme in this volume on the judiciary.

hours before a new adjournment is given. Such non-consecutive trials add significantly to the delays in the criminal system.

These observations underpin the difficulty of bringing to justice a large number of perpetrators from the former regime – and to record for history the crimes of Mengistu's reign – by a domestic judiciary. This ambitious, twofold agenda is on top of the judiciary's ordinary caseload which they were already unable to manage. The institution of the Red Terror trials in 1994 added significantly to the judiciary's problems throughout the country, and it simply became impossible for the judiciary to secure the minimum rights of detainees and accused both in the Red Terror trials and in ordinary criminal cases.

The slow pace of the Red Terror trials was illustrated by the fact that, in the main Red Terror trial *(Special Prosecutor v. Colonel Mengistu Hailemariam et al.)*, the Court had heard only 720 of the prosecution's witnesses from November 1995 until the beginning of 2001. Subsequently the SPO submitted documentary and visual evidence to the Court. When the prosecution concluded its presentation of evidence, the High Court – according to Ethiopian Criminal Procedure – reviewed the case and assessed whether the accused had cases to answer. This review by the Court lasted for most of 2002. It was not until January 2003 that the High Court was able to rule that the accused former top Derg officials had cases to answer.

In accordance with court practice in criminal cases, the defence was not given access to the documentary evidence until it was submitted to the court by the prosecution, i.e. after the hearing of witnesses was concluded. Thus, defence lawyers had to start the time-consuming work of acquainting themselves with the documents at a very late stage of the proceedings. Indeed, the defence lawyers requested to have access to the documents already at the start of the proceedings, but the court decided against the defence in this matter. The defence concluded its presentation of evidence in the beginning of 2006. In March 2006 the Court announced that a verdict would be handed down on 23 May 2006. This was, however, again delayed, and the verdict was handed down in December 2006.[48] The proceedings in the main Red Terror trial and other similar trials were extremely delayed, especially when taking into account the fact that the defendants were detained throughout the proceedings.

The right to a hearing before the adjudicating court
It is an essential element in the fair trial guarantees of Article 14 of the ICCPR that the accused shall be confronted with witnesses in a hearing before the judges that will ultimately decide on the case. This element of the fair trial guarantee is formulated clearly by the European Court of Human Rights:

An important element in criminal proceedings is also the possibility of

---

[48] See conclusion in this volume on verdict and sentence of the main Red Terror trial.

an accused to be confronted with the witness in the presence of the judge who ultimately decides the case. This principle of immediacy is an important guarantee of fairness as the observations made by the court about the demeanour and credibility of a witness may have important consequences for an accused. A change in the composition of the trial court after the hearing of an important witness should therefore normally lead to the rehearing of that witness.[49]

Due to the prolonged trial, there were many changes on the bench of the Federal High Court hearing the Red Terror cases. In general, the work in the divisions dealing with the Red Terror cases (the First and the Sixth division of the Federal High Court in Addis Ababa) was not popular among the judges. Information from the President of the Federal High Court[50] indicated that one or two judges could be removed from the bench every second year. Also some judges retired, some were promoted to the Supreme Court and some left the division for other reasons. This demonstrates that the final set of judges in the trials had not heard the case as from the start. It is clear that the witnesses were not reheard in front of the new judges. One example illustrates the discontinuity of the situation: one judge sitting on the bench of First Criminal Division of the High Court left the Court in January 2003 to pursue postgraduate studies at the Civil Service College, yet, after finishing his studies, he resumed his position as a judge on the same bench in January 2005. The defence had by then started to present their evidence approximately a year earlier.[51] The same situation also occurred in the regional supreme courts. Thus, the Red Terror trials exhibited a serious breach of the fair trial guarantees that envisage the uninterrupted presence of all parties involved in the case until the final decision is passed.

The right to counsel
A basic right of the accused is the right to counsel. The FDRE Constitution and international human rights treaties ratified by the country provide that the accused have the right to legal counsel. In cases of serious offences, the FDRE Constitution provides that the state should assist an indigent defendant in the provision of legal counsel.[52] In the case of the Red Terror trials, the state provided legal counsel at its own expense to the defendants who asserted that they were indigent and who were accused of serious human rights violations including genocide and crimes against humanity. Initially some of the top Derg officials were better-off than the prosecution, as they were provided with the best lawyers the country

---

[49] Judgment of March 9, 2005 by the European Court of Human Rights in *Pitkänen v. Finland*, para 58.
[50] Information given to Frode Elgesem in an interview with the President of the Federal High Court in Addis Ababa on 3 February 2005.
[51] Information given to Frode Elgesem in an interview with the President of the Federal High Court in Addis Ababa on 3 February 2005.
[52] Proclamation No.1/1995 Article 20.

could provide. However, the majority of the defendants in the Red Terror trials were left to the newly established public defender's office.[53] The public defender's office was a new institution established in 1993 with a few lawyers, most of whom had no formal training and experience in high level proceedings.[54] Public defenders lacked formal skills to deal with the complex national and international legal concepts involved in the trials. Moreover, the number of public defenders involved is completely out of proportion to the number of the defendants who needed the service from the office. The shortage of public defenders in the trials caused the assignment of one public defender to represent defendants with conflicting interests, such as the superior defendant and the subordinate defendant in a given action.[55] Thus, the lack of institutionalized public defence experience in the country and the lack of skilled and efficient human resources had a negative impact on the rights to counsel of the defendants in the Red Terror trials.

The issue of capital punishment
More than 20 defendants in the Red Terror trials have been sentenced to death, but no such punishment has been carried out yet. The Federal High Court passed the first death sentence in *absentia* in 1999 against Getachew Terba, former Derg security officer, for crimes against humanity.[56] In 2002 Zeleke Tilahun was sentenced in *absentia* to death by hanging after being found guilty by the Federal High Court of having 'beaten and executed 12 people'.[57] The Federal High Court also sentenced Colonel Tesfaye WoldeSelasie, the ex-security head of the Derg, and General Legesse Belayneh, former head of the central investigation department of the Derg, to death in August 2005.[58] Furthermore, the Federal High Court handed down the death sentence to Major Melaku Tefera, former administrator of Gondar, in December 2005.[59] In April 2008, the Federal High Court passed death sentences on five top military officers in *absentia* responsible for the atrocious attack on Hawzen village in Tigray in 1980, killing several hundreds of villagers.[60] In May 2008, the Federal Supreme Court imposed death sentences on 13 of the top Derg officials including Colonel Mengistu Hailemariam.[61]

Under international law, the death penalty is not yet fully prohibited.

[53] Trial Observation and Information Project (2000), Reports from the observations made in 1996, p. 10.
[54] Trial Observation and Information Project (2000), Reports from the observations made in 1996, p. 10.
[55] Trial Observation and Information Project (2000), Reports from the observations made in 1996, p. 10.
[56] See http://web.amnesty.org/library/Index/ENGAFR250101999?open&of=ENG-ETH.
[57] *The Reporter*, Ethiopian weekly private newspaper, August 12, 2002.
[58] See http://www.news24.com, 11 August 2005.
[59] See http:// www.int.iol.co.za, 9 December 2005.
[60] See Reuters, 'Ethiopia sentences five Mengistu officers to death', 5 April 2008.
[61] See concluding chapter of this volume.

However, there is a gradual trend towards its abolishment (see Nowak 1993: 114). For instance, Article 1 of the Second Optional Protocol to the ICCPR obligates a state to take 'all necessary measures to abolish the death penalty within its jurisdiction.'[62] Nonetheless, in cases that may entail capital punishment, the procedural guarantees of fair trial must be rigorously observed.[63] Unfair trial in capital cases may entail a breach of Article 6 of the ICCPR, which protects the right to life.[64] Among other things, it is 'axiomatic that legal assistance be available in capital cases' lest the right to life be violated.[65] Supporting this argument, the practice of the UN Human Rights Committee shows that the death penalty may not be imposed on the basis of proceedings that breached any of the minimum rights of the accused such as the right to speedy trial and the right to be promptly brought before the court of law (see Nowak 1993: 118–20).

It has been shown in the above sections that there were serious breaches of the rights of the accused in the Red Terror trials. Ethiopian courts and authorities are under an international obligation to reject or commute the death sentences in order to remedy the breaches suffered by the accused.[66] Thus, following the above argument, the implementation of capital punishment in the Red Terror trials will be a violation of the rights of the accused.

Conclusion

Despite their ambitious beginning, the Ethiopian Red Terror trials have exhibited serious breaches of the rights of the accused. The causes range from the inefficient norms and working methods of the SPO and the courts to legislative restrictions imposed such as the rights of *habeas corpus* and timely access to evidence of the accused.

Detention based on public opinions in the *kebeles*, wide powers for the SPO to detain suspects indefinitely and lack of review of detention by the courts, opened up for arbitrary detention. The SPO was given unduly wide powers to detain suspects, and did not pursue the prosecution with sufficient diligence and speed. The large number of detainees who had been released after years in detention without any charges being brought against them underscores the seriousness of the situation.

The delays led to the violation of the rights of the accused to be brought promptly before a court of law as guaranteed by Article 9(3) of

---

[62] Second Optional Protocol to the ICCPR, entered into force on July 11, 1991.

[63] See e.g. the Human Rights Committee's views in *Pinto v. Trinidad and Tobago*, Case no. 232/1987.

[64] See also Proclamation 1/1995, Article 15.

[65] See the UN Human Rights Committee's views in *Robinson v. Jamaica*, Case no. 223/1987.

[66] See the UN Human Rights Committee's views in *Larrañaga v. the Phillipines*, case no. 1421/2005; See also the conclusion of this volume on the reasoning of the majority of the court on the sentence for rejecting the death penalty.

the ICCPR and Article 29 of the Ethiopian Criminal Code. After the appearance of the detained in the courts, the trial process took too long while the accused were being brought before different judges who had not heard the witnesses and examined the evidence in the cases from the beginning. Thus, the fair trial requirements of Article 14 of the ICCPR and Article 20 of the FDRE Constitution such as the right to speedy trial and the right to be brought before the adjudicating court of the accused were not respected. The seriousness of the violations is exacerbated by the fact that most of the charges carry the death penalty. International law and practice dictate that the Ethiopian courts and authorities should reject or commute the death penalty in the Red Terror trials in light of the series of rights of the accused that were not respected and protected for one reason or another.

References

Proclamation No.414/2004, The Criminal Code of the Federal Democratic Republic of Ethiopia, *Negarit Gazeta*, Addis Ababa.

Proclamation No.1/1995, Proclamation of the Constitution of the Federal Democratic Republic of Ethiopia, August 21,1995.

Proclamation 22/92, Proclamation for the Establishment of the Special Prosecutor's Office, 1992, *Negarit Gazeta*, Addis Ababa.

Transitional Period Charter of Ethiopia, Transitional Conference of Ethiopia, *Negarit Gazeta*, July 22, 1991.

The Civil Procedure Code of Ethiopia, Decree No.52 of 1965, *Negarit Gazeta*, Extraordinary Issue No. 3 of 1965, Addis Ababa.

The Criminal Procedure Code, *Negarit Gazeta*, Extraordinary Issue No. 1 of 1961.

Penal Code of the Empire of Ethiopia, *Negarit Gazeta*, Extraordinary Issue No.1 of 1957.

General Assembly Resolution 260 A (III) 9 December 1948, Convention on the Prevention and Punishment of the Crime of Genocide.

Elgesem, Frode 1998. *The Derg Trials in Context – A study of some aspects on the Ethiopian Judiciary*, Human Rights Report No.1, Norwegian Institute of Human Rights, University of Oslo.

Mehari Redae. 2000. 'The Ethiopian Genocide Trial,' *Ethiopian Law Review*, vol.1: 1-26.

Nowak, Manfred. 1993. *U.N. Covenant on Civil and Political Rights – CCPR Commentary*, Kehl am Rhein.

Trial Observation and Information Project (2000), *Consolidated Summary and reports from observations made in 1996, 1997, 1998, 1999*, compiled and distributed by NIHR's project 'Ethiopia's Red Terror Trials: Africa's war tribunal,' Norwegian Center for Human Rights, Faculty of Law, University of Oslo.

4
The Role of the Special Prosecutor's Office

SARAH VAUGHAN

Introduction

This chapter looks at some of the activities of the Ethiopian Special Prosecutor's Office (SPO) and its relationships with other key players in the prosecution of members of the former Ethiopian government for alleged crimes against humanity and genocide. It is not primarily concerned with evaluating the work done by the SPO. Nor does it assess whether pursuing the particular course of action chosen by Ethiopia in attempting to put down a marker against past impunity has been more or less successful than those adopted elsewhere, be they domestic or international processes. Rather, the chapter confines itself to some observations and reflections on how the SPO set about its work of investigation and prosecution; the extent to which policy decisions about the implementation of its mandate may have constrained a timely process; and how it related to four categories of interested parties: the Ethiopian judiciary, the international community, the executive of the Ethiopian government, and the Ethiopian public. In addition, some space is devoted to detailing different aspects of the work of the SPO, since relatively little has been published to date about the nature of the activities involved.[1]

SPO's establishment – and the crisis of habeas corpus
The Office of the Chief Special Prosecutor of the Transitional Government of Ethiopia, was legally established by Proclamation 22/1992 issued by the Transitional Government of Ethiopia (TGE) on 8 August 1992, a full

---

[1] The chapter draws on commentary and trial observations material, most of which is in the public domain, as well as press releases, newspaper reports, and Ethiopian TV broadcasts. It also draws on the author's experiences – and observations suggested by colleagues – during a period of secondment to the SPO in 1994 (with support from the Danish section of the International Commission of Jurists and Danida). I am grateful to Rodolfo Mattarollo and Roger Briottet for conversations at the time and since.

thirteen months after it had itself been established.[2] This proclamation gave the SPO what has been interpreted as a twofold mandate. Firstly it would

> have the power to conduct investigation and institute proceedings in respect of any person having committed or responsible for the commission of an offence by abusing his position in the party, the government, or mass organisation under the Derg-WPE [Workers' Party of Ethiopia] regime. (TGE 1992: Art.6)

Meanwhile, the preamble of the proclamation also set out a second area of responsibility:

> It is in the interest of a just historical obligation to record for posterity the brutal offences, the embezzlement of property perpetrated against the people of Ethiopia and to educate the people and make them aware of those offences in order to prevent the recurrence of such a system of government. (TGE 1992: Preamble)

Although the SPO was legally established in August 1992, its officials, including the Chief Special Prosecutor, Girma Wakjira, formerly a lawyer in the Chief Prosecutor's Office,[3] were not named until the end of that year, and most of the team of 34 Special Prosecutors were appointed only in early 1993. By this time, many of the 1,980 individuals arrested, either as the EPRDF came to power in May 1991 or over the course of the following months, had already been detained for nearly two years without charge.

The proclamation which established the SPO provided for the suspension of *habeas corpus* provisions in SPO cases for a period of six months (TGE 1992: Art.7.3). By the time the SPO was operational, this period was already expiring, and the Office spent the first six months of 1993 responding to more than 1,200 *habeas corpus* writs and determining the legitimacy of ongoing detention. In this period, 900 of those originally detained by the EPRDF or TGE were released on bail, and a further 220 were additionally arrested. The detainee population was reported to be 1,315 in mid-1994, but had risen again to more than 2,300 by the time of the second round of charging in early 1997. According to the SPO:

> By June 1993, all [detainees at that time] were held legally in accordance with Article 59 of the Ethiopian Criminal Procedure relating to preventive detention. According to the 'remand and custody' provision of this code, if the SPO was able to present evidence implicating the accused in a serious crime it was possible for a preliminary detention to be ordered. Subsequently the SPO has been able to demonstrate to

---

[2] To give a sense of the scope of legislation under consideration at the time, the SPO proclamation was sandwiched between one providing for the 'Establishment of the National Election Board', and another providing for the 'Independence of Judicial Administration'.

[3] One of the few senior lawyers reputed not to have joined the WPE during the Derg period, Girma Wakjira had been appointed Vice Minister of Justice by the TGE during the period 1991–2.

the courts' satisfaction that the investigation is progressing and that sufficient evidence exists against the accused to support a preventive detention in order to allow the investigation to continue. (1994: 5)

The SPO's opposition to *habeas corpus* and the wider release of suspects was supported by the 1993 Supreme Court ruling which reasoned that because of the special nature of the crimes involved 'the SPO detainees should remain imprisoned without a specific time limit – but not indefinitely – until they were charged.' (Amnesty International 1996). The delay was also supported by the legislative power of the SPO which provided that '... the time limit concerning the submission of charges, evidence and pleading to charges shall not be applicable to proceedings instituted by the Office [of the SPO]' (TGE 1992: Art. 7.2).

Due to this situation, the SPO was running to catch up from the outset of its establishment in 1992/1993. It already was operating at or beyond the margins of what was legal; moreover, it was also widely criticized domestically and by the international human rights community for infringing on the rights of detainees, both to know the charges levelled against them and for a speedy trial. It seems likely that the strong early criticism of what, with hindsight, looked like relatively short delays may well have blunted the effect on the SPO and the government of such criticism as it escalated later, when delays gravely protracted the proceedings. The situation certainly curtailed the willingness of some, particularly in the international community, to engage with and give support for the early processes of prosecution (Howland 2000).

The early 1990s: training, investigating, and documenting evidence
A number of governments, however, did provide support to the SPO and its activities, responding to a twelve-month request circulated in July 1993 for assistance in the three areas of computerization, infrastructure, and international technical assistance, for a total sum of just under one million US dollars (ibid.: 419). This was sought to supplement an annual Ethiopian government budget subsidy to the SPO of approximately a third of a million US dollars. A diverse group of North American and European donors responded to the request which was quickly funded to well over 80 per cent. SPO donors include: the Canadian International Development Agency, CIDA; the Danish International Development Administration, DANIDA; the government of France; the International Commission of Jurists, Danish Section; the Governments of the Netherlands and Norway; the Swedish International Development Agency, Sida; the UN Development Programme; the UN Commission on Human Rights, and the US Agency for International Development, USAID. Other organisations which supported the work of the SPO in one way or another include: the American Bar Association; the Black Lion Hospital in Addis Ababa; the Carter Centre, Emory University; the ICRC; the International Human Rights Law Group; the John Merck Foundation; Physicians for

Human Rights; and the Yohannes Weir Foundation (SPO 1994; EAAF 2002).

Generous funding saw a rapid and dramatic influx of computer equipment, vehicles, and expatriate advisors. The support was targeted to help overcome a series of interrelated difficulties which the SPO had identified. First, the Special Prosecutors were dealing with a specialized body of Ethiopian law, of which they – along with most others – had little experience. As in many countries, international law relating to crimes against humanity was not taught in Ethiopia in the early 1990s. Second, the SPO faced a range of logistical difficulties in relation to the collection of evidence on an unusually large scale. The volume of documentary evidence to be collected and analysed was often compared with that gathered in Germany in the wake of the Second World War (SPO 1994: 5). Meanwhile, the accumulation of witness testimony required travel to remote parts of the country and interpretation from a number of Ethiopian languages. Once these logistical obstacles in data collection had been overcome, challenges merely shifted to the analysis, collation, and organization of a huge quantity of evidence. All of these problems were only exacerbated by inadequate levels of infrastructure.

The SPO's strategy for investigation and charging suspects classified the type of crime and the position held by the suspect at the time of the Red Terror into three categories, thereby arranging and ranking the investigations for prosecution accordingly. Group one comprised the policy and decision makers; group two was made up of the field commanders, military and civilian; and group three consisted of the actual alleged perpetrators of many of the crimes. The Special Prosecutors were organized into four groups of teams dealing with (a) high officials, (b) war crimes, (c) forced relocation, and (d) red terror (on this last see the chapter by Frode Elgesem and Girmachew A. Aneme in this volume). Five prosecutors were assigned to investigate those suspected of crimes in the first group who had held positions of high authority within the Derg or WPE. Their work focused principally on the analysis of government documentation, including records of meetings and decisions which may have authorised or ordered crimes. They were also involved in pursuing extradition proceedings relating to the large number of suspects in this category who had fled Ethiopia.[4] The Forced Relocation Team spent a year reviewing and selecting from government documentation relating to this issue and gathering witness testimony. The War Crimes Team of three prosecutors focused closely on the record of the Ethiopian military between 1974 and 1991 and worked in close collaboration with the largest department, the seven Red Terror teams made up of 14 Special Prosecutors, with a further 9 assigned regionally.

[4] Ethiopia was not party to extradition treaties with any of the countries in question, and, despite protracted debate and some correspondence about the case of Mengistu Hailemariam, who had fled to Zimbabwe and remains there at the time of writing, little progress was made in relation to extradition.

Investigative work was divided regionally. In Harar, for instance, 125 high- and low-ranking defendants were investigated for both war crimes and Red Terror related charges. Comprehensive documentation of government activities and decisions over the relevant period provided a wealth of potential evidence. In Tigray, by comparison, cases against 76 defendants were built up with greater reliance on witness testimony, as the documentary record was patchy, primarily as a result of the war in the north.

Evidence collection and analysis was clearly an early priority for the SPO, and the collection of documentation from the Derg government archives dominated its work throughout 1993 and early 1994. By mid-1994, 309,778 pages of relevant government documents had been collected, under a process which became an urgent and high-security operation. Over 300 contract data collectors were recruited during 1993 and 1994, and were assigned throughout the *kebeles*[5] of Addis Ababa, Nazreth, South Shoa and Arssi, as well as the more remote parts of the country to compile material. They worked under the scrutiny and co-ordination of Special Prosecutors. Along with the SPO, the Ministry of the Interior and the non-governmental Anti-Red Terror Committee were involved in the selection of contract staff, monitoring the process on behalf of the government and of victims and their families. Special measures were put in place to ensure the security of documents and integrity of evidence collected. Teams, including representatives from each of the monitoring bodies, 'were put together in such a way that their members were not previous personal acquaintances' (SPO 1994: 13). Additionally, a complex system of multiple receipts was instituted to keep track of documents removed as evidence.

Security of the SPO's work, and of its Special Prosecutors, was a pressing consideration in the early 1990s when suspects continued to be apprehended in different parts of the country and new suspects were added to the list of those wanted – some of them even members of the TGE. With political tensions still running high, there was widespread fear of threats to destroy or tamper with evidence, or to undermine or unnerve the work of the Special Prosecutors, many of whom were young and inexperienced, and frequently feared for their personal safety. The security of projects to computerise evidence was anxiously discussed. The Chief Special Prosecutor traveled with an armed escort, and visitors to his Office were required to pass stringent security checks. In retrospect it seems likely that these security concerns contributed to the develop-ment of an embattlement syndrome in the SPO. Special Prosecutors were engaged in controversial, demanding and often distressing or dangerous work, and were unable to confide their concerns and fears to outsiders for fear of compromising security. A number of observers have remarked that the SPO was often a difficult place to work. Given the nature and context

---

[5] *Kebele* is the lowest administrative level of the state, similar to ward.

of its work perhaps this should have been less than surprising.

The other substantive area of work undertaken in this period involved training of different kinds, from the training of documentation collectors and computer processors inputting data, to legal seminars and moot court sessions designed to develop the prosecutors' tactics. International consultants were assigned to the war crimes and forced relocation prosecutorial teams to help them gather secondary evidence, evaluate cases, and devise strategies for further research and evaluation. Much time was spent in considering which laws were applicable. As an outgrowth of this an *amicus curiae*, or legal advisory to the court, was drafted and reviewed by a range of legal experts around the world. In 1994 the Chief Special Prosecutor also made a visit to the UN Commission for Human Rights in Geneva.

One of the most successful areas of the SPO's international collaboration throughout its life has been with the Argentinean Forensic Anthropology Team (EAAF), members of which conducted a series of visits to Ethiopia. In 1993 and 1994 they conducted excavations and exhumations at graves in Kotebe near Addis Ababa, and Hauzien in Tigray. They were able to conduct preliminary training in forensic techniques, as 'Ethiopia has no forensic experts, and has relied on international assistance in human rights cases involving forensic analysis' (EAAF 1998: 81). In 1996 and 1997, EAAF extended their work to Butajira and Alaba Kulito in Southern Ethiopia, returning in 2002 to provide testimony about their findings and the evidence it had produced. With Argentinean help, the SPO has been able to create a map of mass graves throughout Ethiopia (ibid.: 80).

The last decade: bringing charges and prosecuting the cases[6]
The trial of the first category of 'high officials' opened in December 1994, with 46 defendants, and a further 24 individuals including former President Col. Mengistu Hailemariam charged *in absentia*. By the end of May 1995, the central High Court began hearing the response of the SPO to counter charges from defence lawyers of the accused former Derg officials in this group. The court soon adjourned the trial until October 1995 'stating that it will close for the rainy season and the remaining one month is too short to reach a decision' (UNEUE 1995). The protracted delays had already begun. By mid-1996 'after frequently adjourned pre-trial proceedings, the trial [was] only at the stage of hearing witnesses for the first charges in the prosecution case' (AI 1996) and Amnesty International renewed its criticism of the continuing detention without charge of thousands of others, which it was feared 'could stretch into the year 2000 or beyond' (ibid.).

More than five thousand additional defendants were charged in early 1997, over two thousand of them in prison, and nearly three thousand

---

[6] See also Frode Elgesem and Girmachew A. Aneme in this volume on the charges.

others *in absentia*. By 2001 there were still over 2,200 former officials in prison awaiting trial (EAAF 2003). Dramatic testimony was given by the Argentine Forensic Anthropology Team in April 2002 in relation to their findings at a clandestine grave in Kotebe on the outskirts of Addis Ababa where 30 bodies were excavated with green nylon cord 'encircling the disarticulated cervical vertebrae' of 29 of the 30 (see EAAF 2003). Work conducted was able to provide positive identification of a total of 13 of the bodies, tying them to a group of prisoners from Kombolcha and Makalawi prisons, who disappeared from the latter on 7 October 1979. EAAF members were able to give evidence about their excavation and investigations in Kotebe, confirming their view that the cause of the deaths was violent strangulation. Unusually in Ethiopian judicial proceedings, forensic evidence, including skeletons, ligatures, and material used to conceal the grave, were displayed in the courtroom, and the court visited the site at Kotebe.

Evaluating the Policy Decisions: Was an SPO the Right Way to Go?

The decision to deal with the alleged crimes of the Derg regime by means of domestic judicial processes has been debated and criticized from two perspectives: first, that the process should not have been a court one, that a reconciliatory rather than an adversarial and punitive process would have been more desirable; and second, that it should not have been a domestic court process, as an international tribunal would have had more legitimacy and credibility. It seems to me that there is something to be said in defence of the principles behind the Ethiopian decisions on both counts.

From a social science perspective, domestic court processes are preferable *per se* to those conducted under international tribunals in the fight against impunity. The sociological logic behind this perspective is as follows: the fight against criminality and impunity is one waged in the arena of social norms, and is only secondarily about following legal rules or pursuing retributive justice. Centrally and fundamentally, domestic court proceedings are about seeking to change collective patterns of belief and behaviour. Entrenching collective patterns of belief which condemn criminality and impunity requires more than just enforcing laws. It requires constant iteration of such enforcement, and the fostering of a sense of *collective* ownership and approval of such processes, and disapproval or rejection of their contravention. Tribunal or reconciliation processes which are driven from outside a country or a community's borders are less likely to be effective in entrenching social change than domestic processes. This is especially likely to be true where domestic processes are widely watched, endorsed, debated, and regarded as legitimate and fair.

The problem with domestically held judicial proceedings – even those held under international auspices – is that they can usually only be undertaken after those against whom they are brought have been conclusively ousted from power, normally by being defeated in war. As a result, court proceedings from Nuremberg to Rwanda have been critiqued as 'victor's justice,' an accusation which in itself potentially does much to vitiate their perceived legitimacy. In this situation, legal and human rights debates about the quality, probity, and speed of proceedings influence decisions about their overall legitimacy. A sociological response, however, might nevertheless continue to emphasize the important role of domestic proceedings – even where less than perfect – in changing national norms and attitudes for the future. The extent to which opportunities to do this were pursued in the Ethiopian case are discussed in subsequent sections.

The way the Red Terror trials were set up and the SPO established in Ethiopia may perhaps have fed particularly strong tensions between the achievement of just (and speedy) trials of individuals, and the enhancement of collective national processes of coming to terms with the past and changing the future. The so-called dual mandate of the SPO is often seen as creating particular tensions and problems for the pursuit of justice and the rights of the defendants.

Many commentators, including some in this volume, have seen this duality as being at the root of the difficulties which have beset the SPO and the Red Terror trials.This is particularly relevant to the problems of speedy trial discussed by Frode Elgesem and Girmachew A. Aneme in this volume. Even the SPO itself has described the mandate for investigation/prosecution and for the creation of an historical record as 'broad and ambitious':

> Implicit in it is the acceptance by the TGE of its international legal obligation to investigate and bring to justice those involved in heinous crimes. However, the mandate goes further than this: it represents a policy choice as to how a society should best deal with past abuses to create a more democratic future. The policy choice which has been made in Ethiopia is to expose those involved in abuses and to sanction them. (SPO 1994: 3)

However, as indicated above, it might be argued that the twofold mandate, so far from representing a unified policy choice, potentially set up an inherently problematic dichotomy, with activities to promote the second part of the mandate (a historical record) undermining the successful attainment of the first (just trials). However, an alternative argument must be considered against the notion that the delays were the result of working with a particularly ambitious or dual mandate. Many of the problems of a speedy trial would seem likely to have been encountered even without the second component of the mandate. In fact, at the time of writing, the SPO has made little apparent progress in implementing this second component in establishing a public historical record of the events of the Red Terror and Derg period.[7] Given the circumstances of the Ethiopian proceedings, and the nature and scope of the crimes in question, it is arguable that any just approach to the primary element – that of investigating, charging, and prosecuting alleged perpetrators – was already inherently likely to jeopardize such rights as that of a speedy trial. This is an argument successfully made by the SPO in a request to the international community for support as early as July 1993:

> Whilst it is possible to charge certain defendants today, the SPO is reticent to do so. Frankly, the individuals we would charge today would be charged simply because a particular file cabinet was searched first, as opposed to a policy decision based upon a full understanding of the environment in which the prosecutions will be held. Given the present climate in Ethiopia and our desire to base our decisions on the rule of law and sound policy, charging those we simply have encountered evidence on would be arbitrary (SPO 1993).

If the problems associated with the slow progress of trials in Ethiopia cannot be pinned on the dual mandate given to the SPO, is there then an argument that formal legal proceedings were the wrong way to proceed in these circumstances? After all, they could not be carried out in such a way as to respect the rights of the accused, most of whom had been in prison for three or more years by the time they were charged, and for a minimum of five or six years – in many cases much longer – by the time they were sentenced.[8]

In this volume Charles Schaefer argues that there are traditions of reconciliation in Ethiopian political history and culture which could have offered precedents for a non-adversarial approach to dealing with the past. Whilst this is undoubtedly so, there are also strong cultural, historical and political factors which made the selection of anything other than a formal court process highly unlikely in the Ethiopian case. In 1991 at the end of a long and divisive period of civil war, and in the context of the *de facto* secession of Eritrea, the TGE needed to reassert Ethiopian statehood. Prosecutions designed to recast the Ethiopian state's former rulers as its new 'outlaws,' served this purpose well, simultaneously evoking a return to a more 'legitimate' period of Ethiopian statehood, during which, for instance, the country had been one of an elite group of original signatories to the Nuremberg Charter in the wake of the Second World War (a point discussed further by Kjetil Tronvoll in this volume).

---

[7] It is arguable that the description of the SPO's mandate as dual is, in any case stretching the interpretation of Proclamation 22/1992. Whilst the desirability of establishing a historical record is referred to only in the Preamble, Article 6, specifying the Powers of the Office, confines itself to 'the power to conduct investigation and institute proceedings' against relevant individuals.

[8] See Frode Elgesem and Girmachew A. Aneme in this volume.

In Ethiopia, access to the courts to determine property rights and resolve divorce cases has long extended beyond the urban elites and intelligentsia to peasant communities who have been enthusiastic litigants of legal disputes throughout Ethiopian history.[9] The formal judicial resolution of disputes suits a socio-political culture characterized – particularly in highland areas – by a vertically stratified approach to social stability, and a strong adherence to hierarchy in governance. In this context, political authority has been constructed from the demonstration of powerful leadership, perhaps involving a degree of magnanimity towards the defeated, but rarely through the kind of compromise, conciliation, or power-sharing with adversaries, traditionally perceived as symptoms of weakness or anarchy.

In the still militarized and tense situation of the early period of the TGE, the adoption of a 'truth and reconciliation'-style process would have been surprising, politically risky, and potentially open to popular dismay. It is likely that a non-punitive process would have been regarded as a betrayal by many of those whose family members were victims of Derg-era crimes. Discussion about the 'truth' of the past, and the legitimacy of reconciliation, would have risked opening infinite debates about revolutionary justification, territorial integrity, and the nature of the Ethiopian state which, framed in the context of crimes against humanity and genocide, could be confined within the relatively fixed terms of the legality or extra-legality of specific actions. Political constraints – and political expediency – clearly influenced the choice of legal options which were open to the TGE.

There is clearly a debate as to the best way to pursue the transformation of social norms to entrench a new collective intolerance of impunity, in a situation where impunity has become the expected and all-too-tolerated norm (see Elsa van Huyssteen in this volume). The risk in the Ethiopian case is that the pursuit of a strategy which 'fitted' existing patterns of an often hierarchical and 'zero-sum' adversarial political culture, itself served to entrench these elements. Nevertheless, it seems unlikely that the adoption of a strategy which took no account of existing patterns of political and judicial culture would have met with much acceptance or understanding. Eventually, any assessment as to whether or not domestic trials were the right choice must return to the nuances of their implementation, rather than the overarching questions of principle at play. Here, there is perhaps less to defend in the Ethiopian process. In this context it is useful to consider in more detail the relations which developed between the SPO and key groups of stakeholders.

---

[9] A point also stressed by Prime Minister Meles Zenawi as one of the reasons why the EPRDF opted for a juridical process. Cf. interview with Prime Minister Meles by Kjetil Tronvoll, 16 January 2002, Addis Ababa.

The SPO in the Wider Context of the Red Terror Trials and its Relations with the Ethiopian Judiciary

The SPO was housed in offices at *Sidist Kilo*, the administrative hub of the capital city of Addis Ababa, in a compound shared with both the Federal Supreme Court and the Public Defender's Office (PDO). The compound offered a high level of security for evidence and for the Special Prosecutors, and a formal procedure for the admission of witnesses and the public when necessary. Somewhat less usual was the close proximity of the SPO to the Public Defender's Office, the latter body having been established following a request for funding put forward by the SPO itself. The determination of the law applicable to the proceedings emerged as a particularly important matter of contention, with the prosecution and defence naturally seeing their interests in this matter rather differently.

Given the relative unfamiliarity of much of the relevant international and national law on genocide and crimes against humanity to many of Ethiopia's High and Supreme Court judges, a range of programmes of training for judges was offered by legal experts both Ethiopian and international, relating both to the application of the Ethiopian Penal Code and to the incorporation of international law. These training programmes naturally became a focus of competition between the SPO and PDO, with each side attempting to 'capture' the expert education on these matters which was given to the judges.

Occasionally competition broke out between the courts and the SPO, as the high levels of external resources flowing into the SPO in 1993 were a focus of court interest and jealousy. During the early and mid-1990s, a number of international experts who had been working within the SPO moved from the SPO to the courts and/or to the PDO. Whilst in the short term this raised some concerns within the SPO about security of information and evidence, it seems to have had little impact on longer-term relations.

The competition between the SPO and the courts at times also took a personal twist. In July 2000, the Chief Special Prosecutor (CSP) was sentenced by the Sixth Criminal Division of the Federal High Court to one month's imprisonment for contempt of court. The sentence was passed after the CSP sent a letter to the Ethiopian News Agency alleging irregularities in the conduct of the trials and the involvement of one of the judges of the Sixth Bench 'in the offences committed by the Derg officials, and his membership in the defunct Workers' Party of Ethiopia' during the Derg regime (*The Reporter* 2000:1). Whilst a number of observers complained that, given the seriousness of the offence, the sentence was light, many were surprised that the CSP was sentenced at all and even served part of the detention.[10] The CSP's imprisonment marked the

---

[10] The CSP was later released after two days by the Supreme Court on appeal.

culmination of a period of increasing irritation between the SPO and the courts.

The issue of the alleged former WPE membership of judges was a particularly sensitive one. One of the TGE's first acts in 1991 was to exclude WPE members from appointment in a number of areas of public life, including the military, parliament, and the judiciary (see Chapter 1 of this volume). Given that WPE membership had effectively been almost a prerequisite for any sort of judicial career in the period up to 1991, the decision saw the dismissal of a very large proportion of senior judges, causing a crisis of capacity only partially resolved by the recruitment of young, inexperienced, and sometimes very summarily trained judges in subsequent years (see Frode Elgesem and Girmachew A. Aneme in this volume). The contraction of judicial capacity became a focus of middle-class resentment during the 1990s, with frequent allegations of corruption and incompetence. These perceptions did little to enhance the legitimacy of the SPO.

Relations with the international community
The relations between the SPO and the international community have often been more critical, fractious, and erratic than might have been hoped, perhaps not least because of failures of expectations on both sides. A range of western embassies in Addis Ababa were, as mentioned above, quick to respond to requests for support in 1993, and substantial amounts of money and technical assistance flowed into the SPO, with perhaps little consideration for the absorptive capacity of a new and in-experienced institution, charged with a series of weighty, complex and highly sensitive tasks. The first of the SPO's expatriate experts arrived in June 1993, and from December 1993 to March 1994 as many as eleven international technical staff were working in-house. Meanwhile, the SPO was hosting a stream of international visitors and regular visits by forensic scientists. By June 1994 all but one or two of the advisors had left (SPO 1994: Annex II), with a number expressing frustration about difficult working relations. Whilst there was undoubtedly a range of problems encountered on all sides, perhaps in retrospect it is clear that the central one was work overload. In the haste to recruit assistance with a competing plethora of urgent tasks, too little attention was given to the social, cultural, and managerial requirements of harnessing the skills, expertise and expectations of a range of individuals with a spectrum of global experience and backgrounds, and of integrating their skills and resources to suit the capacity and the development of the SPO.

Continuities in technical assistance were not assisted by donor funding strategies, which kept support to the SPO under constant review, often shifting funds between different institutions within the justice sector. The SPO was an increasingly controversial recipient of assistance by the mid-1990s, as delays in presenting charges and bringing cases to court were constantly postponed. As such, the SPO became particularly vulnerable to cuts and interruptions to its funding. It was often the first in line when donor governments shifted uneasily at any perceived deterioration in the wider human rights picture in Ethiopia, as, for instance, around the time of the 1994, 1995 and 1996 elections (respectively constituent, federal and local elections). This suggests that, despite many protestations of commitment to the principles of the fight against impunity, many donors viewed the SPO less as a technical or professional institution than as a political one, with support to it bound up with wider considerations about fluctuating levels of political support or approval given to the Ethiopian government (see Howland 2000: 423–5). This was particularly true regarding requests for support for the establishment of a historical public record of the events of the Red Terror, which proved especially difficult to fund.

International interest in the Red Terror trials, and the activities of the SPO, tailed off significantly from the mid-1990s, with even the moments of relative courtroom drama of the last few years warranting little international interest or commentary. Whilst a number of western embassies in Ethiopia continue to commission regular internal updates on the trials, even trial observation has become an erratic commitment for the international community over the past decade. The extent to which enthusiasm and interest have waned stands out starkly when one reviews the project ideas, aims and expectations of the early 1990s. Loss of interest, and arguably also of legitimacy, seems to have impacted particularly negatively on the capacity of the trials to change international views of Ethiopia, and (as was originally hoped) even to inform, develop and help pioneer norms of international law and legal custom. It can even be argued that the loss of enthusiasm for the SPO's activities extended to the executive of the Ethiopian government.[11]

Relations with the Ethiopian executive
Under the terms of its establishment, the SPO is 'accountable to the Prime Minister' (TGE 1992: Art.1) for a term of office 'which terminates on the accomplishment of its task' (ibid.: Art.4). As suggested above, considerable sensitivity was attached to the SPO and its activities under the TGE, and this was reflected in elevated accountability and reporting arrangements which by-passed the Ministries of Interior and Justice, passing straight to the central political authority of the Prime Minister's office. Partly as a result of this formal arrangement, the CSP and SPO have often been viewed by outsiders as being extremely close to the executive, and therefore lacking independence from government and effectively carrying out the bidding of the EPRDF. In fact, observation of the SPO, at least in its early days, would tend to suggest that the opposite may have been true: that the CSP operated with considerable if not absolute autonomy.

[11] Also acknowledged by PM Meles in interview with Kjetil Tronvoll, 16 January 2002, Addis Ababa.

Observers have argued that, in a number of instances since 1991, the EPRDF government has shown a tendency to confuse the need to respect the independence of the judiciary with a failure to engage, even when this would be both legitimate and desirable, to improve the strategic, managerial, or administrative efficacy of judicial bodies. This confusion has dogged a number of attempts at judicial reform over the last 15 years. It seems to lie behind the marked reticence of the government to involve itself in the affairs of the SPO, even when, as in mid-1994, the Office was drawing considerable international pressure to present charges against those detained for up to three years without charge. Government reluctance to intervene may have been influenced by awareness that the considerable pressure placed on the SPO during 1993 had resulted in an unwieldy programme of international technical support, something which had generated problems of its own. Having placed its faith in the SPO and having retained little managerial involvement in its internal workings, it became increasingly difficult for the executive to intervene to influence the investigative policy behind the unwieldy course of the proceedings or the speed of its implementation.

Indications are that the CSP and SPO had continued to operate with considerable if not absolute autonomy throughout the trials. There is, however, one important instance in which widespread concerns about this independence have been raised. This relates to a number of the SPO defendants against whom charges were dropped for lack of evidence. Notably, several senior members of the Derg military were released as part of a larger group on Ethiopian New Year's Day in September 1998, coincidentally following the outbreak of the war with Eritrea (see the discussion by Kjetil Tronvoll in this volume). Popular suspicion is that charges were abruptly dropped as their specialised military know-how became 'a higher government priority than the pursuit of justice'. Furthermore, new arrests of people allegedly connected to the Red Terror took place during the internal EPRDF dissent process following the war in 2001, where reportedly certain individuals siding with the dissenters were detained for shorter or longer periods. If these incidents are true, it goes a long way in undermining the legitimacy and credibility of the SPO trials.

Little government attention seems to have been paid to the proceedings in recent years, almost as though their extreme prolongation and the demands of the Ethio-Eritrean war have turned them from a source of pride into an embarrassment. However, large segments of the Ethiopian public still continue to tune in to the televised broadcasts of trial footage which are regularly aired on Ethiopian TV.

Relations with the Ethiopian public
Given the difficulties which the Special Prosecutions have faced in overcoming their reputation as a political as much as a judicial project, public perspectives on the trials have remained deeply polarized. Most

Ethiopians have remained supportive or not; interested or not, according to political loyalty and family biography. There is relatively little in the manner of the investigation, charging the defendants, judicial proceedings, and the dissemination of information about these activities which has won over the sceptical public. This is perhaps the most important respect in which the SPO has failed to deliver upon the promise of its broad and ambitious mandate. The SPO has failed to generate a public awareness and determination that the crimes of the past should never be allowed to happen again.

The combination of the length of time before the trials came to court and the failure to establish and publicize a historical record of the events of the Derg period has meant that, for a large proportion of Ethiopia's overwhelmingly young population, the proceedings have an almost surreal air, something from another, and little intelligible, world. This situation is very different from 1992 when legislation mandating the SPO was drawn up. In an attempt to influence urban populations who had seen little of the war in the north, the TGE took the initiative of screening a highly distressing video of the bombardment of the port of Massawa, and through the summer months of 1991 televised the emotional and cathartic debates, led by the Anti-Red Terror Committee, as victims' families relived their traumatic experiences for the first time on television.

The national Anti-Red Terror Committee was established in 1991 as an NGO to represent the victims and families of victims of torture and human rights abuses perpetrated during the Red Terror. The Committee worked from the offices of the SPO and sought to complement the SPO's efforts to bring to justice past officials. It was registered with the Prime Minister's Office and the Ministry of Justice (formerly Ministry of Interior during the TGE). The Committee had 21 members who worked on a volunteer basis and an executive of seven, which was elected by the members. Its activities included collecting information on the Red Terror, campaigning for compensation for survivors, and assisting them in the process of recovering confiscated property (see Nwankwo 1994).

It is important not to underestimate the importance of the Special Prosecutions for families and communities whose members were victims of Derg-era crimes. What is frustrating, however, has been the failure of the SPO to engage with a wider Ethiopian public, and to cross political and generational divisions in forging a national consensus in the fight against impunity. Here again, it is possible to argue that the double mandate of the SPO has been problematic: that the need to respect the integrity and legal privilege of judicial proceedings was always incompatible with the project of disseminating an awareness of the past; and that the simultaneous implementation of the two components of the mandate was impossible.

Conclusions

In 1992, the Office of the Special Prosecutor was established amidst great optimism about the importance of the principles invoked and the prosecutorial processes, not only for political transformation within Ethiopia, but as a potential model for such proceedings throughout Africa and in breaking new ground in international legal precedent. After more than a decade, with the trials of many defendants still continuing, little of the wider potential of this set of opportunities seems to have been fulfilled. Problems of capacity within the judiciary combined with inadequate political management of the investigation and prosecution processes resulted in an exceptionally slow timetable for the charging and trial of defendants. What is understood by many to have been the release of some defendants on political rather than judicial grounds has served to undermine confidence in the basis for the continuing – and now extremely protracted – detention of the rest. Both of these problems have been compounded by failures to engage in projects of public education and historical documentation about the past. As a result of this combination of factors, the potential moral and political weight of the Ethiopian Special Prosecutions as a force in the fight against impunity, both globally and within Ethiopia, has been tremendously blunted. There is a risk that when they come finally to be assessed by historians, these processes will emerge as 'victors' justice' of a much less acceptable kind than the groundbreaking precedent provided at Nuremberg. If this is the case, an invaluable opportunity to demonstrate the legal, political, and moral potential of domestic judicial proceedings in Africa will have been lost.

References

Amnesty International (AI). 1996. *Ethiopia: Human rights trials and delayed justice: the case of Olympic gold medallist Mammo Wolde and hundreds of other uncharged detainees,* July 1996, AI index AFR/25/11/96 available at: http://web.amnesty.org/library/print/ENGAFR250111996

Amnesty International. 2003. *Annual Report.* London: Amnesty International.

EAAF. 1998. *1996–97 Biannual Report of the Argentine Forensic Anthropology Team – Ethiopia,* Buenos Aires: EAAF, pp.77–81.

—— 2003. *EAAF 2002 Annual Report – Ethiopia,* Buenos Aires: EAAF: 66–73.

Howland, Todd. 2000. 'Learning to Make Proactive Human Rights Interventions Effective: The Carter Center and Ethiopia's Office of the Special Prosecutor,' *Wisconsin International Law Journal* 18: 407–36.

Nwankwo, C. 1994. *The Status of Human Rights Organisations in Sub-Saharan Africa,* at http://www1.umn.edu/humanrts/africa/ethiopia/htm, Human Rights Library, University of Minnesota.

SPO. 1993. *Request for International Assistance,* 8 July 1993, Addis Ababa: SPO/TGE.

—— 1994. *Progress and Activity Report covering the period July 1993 to June 1994.* Addis

Ababa: SPO/TGE, 15 August.

TGE. 1992. 'Proclamation 22/1992,' *Negarit Gazeta*, vol. 51 no. 18, 8 August 1992, Addis Ababa: Transitional Government of Ethiopia.

The Reporter. 2000. 'Sentence against Chief Special Prosecutor light: Lawyers,' *The Reporter*, vol. 4, no. 202: 1, 11.

UNEUE. 1995. *Situation Report for May 1995*, Addis Ababa: UN Emergencies Unit for Ethiopia.

United Nations Integrated Regional Information Network (UN IRIN). 2003. 'Ethiopia: Defence Trial of Ex-president Begins,' news item, 4 November.

5

The Red Terror Trials ▓ versus Traditions of Restorative Justice in Ethiopia

CHARLES SCHAEFER

Introduction

After marching into Arat Kilo, the government headquarters in Addis Ababa, the Ethiopian People's Revolutionary Democratic Front (EPRDF) declared victory over Mengistu's Marxist regime and committed itself to restoring human rights, ensuring the rule of law, initiating representative government and pursuing capitalist development. Expectations were exceedingly high in the early 1990s. Among the immediate problems facing the EPRDF in 1991 was what to do with the high-ranking Derg officials who carried out the Red Terror and were accused of committing genocide against students, intellectuals and other persons deemed threatening to the survival of the military junta. Resolving these gross human rights abuses was considered central in the Transitional Government of Ethiopia's (TGE) attempt to move beyond the immediate, bloody past and bring about reconciliation between parties and ethnic factions. Certainly there are numerous examples of reconciliation in Ethiopian history. At the state level, conflict resolution is as prominent a feature of the imperial chronicles as is warfare. Both modern and religious educational curricula dwell upon the country's peace treaties emphasizing levels of financial restitution and a wide range of charitable acts towards defeated foes with the aim of promulgating Ethiopia's efforts at peace building by emphasizing various methods of restorative justice. What is perplexing is the basic disregard for traditional restorative justice methods that the EPRDF was aware of, yet rejected in favour of a trial when contemplating what to do with Derg officials.

That the top leadership of the EPRDF debated this issue is clearly stated by Prime Minister Meles Zenawi in his interview with an editor of this volume, Kjetil Tronvoll. In the interview, PM Meles recounts the decision 'that a legal accounting of what happened was the best way to go' was taken during the last stages of the war against the Derg when it was apparent that the TPLF/EPRDF had seized the upper hand.[1] PM Meles listed three factors for the EPRDF's choice of a trial: first, that the scope of human rights abuses and genocidal killings was so heinous as to be outside the boundaries of Ethiopian political decorum; second, because of the 'irrational, uncontrolled, unaccounted use of power', a line needed to be drawn demarcating the present from the past; and third, that a court trial was a legal process that all Ethiopians were accustomed to and for which its judgment would be respected and perceived as nonpartisan (PM Meles interview).

This chapter attempts to unpack the reasons why the EPRDF chose a trial when, indeed, a trial at this elevated state level was something unique in Ethiopian history. Historically, the Ethiopian state opted for traditions of restorative as opposed to retributive justice since the goal had been to bring about reconciliation and national healing. This chapter assesses the flagship event of modern Ethiopian history, the Battle of Adwa, in order to illustrate strategies of restorative justice applied after Ethiopia's victory by Emperor Menilek to bring about reconciliation. The analysis below does not impute that Ethiopia's history is replete with examples of restorative justice that brought about national reconciliation, for the historical record is full of contradictions – the magnanimous to the malicious – and in certain instances inconclusive examples; yet scrutiny reveals indigenous options that the EPRDF could have considered. By PM Meles' own admission, because of the protracted nature of the trial 'the exercise became more and more irrelevant' (PM Meles interview), and it is unclear whether it has led to the desired outcome – to air grievances and heal societal wounds.

Historical Background to the Red Terror Trials

Without a doubt, EPRDF credibility and prestige were at stake in the first months after taking over in 1991. The international community watched closely to see how the EPRDF would handle the officials of the Derg regime. The EPRDF's decision to prosecute the Derg officials in a trial was a bold step that needs to be historically contextualized on two counts, first internally and second in terms of international pressures.

PM Meles was right when he stated that Ethiopians 'have had courts for many years, for thousands of years' and inferred that the only court that may have had a longer lifespan was 'the court in the sky' (PM Meles interview). The prominence of courts in Ethiopia is woven into the land tenure system in the highlands – the very fabric of society. A voluminous, ethnographic literature exists depicting rather weak usufruct rights to

---

[1] Interview by Kjetil Tronvoll with Prime Minister Meles Zenawi, 16 January 2002, Prime Minister's Office, Addis Ababa.

land and intense competition to ensure those rights to the land.[2] One of the more common yet complex land tenure structures was the ambilineal descent system whereby both male and female descendants of a 'primal' first-settler could claim use rights to a specified piece of land. Multiply countless generations of claimants, irrespective of geniture and gender, and the number of disputes can only be imagined. In this environment local courts were developed that heard cases and determined which party had the strongest claim to said property. Ethiopia was and remains one of the most litigious countries in the world. As part of a young man's traditional education, Blatten-geta Mahteme-Selassie Wolde-Maskal asserts that all Ethiopians were taught to plead their cases clearly and skilfully in a court of law (1970: 64). For everyone, appearing in a court to contest a piece of land or defend it against another claimant was about as universal as baptism and almost as common as communion.

PM Meles' insinuation that a 'fair judgment' in a court would bring consensus may be overly optimistic. Within local land courts, bribes and all other forms of juridical abuses were commonplace; nor was a court's ruling irrevocable for there were mechanisms for litigants to appeal to higher courts or feudal lords. Consensus was rarely achieved and, in fact, the court system may have fostered disputes because of a perception that courts more often rendered unfair judgments (ibid.). One more point needs to be considered: courts did not render opinions on issues of national interest at the state level. That was the prerogative of the emperor or for the highest levels of the aristocratic council.

In regard to the second point, there was also strong international pressure on the EPRDF to disregard the arguments in favour of granting a general amnesty for high-ranking Derg officials and instead charge them with crimes against humanity to be tried in an Ethiopian court with Ethiopian judges, prosecutors and defence lawyers. The time period of the early 1990s was one of intense pressure, for the TGE emerged at precisely the time when the international community was reinventing itself and setting up universal political/judicial standards to which all countries were theoretically held accountable. Gone was the notion that there were no international rules governing states' response to gross human rights violations. The 1980s were somewhat of a step back from the spirit of the Geneva Conventions and marked the heyday of conflict resolution specialists who argued that stopping conflict at all costs, including granting amnesty, was the most effective way to restore national unity and promote development. Conversely, the 1990s were a period when

---

[2] Virtually every anthropologist dealing with agrarian society in Ethiopia has written about *rist* and *gult* rights to land which imply a feudal hierarchy, though with some unique characteristics, the primary of which is the unstable nature of class ties and the prospect for social mobility as a direct result of ambilineal claims to usufruct rights. Among the classic texts is Allan Hoben (1973). For perhaps the latest word on the relationship between ethnology and history see Donald Crummey (2000); however, Gene Ellis (1976) should not be overlooked for a concise examination.

jurists had the upper hand and international legal opinion weighed heavily in favour of retributive justice.[3] In this new era of democracy there was a simultaneous commitment to transparency and accountability in political as well as judicial affairs. New players, the TGE included, had to play by those rules to gain the West's clientage and receive Bretton Woods financial support. Basically the TGE had two options that met the internationalist's criteria: set up a truth commission or try the offenders in court.

South Africa's Truth and Reconciliation Commission (TRC), though perhaps in the planning stages, was unknown to the Ethiopian leadership. Moreover, its emphasis on restorative justice, encapsulated in the concept of *ubuntu,* was a one hundred and eighty degree tack against the prevailing winds of the period, and perhaps partially explains why the TRC is considered that formative event inspiring renewed interest in restorative justice. The forgiving and forgetting option that is often inappropriately associated with truth commissions appeared to be off the table no matter how vociferously policy analysts and academicians argued in the previous decade that it was the best alternative for fragile transitional states. The selection of a trial over a truth commission may in fact be more of a statement about the EPRDF's confidence and cockiness than a measured assessment of how best to account for past abuses. The main party making up the EPRDF was the Tigray Peoples' Liberation Front (TPLF) that gained victory in battle; they were confident and disciplined as evidenced by the way in which the rank and file soldiers, both men and women, comported themselves in the first months after their victory. Self-assured they were, but hidden in the recesses was, perhaps, a fear that a truth commission was potentially too chaotic and that revelations about the TPLF's own human rights abuses might surface. The courtroom may have seemed safer.[4]

Two other criteria must be considered. As a new government that inherited the collection of treaties previous governments had signed, including the Genocide Convention that obligated the EPRDF to prosecute the crime of genocide, the EPRDF felt an enormous responsibility to the international covenants that may have tipped the scale in favour of a trial. Finally the Marxist-Leninist foundations of the TPLF, and thus the leadership of the EPRDF, cannot be discounted. Axiomatic to their adoption of Marxist-Leninism was their rejection of the feudal traditions of the *ancien régime.* For many of the current leaders of Ethiopia, including Prime Minister Meles Zenawi, the injustices of the Haile Selassie

---

[3] The culmination of the international jurists' agenda is seen in the creation of the International Criminal Court, but already most of the judicial momentum was well under way a decade earlier.

[4] What is confusing is the apparent attempt by the EPRDF to split the difference between trials and truth commissions by giving the Special Prosecutors Office (SPO) a dual mandate: to mount a prosecutorial investigation and proceedings, and to establish a historical record 'to educate the people and make them aware of those offences in order to prevent the recurrence of such a system of government,' see Proclamation No. 22/1992.

regime were so egregious that they committed themselves to a 'progressive' socio-political order that rejected all traditions in favour of a new ideology they believed would better serve the interests of the Ethiopian people. This, of course, was Marxism at least through 1989, when the collapse of the Soviet Union forced them to quickly retool and learn the democracy-and-capitalism discourse acceptable to the West. Spending their formative years as avid Marxists may have precluded the EPRDF leadership from accepting, much less integrating, elements of the *ancien régime* into their worldview.

What was notably absent was consideration of Ethiopian traditions of post-conflict reconciliation other than the Penal Code of the Empire of Ethiopia of 1957. The Penal Code was the extent of the EPRDF's reference to Ethiopian history. The code incorporated 'rules of customary international law in the form of provisions to genocide, crimes against humanity, and the grave breaches of the Geneva Conventions' (Mayfield 1995). Moreover, the provisions of Article 281 of the Penal Code of 1957, which concern genocide and crimes against humanity, expanded the Genocide Convention's identification of national, ethnic, racial or religious groups subject to genocide to include political groups – although there remains controversy over this last inclusion when the Amharic version is consulted (see the concluding chapter of this volume). The High Court used this provision to strengthen its contention that the trial should be staged in Ethiopia using domestic laws and not be subject to international law (see the concluding chapter in this volume). Besides this, virtually no consideration was given to other methods of justice from Ethiopia's past.

Ethiopia has a longstanding tradition of granting clemency to political and military dissidents, yet as this chapter demonstrates, clemency was conditional and bridged the dichotomy between retributive and restorative justice in ways that ensured accountability and, perhaps more effectively than current internationally inspired methods, healed national wounds. Briefly this chapter assesses the aftermath of the Battle of Adwa as that crucial juncture that highlights the virtues of restorative justice.

Magnanimity after the Battle of Adwa

By noon of 1 March 1896, Menilek's army had routed an Italian army that had set out the night before, 29 February, to mount a surprise attack that went awry. Conservative estimates claim 4,000 Italian and 2,000 *askari* (Eritrean soldiers under Italian command) casualties, while at least another 2,000 were captured.[5] News of the Battle of Adwa took a day or

[5] The figures are given by Harold G. Marcus (1975) around which a general consensus has emerged, p. 173. It should be noted that about an equal number of Ethiopians died in the fierce fighting but as a percentage of the total fighting force the Ethiopian casualties were less devastating.

two to become headline news throughout the world. The majority of Western newspaper editors cast it as Italy's shameful defeat; for black and Third World presses it was celebrated as Africa's victory over colonial aggression. That the victory was a signature event was beyond doubt, but equally noteworthy were Emperor Menilek's charitable acts towards the defeated Italians afterwards. As Harold Marcus states, 'Why the emperor acted so magnanimously is still open to conjecture' (1975: 176). His magnanimity, however, needs to be unpacked. First, debate still rages over why Menilek did not follow up his victory by pushing the retreating, confused and demoralized Italian army into the sea and retake Eritrea. To many, this failure to achieve outright victory is popularly attributed to Menilek's 'soft' character;[6] on the other hand, his reluctance to pursue outright victory may indicate his preference for following time-honoured Ethiopian traditions of post-war conflict resolution, which emphasized leniency. Second, his treatment of the 49 Italian officers and 1,656 soldiers taken prisoner says much about how historically Ethiopian victors treated the vanquished. The third issue concerns the controversy over repatriating the Italian prisoners of war. The repatriations speak to Ethiopia's laws of war, including post-war politicking, all of which were intended to promote national reconciliation. Fourth, his mutilation of the Eritrean *askari* appears to contradict all this talk of magnanimity yet, as will be demonstrated below, it too fits into widely accepted conceptions of restorative justice practised in Ethiopia.

Reluctance to pursue outright victory
Menilek's reluctance to drive the Italian army out of Eritrea and pursue outright victory was a longstanding tradition for ending hostilities in Ethiopia. Turning to the historical record of clemency as an act of magnanimity, to grant amnesty to officers and soldiers after, perhaps, premature secession of hostilities was tantamount to the rules of war in pre-twentieth-century Ethiopian history. The literature on the *zamana mesafint* (also known as the 'era of the princes' and a period of incessant war from approximately 1769 to 1855) leaves the impression that one of the reasons imperial aspirants were continually resurrecting themselves to fight another day was the result of the terms by which victory was declared. In other words, seldom were armies vanquished. Often defeated feudal princes were allowed to escape or when captured were forced to sign treaties or other notes of non-aggression and then after an indeterminate time were permitted to return to their own provincial bases. There was a sense of cordiality and chivalry given to rivals reminiscent of feudal Europe. Wars were waged within an aristocratic fraternity where leniency was considered good form.

Kasa Hailu, who was later crowned Emperor Tewodros II, was

---

[6] Augustus B. Wylde (1970), writing shortly after the battle and having been in a position to observe the whole war and its aftermath, concludes that Menilek was simply militarily savvy in that he lacked provisions to continue moving his army into Eritrea, p. 212.

considered an outsider for two reasons: first, because of his questionable familial background, and second, because he did not exhibit aristocratic restraint on the battlefield or afterwards (Taddese Beyene *et al.* 1998). Granted he stopped the *zamana mesafint* and inaugurated modernization efforts in Ethiopia, in fact, in his early campaigns to restore imperial power 'he exercised the utmost clemency towards the vanquished, treating them rather as his friends than his enemies' (Dufton 1867: 134). Unfortunately, Tewodros lost his 'character for justice and probity' (Johnston 1844: 189) when he began to use unbridled force and treated rivals with vindictiveness.[7] The Ethiopian aristocracy quickly came to view him as an outsider – one who did not embody the characteristics of a true king. By contrast, Menilek was a model emperor. Examples abound concerning the lengths to which Menilek went to show magnanimity. Prior to mobilizing against the Italians, Menilek reconciled past disputes between himself and the Tigrayan Rases Mangasha Yohannes, Sebhat Aragawi, Alula Abanega and Bahta Hagos who had all sworn oaths of solidarity with the Italians at one time or another. Yet in finding common cause, honouring provincial suzerainty and only insisting on rather perfunctory acts of submission to the Showan throne, Menilek managed to regain the allegiance of his wayward Rases and count on their support and that of their armies at Adwa (Erlich 1996: 161–96). Menilek could have been hot-headed, like Tewodros, and punished the Tigrayan Rases, but instead chose to restore them into the body politic.

Menilek's decision to grant amnesty to the Italian officers and soldiers was not unusual. Originating in biblical times, but certainly practised throughout the Occident and Orient until at least the eighteenth century, was a tradition of clemency for militias and recruits. This tradition recognized demographic realities and labor requirements of pre-industrial societies and sought to re-deploy these men back to their farms or trades as soon as possible. Even Western rules of war are based on swift reintegration and are codified in the whole practice of prisoner-of-war exchanges. Ethiopia was no different. As Tsegaye Tegenu states, military recruitment and demobilization recognized the seasonal demands of agriculture cycles and made efforts to repatriate soldiers to their homesteads for planting and harvesting (Tsegaye Tegenu 1996). Pre-industrial rulers basically recognized that their existence and that of the whole state hierarchy depended on producers; moreover, they honoured the neutrality of peasant soldiers to serve whoever may be dominant in their locale.

---

[7] Clement Markham (1869), as background to his unflattering comments on the cruelty of Tewodros, describes the ideal Ethiopian sovereign as being 'most merciful' and 'a great favorite with [the peasants] because he administered justice, and protected them from oppression', p. 51. By contrast Tewodros, after having granted clemency to about a hundred prisoners personally killed three others and had approximately another 280 'hurled alive over a precipice; any who showed signs of life afterwards were fired upon by the guards.' All this simply because the 280 pleaded for their own amnesty and in so doing woke him from a drunken stupor, (Holland and Hozier 1870: 57).

Arnauld d'Abbadie writes, 'Ethiopian soldiers are so secure in the solemnity of warfare that these beliefs contribute to their ability to give clemency to the vanquished. One observes the victorious and the defeated recognizing each other, embracing, inquiring with concern about the wellbeing of recent adversaries, or interposing in order to improve the fortunes of friends' [interpretation mine].[8] It appears inconceivable that soldiers could be fighting, for, at the conclusion of a battle, rank-and-file soldiers would embrace, attend to one another and even recount their versions of the battle. Moreover, it was customary for victorious leaders to quickly decide upon the few who were to be taken prisoners and to release all other defeated combatants within twenty-four hours. To offer to release Italian prisoners after the Battle of Adwa, as Menilek had already done with Italian prisoners after the siege of Meqele in December 1895, was standard procedure.

A complementary issue that needs to be addressed with reference to the Battle of Adwa is: on whom was the decision to be either magnanimous or vengeful conferred? Clemency and other judicious actions were uniformly accepted by the Ethiopian aristocracy and population when the emperor possessed undisputed legitimacy and internalized the piety and prowess of leadership that most Ethiopians upheld as their ideal. The Old Testament contained numerous paragons of justice, not least of which was King Solomon, and literally hundreds of examples that required judges or kings to mete out justice, sometimes requiring a heavy hand, other times a compassionate heart. The biblical narrative served as the political and judicial model for the Ethiopian state.[9] Christianity and the mythology of the *Kebra Nagast* (the national epic about Ethiopia's Queen of Sheba meeting the Old Testament's King Solomon) linked Ethiopia to Israel providing it with examples of when to be vengeful or forgiving and the rationale and consequences of both. But equally important, the biblical narrative devoted much attention to governance and the ideal ruler.

According to the *Kebra Nagast*, 'the Queen of Ethiopia, gave the kingdom to her son David [Menilek I], the son of Solomon, the King of Israel, and she said unto him, "Take [the kingdom]. I have given [it] unto thee. I have made King him who God hath made King, and I have chosen him whom God hath chosen as the keeper of His Pavilion."' (Budge 1922: 148). A king's duties were also scripted in the *Kebra Nagast* and royal chronicles that preceded it; they included defence of the country, main-

---

[8] 'Les soldats éthiopiens sont convaincus de la versatilité des positions, et cette croyance contribue à les render cléments envers les vainc?s.' To the extent that, 'On voit des vainqueurs et des vaincus se reconnaître, embrasser, s'informer avec solicitude de leurs récents adversaires ou s'interposer auprès d'un compagnon afin d'améliorer le sort de quelque ami.' d'Abbadie, (1980), p. 455.

[9] This was noted by Henry Salt (1967) travelling between 1809 and 1810, 'The reader conversant in Scripture, cannot fail, I conceive, to remark in the course of this narrative, the general resemblance existing throughout between the manners of this people and those of the Jews previously to the reign of Solomon,' pp. 305–6.

taining political order, functioning as the court of final appeal, and protecting the ecclesiastical and doctrinal identity of the church. To defy the will of the king or to view his decisions as open to discussion went against Ethiopians' strict adherence to superior-inferior personal relationships.[10] All subjects were to revere the king, for as God's chosen, God would not tolerate insurrection. 'It is not a good thing for any of those who are under the dominion of a king to revile him, for retribution belongeth to God' (ibid.: 64).

In much of the literature on justice and reconciliation the foundations are twentieth-century documents such as the Universal Declaration of Human Rights and the Geneva Conventions, but lately a growing body of literature has begun to reassess the importance religious texts, particularly the Bible, perhaps as a response to the Truth and Reconciliation Commission in South Africa and its heavy dose of biblical metaphor. Appleby (2000), Lederach (2001), Crocker (1999) and Little (1999), as a small sample, use the Christian notions of forgiveness to argue that justice and truth are not irreconcilable. By developing the idea that forgiveness is given with the constraint of accountability attached to it, they weave a matrix through which reconciliation can take place if truth is honestly divulged, with the option of retributive justice to follow as a last resort. In short, they appear to be recycling Old Testament notions of accountability with which Jews, Christians and Muslims are all familiar.

In Ethiopia, though, there is no need to revisit biblical notions of justice, as they were and remain foundational to the judiciary. Admittedly, since the Marxist Derg there have been attempts to couch justice in more scientific or secular terms, but most attempts to appropriate Western discourse are little more than window-dressing and do not resonate with the Ethiopian people. Ethiopians are socialized to think that God, king and courts alternate between wrathful and forgiving; however, ideally the vacillation would be done with an almost divine view of the common good (Mahteme-Selassie Wolde-Maskal 1970; and Molvaer 1995). Menilek was judged to be the best example of the embodiment of the state and everything that was just and merciful about the institution of emperor.

Treatment of prisoners
Concerning how historically Ethiopian victors treated the vanquished, of the approximately 1700 prisoners of war after the Battle of Adwa, fewer than one hundred died of complications in Ethiopia. Those with severe injuries were transported to Addis Ababa and Harar and treated by either Russian or Italian physicians. Others were divided up and given to various victorious Rases (princes) to be sheltered in aristocratic households throughout the kingdom. Many of them were treated well and, at

---

[10] Although Donald Levine (1965) concedes that Ethiopian's unquestioning deference and loyalty to those in authority is not as absolute as in Japan, he nevertheless employs the modality 'superior-inferior' to characterize social relations in highland Ethiopia, pp. 148–237.

the invitation of the aristocrat or of their own volition, stayed in Ethiopia even after the opportunity for repatriation was made available to them. The practice of parcelling prisoners out to various aristocratic households went back centuries and was developed out of expediency at a time when Ethiopia did not have an established capital city and found a roving tent capital suitable to keep an eye on wayward feudal lords. Under those conditions there were no fixed prisons; it was practical to disperse prisoners to distant regions where they could be watched relatively effectively and at little cost because the local population considered them outsiders. According to Arnauld d'Abbadie, some prisoners, often aristocrats themselves, were considered booty to be ransomed off to their relatives or districts as part of the settlement or reparation-package of feudal Ethiopia (d'Abbadie 1980: 454). Others were used as labourers or, if they possessed special skills, were employed for their technical expertise. By 1896 Addis Ababa was taking shape as the national, modern capital thus demanding skilled labourers to construct its infrastructure. With some of these requirements in mind, the majority of Italian prisoners were settled in Talian Safar (Italian Quarters), a neighbourhood on the western side of Addis Ababa, and were allowed to work on engineering and construction projects. On these projects, they were given significant freedom and even authority over hundreds of Ethiopian unskilled labourers. Prisons hardly existed and escape, in past centuries, was considered a remote possibility, for Italians were truly outsiders in Ethiopia. To the chagrin of the Italian statesmen who later tried to vilify Ethiopia's treatment of their prisoners, many of these POWs chose to stay in Ethiopia, some for the duration of their lives (Prouty 1986).

The politics of repatriation
Repatriation became an issue when it was delayed because the Italians began prevaricating over revoking the Treaty of Wichale and tried to use the negotiation process to turn their military defeat into a diplomatic victory. Under these circumstances, Menilek used the prisoners as leverage until the treaty was abrogated and Ethiopian sovereignty recognized. Immediately after a new treaty was negotiated, a convention for the repatriation of prisoners was signed, and by late 1896, all the soldiers were allowed to return to Italy or stay in Ethiopia under a general amnesty. Two sub-issues require further scrutiny. First is Menilek's use of prisoners as pawns in a political chess game that clearly demonstrated that the way in which national conflicts have been resolved have historically accounted for international political realities. The EPRDF's reading of the international community's preference for retributive justice in the 1990s points to radically different historical circumstances from those of the 1890s when Menilek found a more magnanimous option better suited to resolve both internal and international tensions. The second is that granting amnesty to an adversary was an idea the Ethiopian people were familiar with and supported, and that the judgment to be either harsh or

lenient was the emperor's to make for he was the embodiment of the state.

Concerning prisoners as pawns, a fundamental axiom of political theory is that armed conflict is a result of failed politics, and that the latter is never removed from the former. In this context initial negotiations after the Battle of Adwa were conducted as if the outcome of the war was meaningless. The Italian government even pressured Pope Leo XIII to write a letter in the name of Christian brotherhood to release the Italian prisoners before a peace treaty was concluded, thus extricating the Italian government from, in Menilek's words, 'sacrificing the sole guarantee of peace that I have with me'.[11] The audacity of the Italian diplomatic effort – to undo their defeat on the battlefield – probably had never been encountered before in Ethiopian political history. In defeating a European country for the first time, Ethiopia was exposed to new rules of war whereby national interests extended beyond victory or defeat to different arenas where the same political/colonial objectives were simply recycled by employing new tactics. Italy was clearly interested in gaining international recognition for dominion status over Ethiopia regardless of the outcome on the battlefield. Menilek, for his part, realized that if continued pressure was not applied, sovereignty would be lost. In this case, then, the release of Italian prisoners was conditional on Italy's playing by an old set of rules that recognized military victory. But beneath political expediency, Menilek's acts of magnanimity point to restorative justice with provisos, meaning disposed to forgive but not necessarily forget.

Punishment of Eritrean askaris

The problem with the treatment of prisoners after the Battle of Adwa has to do with the way the askaris were treated, not the Italian soldiers. Augustus Wylde, one of the few people to travel into the interior of Ethiopia shortly after the Battle of Adwa, reported:

> The Italian native prisoners, soldiers in the Italian service who had fought against the Abyssinians, were tried by a council of war consisting of all the chief Abyssinian leaders, and the horrible sentence of mutilation was passed; which Menelek sanctioned, after, it is said, great pressure had been brought to bear upon him, he being greatly against any harsh measures being used. The sentence of mutilation – that is, the cutting off the right hand and the left foot – is customary punishment for the offences of theft, sacrilege and treason, of which many of these men were judged to be clearly guilty. (Wylde 1970: 213)

Although mutilation was harsh and could be perceived to contradict the interpretation that magnanimity characterized Ethiopian actions after the Battle of Adwa, within the prevailing cultural and religious paradigms it was nevertheless comprehensible and coherent. Again, the contradiction can be understood from the Biblical perspective. Restorative

---

[11] Translation of Carlo Rossetti, *Storia diplomatica dell'Etiopia durante il regno di Menelik II* (Turin: 1910), p. 196, found in Bahru Zewde (1991), p. 83.

justice implies both blanket amnesties and penalties but in all 'forgiveness' figures prominently. Forgiveness assumes obligation, for although the power to be merciful lies with the forgiver, the one seeking forgiveness is obligated to show contriteness and to be accountable for future actions, in other words, to correct their criminal or in this case treasonous ways. Accountability is one of the components of forgiveness, and if the accounting does not measure up, forgiveness does not mean forgetfulness. Rather, in cases of recalcitrance there is a component of punishment tied into the Biblical understanding of forgiveness. The Parable of the Unforgiving Servant found in Matthew 18: 23–35 describes this. In the parable a king wished to settle accounts with his servants. One servant owed a particularly large amount that he was unable to pay and because of customary law he and his family could be sold into slavery as repayment. Consequently, the servant fell on his knees and pleaded with the king. The king had compassion and forgave him. On exiting and averting this potential debacle, the servant met another servant who owed him far less money, upon which he demanded immediate payment and when the other servant was unable to pay, he had the other servant thrown into prison. The king soon heard about this and summoned the original servant and admonished him saying, 'You wicked servant! I forgave you all that debt because you pleaded with me. Should you not have had mercy on your fellow servant as I had mercy on you?' And then he sent him to jail (other versions say 'tortured') until he would pay his entire debt. Modern exegetes discounts the retributive aspect of forgiveness in this text by arguing that the king refers to God and therefore retribution is divinely decreed and, perhaps, refers to some kind of atonement or judgment day. They argue that the Parable of the Unforgiving Servant comes after Matthew 18: 21–22 where Jesus orders his followers to forgive offenders 'seventy times seven,' which takes precedence (Little 1999: 70).

Certainly Ethiopian priests and high officials were intimately aware of these passages, but they were also familiar with other New Testament verses such as Romans 13: 1–5 culminating in the words 'It is for the servant of God to execute wrath on the wrongdoer.' In cases of recalcitrance, punishment was the stick implied in the symbiotic understanding of forgiveness. In the case of the *askari,* the situation, from the Ethiopian perspective, was one of recalcitrance. Time and again Menilek's forces had warned the *askari* that if they continued to fight on the side of the Italians, they would be viewed as traitors. Augustus Wylde added to the quote reproduced above by saying, 'Those soldiers who had served at the defense of Macalle [Meqele] had been warned of what punishment they would receive if they were again found in arms against Abyssinia' (Wylde 1970: 213).[12] Menilek, like the king in the parable, found the *askari* were

---

[12] Certainly as early as the Battle of Dogali in 1887 the lines of enmity between Ethiopians and Italians and the *askari* who served them had been drawn, see Erlich (1996), pp. 103-6.

unworthy of forgiveness, for they had wilfully fought against their Ethiopian brothers and demonstrated no remorse for their treasonous actions.

Conclusion

Restorative justice has elicited significant attention in recent years, much of it condemning it for having no bite. Critics of restorative justice claim that truth commissions, blanket amnesties and various forms of clemency simply promote the idea of 'forgive and forget by fiat', thus committing a country and its people to the repeated misuse of power and gross human rights abuses. Yet by evaluating the rationale and practices for granting clemency to the vast majority of Italians and Eritreans while punishing some *askari* after the Battle of Adwa gives restorative justice more bite: forgive but not forget.[13] Memory of warnings given or recollection of continued disregard for the precepts of feudal society resulted in the Ethiopian emperor punishing the *askari* for not being accountable to the obligations underlying forgiveness. Society can forget its rich judicial precedents, and that appears to have taken place in the latter part of the twentieth century in Ethiopia. The Derg represented a political as well as cultural rupture with the past, and forgotten were historical methods in which past regimes resolved political upheaval. Perhaps this rupture is the EPRDF's excuse for disregarding Ethiopian models of restorative justice that were exceptionally elastic and able to mould themselves to historical particularities.

The Battle of Adwa highlighted four issues central to opting for some form of restorative justice to bring about national reconciliation. First, and perhaps the most unsubstantiated assertion of this chapter, is that the rationale behind restorative justice advocates returning to a pre-existing period of peace where citizens felt allegiances were honored, support was reciprocal, freedoms were acknowledged and trust was restored. In short, recovery, reconciliation and envisioning a common future are the goals of restorative justice, which includes reintegrating most if not all perpetrators of the atrocity. The Derg period represented such a breech with the past and the new government, led by the EPRDF, repudiated the virtues of the past so wholeheartedly that it may be nearly impossible for the current government to reach back into history to find a period of peace and a scenario for reconciliation.

Second, the Battle of Adwa and its aftermath show how, in times of dynastic turmoil, an emperor who personified the state and its judiciary, could determine the right course for Ethiopia and decree whether leniency or retribution was appropriate. But what about 1991 when there

---

[13] Remarkably Gyude Bryant, Chairman of the National Transitional Government of Liberia (2003-2006), has made this phrase the cornerstone of his attempt to put closure on the decades of Charles Taylor's civil war and bring about reconciliation by considering restorative justice through a truth commission.

was no emperor? Again the historical record shows that, when there was turmoil surrounding dynastic succession, the *makwanent* (the ruling class consisting of nobles, provincial governors and high-ranking military officials) stepped forward to decide the future of the nation in place of an emperor. The *makwanent* traditionally were recognized as representing the public interest when it was determined that the ruler had abused his position; to an extent, the EPRDF occupied this privileged position in the early 1990s.

The plot of the *makwanent* that led to the overthrow of Menilek's heir, Lij Iyasu, culminating in the Battle of Sagale in 1916, shows flexibility on the issue of who could be the arbiter of justice. Iyasu was accused of converting to Islam, though revisionist historians claim he was taking concrete measures to include Ethiopia's Muslim population in the polity. In any event, like Emperor Tewodros before him, Iyasu did not follow imperial decorum, resulting in *Abuna* Mattewos charging him with apostasy, thus releasing the plotters from the oath of allegiance to the ruler (Bahru Zewde 1991: 120–8). Yet after the Battle of Sagale, the same group of nobles followed the old, strict rules of war – and peace – and gave the defeated soldiers amnesty to return to their homes in Wollo province, for as Ras Tafari reputedly said, 'We are all Ethiopians' (Marcus 1995: 24). The *makwanent,* and later on Ras Tafari/Emperor Haile Selassie, also determined appropriate punishments for Ras Mikael (Iyasu's father) and Iyasu, originally showing harshness, then leniency, followed by harshness as circumstances changed in connection with how contrite the prisoners were in abiding by the terms of their confinement (Gebre-Igziabiher Elyas 1994: 367–73). The problem the EPRDF has encountered in assuming the role of the *makwanent* in determining what is best for the nation has been the rise of ethnic politics and the dismissal of opposition parties representing many of the non-Tigrayan ethnic groups. In short, the EPRDF, as stated above, occupied the privileged position of the *makwanent* in the early 1990s. The July 1991 Transitional Conference in Addis Ababa, where all stakeholders participated, was perhaps a modern-day equivalent of convening the Imperial Council of the *makwanent,* bringing together all representative groups to solve the socio-political problems of the nation. But with the elections of 1992 began the political fighting that has monopolized national discourse to the present, such that it is impossible to perceive the national interest asserting itself over the entrenched interests of each and every party. That a modern-day equivalent to the *makwanent* is still sought is clearly seen in the almost universal call for a national referendum and some kind of internationally sanctioned conference to bring all parties together in order to pursue justice and determine how to bring about national reconciliation.

As shown above, treatment of defeated foes after the Battle of Adwa varied widely, pointing to Ethiopians' understanding that forgiveness involves an ongoing evaluation as to whether or not the one seeking forgiveness is living up to the terms of those giving it. This third point could have been useful for the EPRDF to consider, for it measures accountability and yet is malleable; in other words, a judgment such as amnesty can be overturned if new circumstances – lack of contriteness or volition to continue committing abuses – warrant imprisonment or some other form of punishment. In Ethiopia 'forgive and forget' justice never existed; when stacked up against the record, history shows that forgiveness was conditional and that actions had consequences regardless of the propensity to be magnanimous. The mandate of the SPO to create a permanent record of the abuses committed by the Derg during the Red Terror partially fulfills what Ethiopians have been doing for hundreds of years, and that is remembering the infractions of those who abused power to the detriment of the state and citizenry. The problem is that the judiciary was incapable of offering forgiveness and the form of retributive justice, as assessed in other chapters in this volume, is so fraught with inconsistencies that the rank and file Ethiopian looks upon the trials as victor's justice.

The fourth point illustrates that in the aftermath of the Battle of Adwa there were political issues that had to be considered, yet restorative justice was not a straightjacket; in fact, it provided more latitude to manoeuvre along the whole continuum between vengeance and forgiveness. Both internal politics and foreign policy were taken into account in determining whether to be magnanimous to some and/or harsh towards others. In essence, by taking the judgment out of the hands of advocates and judges in the restricted space of a courtroom and putting it into the hands of the emperor, his verdict was recognized in the "court of public opinion" as best for the future of the nation. The EPRDF, as inheritors of sovereignty, may have done well to consider these issues.

References

Appleby, R. Scott. 2000. *The Ambivalence of the Sacred: Religion, Violence, and Reconciliation*. New York: Rowman & Littlefield.

Bahru Zewde. 1991. *A History of Modern Ethiopia, 1855–1974*. London: James Currey.

Budge, Wallis. 1922. *The Queen of Sheba and Her Only Son Menyelek*. Trans. London: Medici Society.

Crocker, David A. 1999. 'Reckoning with Past Wrongs: A Normative Framework,' *Ethics and International Affairs* 13: 43–64.

Crummey, Donald. 2000. *Land and Society in the Christian Kingdom of Ethiopia: From the Thirteenth to the Twentieth Century*. Addis Ababa: Addis Ababa University Press.

d'Abbadie, Arnauld. 1980. *Douze Ans de Séjour dans la Haute-Éthiopie(Abyssinie)*. Reprint. Vatican: Biblioteca Apostolica Vaticana.

Dufton, Henry. 1867. *Narrative of a Journey through Abyssinian 1862–3*. London: Chapman & Hall.

Ellis, Gene. 1976. 'The Feudal Paradigm as a Hindrance to Understanding Ethiopia,' *Journal of Modern African Studies* 14: 275–95.

Erlich, Haggai. 1996. *Ras Alula and the Scramble for Africa*. Lawrenceville, NJ: Red Sea Press.

Gebre-Igziabiher Elyas. 1994. *Prowess, Piety and Politics: The chronicle of Abeto Iyasu and Empress Zewditu of Ethiopia (1909–1930)*. Translated by Reidulf Molvaer. Köln: Köppe.

Hoben, Allan. 1973. *Land Tenure Among the Amhara of Ethiopia: the Dynamics of Cognatic Descent.* Chicago: University of Chicago Press.

Holland, Trevenen and Henry Hozier. 1870. *Record of the Expedition to Abyssinia.* London: War Office.

Johnston, Charles. 1844. *Travels in Southern Abyssinia through the Country of Adal to the Kingdom of Shoa.* London: J. Madden.

Lederach, John Paul. 2001. 'Five Qualities of Practice in Support of Reconciliation Processes' in *Forgiveness and Reconciliation: Religion, Public Policy, and Conflict Transformation.* Raymond G. Helmick, S.J. and Rodney L. Petersen (eds). New York: Templeton Foundation Press.

Levine, Donald. 1965. *Wax and Gold.* Chicago: University of Chicago Press.

Little, David. 1999. 'A Different Kind of Justice: Dealing with Human Rights Violations in Transitional Societies,' *Ethics and International Affairs* 13: 65–80.

Mahteme-Selassie Wolde-Maskal. 1970. 'Portrait Retrospectif d'un Gentilhomme Ethiopien,' in *Proceedings of the Third International Conference of Ethiopian Studies.* Addis Ababa: Institute of Ethiopian Studies, Haile Selassie I University.

Marcus, Harold G. 1975. *The Life and Times of Menelik II.* Oxford: Clarendon Press.

——. 1995. *Haile Sellassie I: the Formative Years 1892–1936.* Lawrenceville, NJ: Red Sea Press.

Markham, Clement. 1869. *History of the Abyssinian Expedition.* London: Macmillan.

Mayfield, Julie V. 1995. 'The Prosecution of War Crimes and Respect for Human Rights: Ethiopia's balancing act.' *Emory International Law Review.*

Molvaer, Reidulf. 1995. *Socialization and Social Control in Ethiopia.* Wiesbaden: Harrossowitz Verlag.

Prouty, Chris. 1986. *Empress Taytu and Menilek II: Ethiopia 1883-1910.* Trenton, NJ: Red Sea Press.

Salt, Henry. 1967. *A Voyage to Abyssinia and Travels into the Interior of that Country.* Reprinted. London: Frank Cass.

Taddese Beyene, Richard Pankhurst and Shiferaw Bekele (eds). 1990. *Kasa and Kasa.* Addis Ababa: Institute of Ethiopian Studies.

Tsegaye Tegenu. 1996. *The Evolution of Ethiopian Absolutism: the Genesis of the Making of the Fiscal Military State, 1696–1913.* Uppsala: Acta Universitatis Upsaliensis.

Wylde, Augustus B. 1970. *Modern Abyssinia.* Reprint. Westport, CT: Negro University Press.

6

The Quest for Justice or the Construction of Political Legitimacy?

The Political Anatomy of the Red Terror Trials

KJETIL TRONVOLL

Introduction

In May 1991 the Ethiopian Peoples' Revolutionary Democratic Front (EPRDF) assumed power in Ethiopia in the wake of a protracted war of resistance where ethnically organized insurgents' movements were pitched against one another in the struggle to defeat the authoritarian and violent central government of the Derg military junta. At that time the Ethiopian people were shattered by the societal consequences of the implementation of rigid, authoritarian ideological doctrines and the wanton disregard of basic human rights. The new revolutionary front which seized power after the collapse of the Derg regime promised substantive changes in that regard, saying that henceforth the central government in the country should be the servant of its people and not its master.

After nearly two decades of internal conflict involving a number of military fronts fighting the central government and each other and massive human rights abuses committed by, but not exclusive to, government, the Ethiopian people held multiple and contradictory perceptions of 'who was to blame', as popular memories of an authoritarian past are multi-layered, fluid, indeterminate, fragmentary and contextual (cf Wilson 2001). Thus, an important priority for the new EPRDF-led government was to establish a common and uniform interpretation of the Derg era, by fixing memory and institutionalizing a view of the past conflict.[1]

New regimes will try to re-create the 'nation' in their own image in order to give legitimacy to political change by re-inventing history according to their own ideologies (Hobsbawm and Ranger 1992). The main institutional change in this respect was to abolish the unitary state structure and adopt an ethnic federal system in Ethiopia. A unitary state and a strong central government were used as explanations for human

---

[1] This point was also stressed by Prime Minister Meles Zenawi in an interview with the author, 16 January 2002, Addis Ababa.

rights violations during the Derg period and the imperial reign. Thus, by delegitimizing and dissolving the ancient Ethiopian 'empire,' the EPRDF established a constitutional breach with the old order of the country. With the establishment of the Federal Democratic Republic of Ethiopia (FDRE) after a three-year transitional phase, a new start was declared for the re-created Ethiopian polity. Furthermore, by creating the Special Prosecutor's Office with a broad mandate to prosecute violators and gather historical evidence of past abuses, the EPRDF hoped to further cement the political discontinuity with the past.

To assume power after an outgoing regime accused of committing genocide and other gross human rights abuses, offers several interlinked challenges. First, how can one create a breach with the past and institutionalize a new human rights-respecting political culture in the country? Second, what should the new power-holders do with the perpetrators of past violations? Third, how can a new government that has been an important military actor in a bloody internal conflict create legitimacy for a 'civil' political platform? This chapter will seek answers to these questions within the Ethiopian context.

The Red Terror trials shed light on a wide range of juridical and political issues related to regime transitions and the assignment of political responsibility for human rights violations in posterity. This chapter, however, will be limited to addressing how the trials are used as a political tool in order to try to create a decisive breach with the past and the old political order, concomitantly giving legitimacy to a new system of federal government and its ethnic policies. As other chapters in this volume have elaborated upon the juridical framework, the focus here will be on the political dimensions of the trials. First, the introduction of the new ethnic federal system will be briefly explained, since this chapter argues that the Red Terror trials are used as an instrument to give legitimacy to this new system of governance. Thereafter, the context of human rights in the country – past and present – will be addressed. Human rights are vital in constituting the political legitimacy of the EPRDF government, and any accusations of current violations may thus decrease the government's political capital and undermine its self-appointed role as prosecutor of the Derg regime. The chapter will subsequently analyse the Red Terror trials along three key principles of transitional justice: the whole truth about the atrocities committed in the past must be revealed; any politico-juridical process must reflect the will of the people; and lastly, an incumbent regime must itself respect and up-hold human rights during the process of transition. By embedding the Red Terror trials in Ethiopia's current political and human rights context, the trials' political anatomy will be unpacked. This chapter thus concludes that the trials go beyond simply representing a juridical accountability; they act as a symbol of repressive continuity, accentuated by a politically controlled judiciary and contemporary human rights violations.

Reconfiguring the State – Reconceptualizing Human Rights Abuses

Since the resistance towards the authoritarian unitary Ethiopian state and the Derg regime was predominantly launched by ethnic and ethno-nationalistic movements fighting for independence or politico-cultural autonomy, the main challenge for the EPRDF when forming a government in 1991 was to address the ethnic order of the *ancien régime*. The solution – according to the EPRDF – was to dissolve the repressive, unitary Ethiopian state and to reconfigure it into an ethnic federation composed of nine ethnic, autonomous regional states, excluding Eritrea which was simultaneously allowed self-determination and independence.

The new Ethiopian constitution adopted in 1995 devolved wide powers to the ethnic regional states and even guaranteed the regional states – and in principle every ethnic group in the country – the right to self-determination and secession from the Ethiopian federation if so wished by the majority of the population within the regional state or ethnic group. Article 39.1 of the constitution reads: 'Every Nation, Nationality and People in Ethiopia has an unconditional right to self-determination, including the right to secession.' The stated intention of the EPRDF in introducing this radical constitutional model was to defuse ethnic tension by guaranteeing ethnic rights. It was believed that in order to create confidence and legitimacy among the many ethnic groups in the country, they needed a constitutional guarantee of political and cultural autonomy and secession, if so desired, from a potentially authoritarian and suppressive central government. Only with such a constitutional guarantee would minority or ethnic groups overcome the fear of belonging to the Ethiopian polity.[2] Concomitantly, it was believed that the granting of extensive political rights and autonomous arrangements to ethnic groups in the country, would serve as checks and balances against a possible human rights-abusing central government. This solution was a clear breach with the historic-ideological concept of 'Greater Ethiopia' and the assimilative practices under the *ancien régime*.

It is within such a context that the EPRDF's speaker of the House of People's Representatives (the Parliament) explained the introduction of the new ethnic federal system during the first elections for regional and national parliaments in 1995:

> The EPRDF is challenging the political environment of Ethiopia. We do not have loyalty to history, it has proved to fail. We do not either perceive containing Ethiopia as an absolute entity as our main goal, hence we also accepted Eritrean independence. We must find a solution which is beneficial for the Ethiopian people today, therefore

[2] See Tronvoll (2000) for a description of the implementation of the constitutional framework.

history will not provide the answer. History has been used as a veil, covering up differences within Ethiopia. People have believed that we have had unity in this country, but this has never existed. What they call unity was a geographical entity dominated by one ethnic group. An Amhara peasant had never met an Eritrean; likewise an Afar nomad had never heard of a Nuer, let alone seen one. And this they call unity! At the stage Ethiopia is now you cannot force people to form a unity.[3]

The Red Terror trials against human rights perpetrators from the Derg regime must be analysed and interpreted as an integral part of this process of re-creating a new Ethiopia. By publicizing the atrocities committed in order to defend 'Ethiopian unity' and the territorial 'integrity' of the country by the Derg regime against 'anti-state,' 'anti-peace' and 'anti-revolutionary' elements (as, *inter alia*, the EPRDF forces were called), this might be understood as legitimizing the ideology and actions of the victims of the Derg regime, hence giving legitimacy to the new state order and political capital to the new political front in power.

Human Rights Accusations of the Past and Current Violations

In the beginning, the Red Terror trials attracted both national and international attention. However, the prolongation of the trials affected people's perceptions, since people's attitudes and understandings are, of course, influenced by the current political and human rights context in Ethiopia. The status and independence of the judiciary and law enforcement are extremely important, since they are vital in shaping people's perceptions of a just and fair legal process. In this regard, it is appropriate to question the independence of the judiciary and police in Ethiopia under EPRDF rule (see also Girmachew Alemu Aneme in this volume). Due to historical reasons – and particularly during the Derg regime – the Ethiopian judiciary did not perform its duties independent of executive political powers. This author has been made aware that many Ethiopians today too are of the opinion that the civil service is still politicized. Civil servants in the courts, prosecutor's office, and government bureaucracy may have leanings towards the ethnic policies of the incumbent, and are not concerned with the quest for justice alone. This issue is accentuated by the fact that grave human rights violations are still taking place in Ethiopia. Amnesty International draws the following parallels:

The process [Red Terror trials] also risks being undermined by the authorities' failure to punish many human rights violations committed since the new government came to power in 1991. These include

---

[3] Interviewed 26 April 1995 in Addis Ababa.

torture, extrajudicial execution, 'disappearances', unfair political trials and arbitrary detentions [...] These violations are still going on. There has been a substantial gap between the government's publicly stated commitment to human rights and the actual practice. (Amnesty International 1996: 5)

During the decade when the trials were in process (1995–2005), there was an increase in reported human rights violations in the country (Tronvoll 2008). Many Ethiopians are hence of the opinion that the Derg violations are no longer socially or juridically relevant to their everyday life. They argue that the focus be shifted onto individuals responsible for the current human rights violations in order to make them accountable. However, the Ethiopian government is unwilling to admit or take responsibility for the wide variety of human rights abuses reported today. As such, it has developed a threefold strategy to counter any human rights accusations. One strategy is to deny any responsibility for violations occurring in the rural parts of the country, since the central government claims that they do not have direct control over local civil servants or cadres in the regional states. Usually these violations are blamed on over-zealous cadres and officials, who do not 'understand' the new liberal policies of the government. A second strategy, which is widely used, is to label any accusations as fabrications by the opposition or foreign elements trying to destabilize the country. And lastly, the government may admit that certain human rights violations are occurring, but these violations are regarded as exceptions to the rule, and are blamed on 'counter-forces' within the state apparatus – or 'remnants of feudal Ethiopia' as a former high-ranking EPRDF official described them to the author.[4]

States in transition are politically fragile, thus the discourse on human rights and democracy tends to become extremely sensitive. Accusations of violations will be used by many actors to de-legitimize the position of the adversary. In Ethiopia the political debate is confrontational and polarized. The political actors do not agree on a common understanding of the human rights context in the country and finding the 'truth' about current human rights violations is usually not an objective in itself but an instrument in the struggle to position oneself in the political arena. The EPRDF government has demonstrated little willingness to enter into a dialogue on the circumstances surrounding the political development of the country. The political struggle, therefore, turns into a fight for the optimal position in a zero-sum game. Within this context, human rights are infused with profound political symbolism. Human rights become key concepts and notions which the government, opposition, civil society and international actors are struggling to define in order to legitimate or de-legitimate the EPRDF's political powers and rights to govern the country (Pausewang 1996; Tronvoll 1997; Vaughan and Tronvoll 2003). In this struggle, the authorities employ harsher and harsher

---

[4] Interviewed 10 July 2001, in Addis Ababa.

measures, summarized by the US State Department with regard to the violations occurring in 2005:

> Although there were some improvements, the government's human rights record remained poor and worsened in some areas. ... in the period following the elections, authorities arbitrarily detained, beat, and killed opposition members, ethnic minorities, NGO workers, and members of the press. Authorities also imposed additional restrictions on civil liberties, including freedom of the press and freedom of assembly. (US State Department 2006)

EPRDF government spokespersons strongly condemn the former Derg regime and its human rights abuses, a condemnation which is fully understandable both in a juridical and political context. Prime Minister Meles Zenawi has explained that, 'It is very important to prove to Ethiopians that those who mess around with the law, human rights law, those who consider themselves above the law, are not really above the law, that there will be some day of reckoning.'[5] Such a statement discloses the inherent paradox in the policies of the government: while the Ethiopian government invests political capital and spends huge resources on persecuting past human rights violators within an overloaded judiciary, current human rights violations are perpetrated with impunity.

The Red Terror Trials and the Administration of Political Legitimacy

In a review article on the principles and political limitations of settlements of human rights violations of former regimes, Zalaquett (1995: 6–10) lists three conditions that must be met in order to secure judicial legitimacy and popular support for the settlement. First, and most important, is the principle that the whole truth about the violations must be known; second that the preferred policy must represent the will of the people; and third that the chosen policy must not violate international law related to human rights. The failure to implement these three conditions, in whole or in part, illustrates why and how the Ethiopian Red terror trials are considered by many to be 'victor's justice'.

The importance of revealing the whole truth
As related to the first principle, one of the objectives of the Special Prosecutor's Office was to investigate the Derg's human rights violations in their historical and political context, in order to establish a documentation centre which can operate as a national, collective memory bank about the atrocities committed and their victims. In this regard, it is

---

[5] Andrew Lycett, 'Mengistu's henchmen face trial', *New African*, September 1994.

important to emphasize that the mandate of the SPO does *not* include the investigation of *all* atrocities committed by *all* warring factions and movements during the 1974–91 Derg era, but, notably, only the atrocities committed by the vanquished.[6] The investigation concentrated on violations committed during the Red Terror campaign, where Mengistu Hailemariam targeted the Ethiopian Peoples' Revolutionary Party (EPRP) as the main enemy due to its 'contra-revolutionary activity'.

The Red Terror was urban warfare that had the Derg, EPRP and *Ma'ison* as main actors (see Bahru Zewde in this volume). At the end *Ma'ison* was annihilated while the armed wing of the EPRP (EPRA) withdrew to the highlands of Tigray to continue the armed struggle against the Derg. However Tigray was also home base for the TPLF, the core party that established the present ruling party, the EPRDF. The TPLF-EPRP relationship had been difficult since the establishment of the TPLF in 1975. Coordination meetings were held between the two fronts from 1975 to 1977, but no firm agreement of cooperation was achieved. In a TPLF publication it was concluded that 'from the very beginning, it was reflected that the EPRP was a national chauvinist petty-bourgeois organisation that is inimical to the Tigrayan people' (cited from Kiflu Tadesse 1998: 392). The TPLF considered that the EPRP's activity and base in Tigray was a threat to its own attempt to achieve territorial control and hegemony in the region. Additionally, the TPLF was interested in neutralizing the EPRP as an ideological adversary, since the latter defined the war against the Derg regime as a class struggle, in contrast to the TPLF who viewed it as a nationality (ethnic) struggle. In this respect, the EPRP had a much broader potential for recruitment of supporters than the TPLF, since it was defined as a pan-Ethiopian movement, soliciting support beyond narrow ethnic confines. This made the EPRP a great political and military threat to TPLF's regional domination and ideological hegemony.[7] Hence, in the view of the TPLF struggle, the EPRP had to be eliminated as an organizational structure. In March 1978, the TPLF thus launched a full-scale war against the EPRP forces in their ethnic homeland, and in a matter of a few weeks many of the operators were killed and the organization was driven out of Tigray.

Since the EPRP and *Ma'ison* are implicated in the Red Terror, the TPLF/EPRDF could have brought EPRP and *Ma'ison* members to court together with the Derg-WPE officials on the same charges.[8] This did not happen. The trials – possibly wrongly – portray the EPRP and *Ma'ison* as

---

[6] In accordance with article 6 in Proclamation 22/1992, stating that the investigation shall be focused on any person 'abusing his position in the party [WPE], the government [Derg] or mass organization under the Dergue-WPE regime.'

[7] See Andargachew Tiruneh (1993), Markakis (1990: 254-7) and Markakis and Nega Ayele (1986: 146–77).

[8] The status of EPRP as a dangerous opposition party did not change after the TPLF/EPRDF takeover of power in 1991. Amnesty International reported on arrests and disappearances of central EPRP cadres after 1991 (Amnesty International 1995: 26–7), and the political harassment continues until today. (Interview with Iyasou Alemayehu, EPRP leader, in Paris 29 June 2001.)

victims only – and not as perpetrators too.

Moreover, the present trials focus on the massive violations committed mainly during the Red Terror. For instance, the main Red Terror trial against the Mengistu Hailemariam and the top Derg officials did not hear war crimes charges. If war crimes charges were part of the main trial, all the insurgent groups that fought the Derg (including the TPLF, OLF, EPLF, etc.) would have been implicated.

This confusing context of overlapping conflicts – where perpetrators are also victims and vice versa – illustrates the difficulty of the Red Terror trials to bring forth the 'whole truth' about the gruesome internal warring in Ethiopia during the turmoil in the 1970s and 1980s. This is also essentially admitted by a former key cadre of the TPLF who explained to this author that: 'If the TPLF is accusing the Derg for the war against the EPRP, they should also put themselves on trial. If the issue is the atrocities conducted during the war, we should all be on trial.'[9]

Transitional justice must reflect the will of the people
The second principle needed to establish a legitimate process of making former human rights violators accountable is to make sure that the trial truly represents the will of the people. The new government's approach and strategy to tackle the past policies of systematic human rights abuses under the Derg regime should create resonance among broader segments of the population in Ethiopia. However, to generalize and stereotype one understanding of how the Ethiopian people consider the Red Terror trials is of course impossible. Different individual experiences and historical, political and ethnic backgrounds create individual perceptions and attitudes to the trials. Nonetheless, a general observation in current Ethiopia is a growing opposition towards the EPRDF government, a trend which may also be reflected in people's understanding of the trials.

The former Derg Prime Minister, Fikreselassie Wegederesse, is one of the most prominent leaders of the first group of the accused. His stand with regard to the trials reflects an ethnic-political understanding: 'These people – the Tigrayans – are an ethnic minority. They should not be ruling. They are not competent to try us' (Ryle 1995: 61). Prime Minister Meles Zenawi rejected such an accusation, and explained: 'We are not motivated by a desire for vengeance. The absence of a rule of law was the reason we had these tragic events. We had to come to terms with the events of those years. The only legitimate way was a trial' (ibid.: 52). Furthermore, in an interview with this author, PM Meles emphasized that a juridical trial would prove the best bipartisan and objective way to demarcate and reach a consensus on this distinct period of the country's history, since the courts and processes of litigation in Ethiopia are historically highly valued.[10]

[9] Anonymous, interviewed 21 September 2001.
[10] Recorded interview by Kjetil Tronvoll with PM Meles Zenawi, 16 January 2002, PM's Office, Addis Ababa.

We should be careful to evaluate individual expressions in favour of or against the Red Terror trials as representative of the majority of the Ethiopian population. Professor Beyene Petros, one of the key leaders of the legally registered political opposition in Ethiopia, has a very critical judgement of the EPRDF government's policies and human rights practices. His evaluation of the Red Terror trials as a power play and creation of political legitimacy might give an adequate explanation to the trials.

> There are two opinions about the trials. An extreme one is that this government has no legal or moral right to put these people on trial. Those who hold this view accuse it [EPRDF] of atrocities comparable [to] those of the Derg. Myself, I hate the self-righteous attitude of the EPRDF guys – as though they were performing some miracle. And I don't think the fact that they are bringing the Derg to court clears them. But our position is that the trials should go ahead: and the trials should get to the abuses of the Tigrayan People's Liberation Front itself, past and present. (Ryle 1995: 59)

Other Ethiopians have expressed a wish to put the history of the Derg regime's atrocities to rest and rather look to the future. The fact that the trials received comparatively little attention among ordinary Ethiopians was a surprise to many observers of the trials, and can be difficult to understand for foreigners accustomed to the publicity surrounding the South African Truth and Reconciliation Commission. However, one of the reasons for the lack of public interest in the trials may be that everyday political, social and economic challenges faced by the Ethiopian people eclipse the accounts and images of the trials. Thus, if a trial is not called for, it is also doubtful that it will bring about its stated objectives of justice and reconciliation. This was partly acknowledged already in the mid-1990s by Dawit Yohannes, Speaker of the House of Representatives and prominent EPRDF spokesperson: 'The ordinary man may have lost hope in the Derg trials process. But the process must necessarily take time, and we will not cut any corners.'[11] PM Meles Zenawi later in 2002 also acknowledged the failure of the trials to be an inclusive, publicized and popular process in order to bring about reconciliation and explained that: 'One of the main reasons is that this has taken so long. I think we sort of swallowed more than we could chew. The judicial system in our country was not structurally capable of managing such an exercise [Red Terror trials] quickly. And as time went by the exercise became more and more irrelevant.'[12]

Most Ethiopians today may agree on the fact that government officials, party cadres and military servicemen, irrespective of which political regime they represent, should be held accountable for their actions which violate national law and international human rights standards. Today's disagreement is rather focused on who is supposed to carry out the trials

[11] Interviewed by the author 30 April 1997, Addis Ababa.
[12] Interviewed by the author, 16 January 2002, Addis Ababa

– a national or international court – and how encompassing the mandate of the court should be: the juridicial truth only, or also granting amnesty in order to reach reconciliation. Another key issue is whether the charges should also have included violations perpetrated by *all* warring factions during the Derg regime, and whether violations carried out after 1991 should be included. The TPLF/EPRDF had decided already prior to the fall of the Derg that Derg/WPE officials should be made juridically accountable for their violations,[13] a stand which was formally adopted by the transitional government in August 1992 (Proclamation 22/1992). Thus, whether or not the basis to decide on a juridical process against the human rights perpetrators of the Derg regime reflects the 'will of the people', is a moot question.

The importance of upholding human rights standards
The third and last principle, noted by Zalaquett, in a popular strategy for making human rights violators accountable emphasizes that the imple-mentation of the strategy must not violate international human rights principles. Many human rights organizations, however, have expressed a concern over the protracted and delayed timetable resulting in the extended detention of the accused prior to going to trial. This critique is further substantiated by Elgesem and Girmachew A. Aneme in this volume. Dawit Yohannes, the former Speaker of the House of Representatives and a senior EPRDF official, has, on the other hand, strongly rejected any criti-cism of the Red Terror trials:

> There is a periodic surge of the same issues [human rights situation in Ethiopia] triggered by the release of new 'reports' with the same 'fact finding' and 'analysis'. What run like a red tape through these hostile criticisms are the facts of double standards, falsification of facts and a hostile attitude to the new federal arrangement under which the right of nations and nationalities is respected. [...] The best example of all is the allegation that the Derg trials are unfair because of the time they are taking. Again, can they tell us how long [a time] trials take in other countries? In Rwanda? In Yugoslavia? With all the resources the Allies had, how long did it take to prosecute the German Nazi and Japanese war leaders? As you can see, these reports are so distorted that it is a waste of time to respond to them.[14]

Hence any critical argument against some aspects of the trials based on human rights law is dismissed as irrelevant bickering by a government spokesperson, as it is interpreted within the context of the struggle for political legitimacy – a context where human rights are used and misused as an arguing point by the 'centralist' and Amhara-dominated political opposition to the EPRDF. Dawit Yohannes explains further that:

[13] Confirmed by PM Meles Zenawi in interview of 16 January 2002.
[14] Written statement by Dawit Yohannes on Pol.Ethiopia e-mail network, 18 December 1997 (pol.ethiopia@wn.APC.ORG).

> They [the Derg officials] do not have a moral standing to talk about human rights even if they become new converts for human rights protection [as] their social friends are doing in Addis right now. In their new status as a humiliatingly defeated political force, with no acceptance among the people, their only motive for raising the banner of human rights is to use it as an instrument to stage their political comeback. They think that they have found the appropriate dress for the present democratic situation. They are wrong. The people know their lies and their new dresses.[15]

Dawit Yohannes addresses here the same issue raised in the beginning of this chapter: Can one reasonably argue that the current EPRDF government is exploiting its political position in a wider context which centres on the perception of the Ethiopian polity as one in which the Amhara elite has traditionally advocated a strong, centralized and unitary state, whereas the TPLF/EPRDF favours the decentralized, ethnic federal system.[16] And does the Red Terror trial play a political role in this power struggle?

The Red Terror Trials: Juridical Accountability or Repressive Continuity?

In all cases of transition from a repressive regime to a non-authoritarian system, the interpretation of history has been an important and disputed subject (see Hobsbawm and Ranger 1992). Even after the fall of a regime, the old ruling elite will still have its supporters and advocates trying to defend, explain away, or excuse the violations that have been committed. If such assertions of innocence are not met and countered, they will undermine the legitimacy of the new rulers and consequently make the transition to a peaceful democracy more difficult. Furthermore, any action taken – juridical and/or political – against the former regime will be used in creating historical discontinuity with the past, as part of the relational dimension of national identity-forming processes (Wilson 2001: 16).

The new rulers of Ethiopia chose to stage a legal procedure culminating in a trial in order to create this breach with the past and to define a new starting point – a year zero – for democracy. The Red Terror trials will, in this context, operate as a political ritual whose function is to legitimate the new system of governance and its rulers. By letting a so-called 'independent' body – the SPO – carry out the task of bringing forward the charges in the trials, in combination with letting presumptive 'indepen-

---

[15] Written statement by Dawit Yohannes on Pol.Ethiopia e-mail network, 31 December 1997 (pol.ethiopia@wn.APC.ORG).

[16] The new treason and attempted genocide trial launched post-election in 2005 in Ethiopia against *inter alia* the leadership of the Coalition for Unity and Democracy (CUD) party, whose strongest constituency is located in the highland Amhara region, may also be related to the cultural-political competition between these two groups.

dent' courts decide the judgement over the old regime based on accepted Ethiopian law, the verdict will appear as the 'objective truth.' The fact that the trials only address one segment of the Red Terror – the violations carried out by the Derg – also fulfils a specific purpose since the verdict will in this way serve not only as a judgement on the Derg regime but, simultaneously, serve as an implicit acquittal of the TPLF and other ethnic resistance movements against the Derg regime. Passing a verdict on nationalistic Derg officials will legitimize the ethnic resistance towards the regime as justified and warranted, thus acquitting the resistance movements for their actions and violations. In this way the Ethiopian population have been forced to accept the trials as a *fait accompli*, since they have not had any chance to influence the mandate or principles of the trials; moreover, the new government has created the necessary link between violation and verdict, as reflected in the difference between the old and new political order.

The attempt to create a decisive breach with the past may also explain why Prime Minister Meles Zenawi has not responded to the request from 33 of the top Derg officials on trial to be given a forum where they may 'beg the Ethiopian public for their pardon for the mistakes done knowingly or unknowingly' during the Derg regime (Girmachew A. Aneme 2006: 67). The letter, signed by former Vice President Colonel Fiseha Desta, former Prime Minister Captain Fikreselassie Wegederesse and Major Melaku Tefera, known as the 'Butcher of Gondar,' explains further that:

> We are the people who remain from the regime, our actions had the support of the majority of the people who benefited, while we believed it was also the cause of the civil war that has consumed the life of the people and destroyed property. [...] Even though we were the sworn servants of the regime of the emperor to protect it, when the people showed their dissatisfaction with the regime, we decided to side with them, instead of protecting it.[17]

The Chief Special Prosecutor has previously touched upon the importance of the accused offering a public apology. In an SPO statement from 1997, he explains:

> It is our knowledge that some people in Ethiopia are not convinced that investigation and prosecuting past human rights violations are necessary, but instead insist on forgiveness. However, forgiveness implies an existing wrong done by the party to be forgiven. Confession precedes forgiveness. The wrongdoer should officially confess the wrong he has done and ask God or the victim for forgiveness.[18]

---

[17] The letter is dated 13 August 2003, but was first published on the web by Independent Online, 1 February 2004 (http:www.int.iol.co.za).

[18] Announcement by the SPO to the Corps Diplomatique, Government representatives, Representatives of the Victims, NGOs and Human Rights Organisations and members of the press', February 13, 1997, Addis Ababa.

This was a position held in the early years of the trial; however, with the extreme prolongation of the process, its initial objective becomes increasingly blurred and diluted. Therefore, the plea from the Derg officials to speak to the Ethiopian population in order to beg for forgiveness, came too late. They would also have taken such an opportunity to present their side of the 'war story'. By contextualizing the Red Terror from the Derg's viewpoint – in the midst of contemporary human rights violations – such a communication by the representatives of the main group of defendants would potentially have made a mockery not only of the trials, but of the EPRDF's human rights agenda as a whole. Obviously, this would have been a dangerous act which could jeopardise the EPRDF's effort to establish the rigid discontinuity with a past of human rights abuses. Thus, in order to protect the victor's interpretation of events, PM Meles Zenawi and the government have remained silent about the request.

Concluding Remarks

In countries carrying out revolutionary transitions from dictatorship to democratic government, questions of transitional justice become a challenge for the new rulers: do they really represent a true democracy with respect for basic principles of human rights, and do they establish a necessary breach with the past and the old order? Strong political pressure for 'victor's justice' over the supporters of the old regime and the necessity to mark a clear breach between the old and new order, may entail that the settlement with the past will be drained of its intended objective and instead filled with contradictory content. In short, rather than healing and reconciling national wounds, 'victor's justice' may broaden and worsen them. This happens most often in countries where a clear compartmentalization of the different political processes is made: when attempts to call for justice and make accountable the former human rights violators are seen in isolation from the contemporary political context and current human rights violations (Kritz 1995: xxi). I argue that this is exactly what is going on in Ethiopia today (cf. Tronvoll 2008). The settlement with the past is eclipsed by contemporary violations and lack of the rule of law. This undermines the legitimacy of the trials, since the difference between the stated policies and the empirical practice of the new government is so universally apparent.

The crucial dilemma of regime transitions – either by implementing a juridical process in order to create a definite breach with the past, or by facilitating a reconciliation process where past experiences are used as stepping-stones to create a peaceful future – is that no matter which strategy is preferred, one cannot isolate it from the contemporary political context wherein it takes place. Since human rights trials are such important politico-symbolic rituals, they must be played out in a context which creates favourable conditions for the growth of understanding and tolerance among the broadest segments of the population. A trial or a reconciliation process against the old political order will lose its legitimacy and be drained of its politico-symbolic capital if the new rulers continue the repressive order. The current EPRDF government in Ethiopia seems to continue the political practice of human rights violations and authoritarianism, paradoxically the same order it symbolically tried to deprecate through the human rights trials of the Derg regime's perpetrators.

References

Amnesty International. 1995. *Ethiopia Accountability Past and Present: Human rights in transition.* London: Amnesty International, International Secretariat.

——. 1996. *Ethiopia: Human rights trials and delayed justice.* London: Amnesty International, International Secretariat.

Andargachew Tiruneh. 1993. *The Ethiopian Revolution 1974–1987: A transformation from an aristocratic to a totalitarian autocracy.* Cambridge: Cambridge University Press.

Girmachew Alemu Aneme. 2006. 'Apology and trials: The case of the Red Terror trials in Ethiopia,' *African Human Rights Law Journal,* vol. 6, no.1.

Hobsbawm, Eric J. and Terence Ranger. (eds.) 1992. *The Invention of Tradition,* Canto edition. Cambridge: Cambridge University Press.

Kiflu Tadesse. 1998. *The Generation. Part II.* vol. 2. Lanham, MD, New York, Oxford: University Press of America.

Kritz, Neil J. (ed.) 1995. *Transitional Justice. How emerging democracies reckon with former regimes. Volume I: General Considerations.* Washington, DC: United States Institute of Peace Press.

Markakis, John. 1990. *National and Class Conflict in the Horn of Africa.* London: Zed Books.

Markakis, John and Nega Ayele. 1986. *Class and Revolution in Ethiopia,* American edition . Trenton, NJ: Red Sea Press.

Pausewang, Siegfried. 1996. 'Ethiopia', in *Human Rights in Developing Countries Yearbook 1996.* P. Baehr, L. Sadiwa, and J. Smith (eds). The Hague: Kluwer Law International.

Ryle, John. 1995. 'An African Nuremberg', *New Yorker.* 2 October.

Special Prosecutor's Office. 1995. 'The Special Prosecution Process of War Criminals and Human Rights Violators in Ethiopia,' in *Transitional Justice. How emerging democracies reckon with former regimes,* vol. III, *Transitional Justice.* N. J. Kritz (ed.). Washington, DC: United States Institute of Peace Press.

Tronvoll, Kjetil. 1997. *Contextualising Human Rights and Democratisation Support: External aid to the NGO sector in Ethiopia.* Norwegian Institute of Human Rights, University of Oslo 6/1997.

——. 2000. *Ethiopia: A new start?* London: Minority Rights Group International.

——. 2008. 'Human Rights Violations in Federal Ethiopia: When Ethnic Identity is a Political Stigma,' *International Journal on Minority and Groups Rights,* vol. 15, no. 1.

US State Department. 2006. 'Ethiopia,' in *Country Reports on Human Rights Practices 2000.* Washington, DC: US State Department.

Vaughan, Sarah and Kjetil Tronvoll. 2003. *The Culture of Power in Contemporary Ethiopian Political Life.* Stockholm: Sida studies, Sida.

Wilson, Richard A. 2001. *The Politics of Truth and Reconciliation in South Africa.* Cambridge: Cambridge University Press.

Zalaquett, José. 1995. 'Confronting Human Rights Violations Committed by Former Governments: Principles applicable and political constraints,' in *Transitional Justice. How emerging democracies reckon with former regimes: General Considerations,* vol. 1. N. J. Kritz (ed.). Washington, DC: United States Institute of Peace Press.

7

Building State & Nation ▓ Justice, Reconciliation & Democratization in Ethiopia & South Africa

ELSA VAN HUYSSTEEN

Introduction

A brutal, repressive regime creates what Vaclav Havel (1991: 391) calls a 'contaminated moral environment' where both state and society are scarred by violence, fear and inhumanity. The consolidation of a new democracy burdened with such a legacy thus requires the creation of '[...] a new type of society, a new form of politics, and a new kind of people' (Parlevliet, 1998: 174), which in turn requires dual processes of the democratization of state and civil society.[1] There is a near-global consensus[2] that this demands a reckoning of some kind with the past, but what form this should take is controversial.

There are two core elements of such a reckoning. The first is the creation of an account of the past, in order to establish a historical record, or a collective memory, of the atrocities committed. In his novel *The Book of Laughter and Forgetting*, Milan Kundera (1980: 3) writes that 'the struggle of man against power is the struggle of memory against forgetting', and the creation of a public memory of past abuse of power is indeed seen as a weapon against future abuse of power. The second element relates to dealing with the perpetrators of the atrocities, and this is the more controversial part of the process. Strategies range along a continuum with the prosecution of perpetrators at the one end and blanket amnesty at the other, and a number of other options in between. Debates about the appropriate strategy for dealing with perpetrators are fundamentally debates about the relative importance of justice and reconciliation in processes of democratizing states and societies. Do these processes require forgiving and forgetting, and therefore the granting of

---

[1] The argument that the consolidation of democracy requires the democratization and transformation of both state and civil society is made by Held (1987) and (1993).

[2] For a discussion of the limited number of exceptions, see e.g. Adam (2000) on Germany, Japan, Spain and other examples of 'amnesia' as a way of dealing with a painful past, and Parlevliet (2000) and Saul (2000) on denial of Swapo atrocities in Namibia.

amnesty to perpetrators, or do they require bringing perpetrators of the brutal past to justice by means of prosecution? Are calls for justice at odds with strategies aimed at reconciliation, or is justice a condition for reconciliation and thus for democratization?

The transitions in Ethiopia and South Africa provide instructive scenarios to investigate these questions. After the transition from the brutal Derg regime in Ethiopia, the new government initiated a process of prosecuting officials of that regime for its atrocities. This was conceptualized as a means of both constructing an official record of that era and bringing perpetrators to justice. After the transition from apartheid to democracy in South Africa, a Truth and Reconciliation Commission was established to write an official history of the past and to give amnesty to perpetrators of that past. Both processes were explicitly aimed at providing the basis for consolidating a new state and society with a new culture of accountability and democracy where the atrocities of the past could never happen again. Both processes have also, however, been contested: in South Africa, by those who call for justice as the basis for reconciliation and democratization, and in Ethiopia, by those who argue that such a conception of retributive justice perpetuates a cycle of revenge and who call instead for an emphasis on reconciliation as the basis for democratization.[3]

This chapter focuses on the construction of notions of justice and reconciliation as part of strategies aimed at dealing with a painful past in order to build a new democratic state and civil society. The central argument of the chapter is that processes of transitional justice can make a meaningful contribution to the consolidation of new democracies if they are designed in such a way that they contribute to the democratization of both state and civil society. Of course, the opposite is also true: transitional justice processes can undermine such democratization and in that way hinder the consolidation of new democracies. An analysis of the cases of transitional justice in Ethiopia and South Africa can provide valuable insight into the design of these processes. The first section briefly investigates the role of notions of truth, justice and reconciliation in democratisation in order to form a backdrop for the discussion and evaluation of the processes of transitional justice and democratisation in South Africa and Ethiopia.

---

[3] I have encountered much resistance among Ethiopians to the attempt to compare Ethiopia and South Africa, on the grounds that the two cases are too dissimilar. This chapter does not argue that the two cases are similar, on the contrary, it is argued that the historical, political and social contexts of the two countries are dramatically different and that this fundamentally shaped the processes of transitional justice. However, a discussion of the two cases is enlightening precisely because such different avenues were taken. In addition, while international literature on transitional justice almost always includes the South African case, the Ethiopian case is virtually completely ignored (see Haile, 2000), and a comparison of the two may contribute to introducing the Ethiopian experience into those debates.

Democratization:
The Role of Truth, Justice and Reconciliation

Why is dealing with the past important for democratization? Democracy requires a particular set of values and practices in both state and civil society.[4] Democratic states are characterized by transparency and accountability of governance and a measure of participation in decision-making processes on the part of citizens. They command a measure of legitimacy among the citizenry, and respect and protect the rights of citizens, including freedom of expression and of association. Authoritarian regimes which govern through violence and brutality, of course, do not meet any of these criteria, and new democracies with such a past therefore lack an entrenched culture and established practices of democratic governance. In this context, democratization thus requires a process of democratizing the state by means of which new forms of governance and politics are established and entrenched. Second, democratic civil society[5] is characterized by values and practices that tolerate diversity, including diversity of opinions and views, that facilitate participation in public debate and other political processes, and that facilitate the respect of the rights of other citizens. The conflict, fear and suspicion caused by brutal regimes destroy these features of public life, and democratization thus also requires a transformation of civil society by means of which a new culture and practice of public life can be established and entrenched.

The democratization of both state and civil society under such circumstances requires that the past be dealt with in some way, and this includes establishing an account of the past (truth) as well as dealing with the perpetrators and consequences of that past (justice and reconciliation), with the aim of both repairing the damage done by past practices, or healing the wounds of that past, and of preventing the recurrence of the atrocities committed.

There are, however, two additional challenges to democratization in societies like Ethiopia and South Africa which may impact dramatically on the success of transitional justice processes, and thus have to be addressed by such processes: ethnic diversity and polarization, and poverty and inequality. First, it is argued that democratization entails the

---

[4] There is, of course, much debate around what exactly these values and practices should be, and a growing consensus that these ideals are rarely concretized in practice, and that '"really existing" democracy does not work as well as it should' (Nash, 2000: 216), to the extent that Trend (1996: 7) can speak of 'democracy's crisis of meaning'. These debates are, however, beyond the scope of this discussion, and this section thus merely briefly outlines a number of uncontroversial basic elements of democratic values and practices.

[5] 'Civil society' is often assumed to be democratic. However, civil society can assume many guises, including forms that are fundamentally undemocratic. See, e.g. Chabal and Daloz (1999) for a discussion.

creation of a 'civic nation' which 'does not derive its identity from some common ethnic and cultural properties, but rather from the *praxis* of citizens who actively exercise their civil rights' (Habermas, 1992: 3). This does not mean the denial or repression of ethnic or cultural identities, but requires that they are exercised in a framework of the tolerance or accommodation of heterogeneity,[6] and the protection of minorities,[7] in order to avoid discrimination and violence. Second, failure on the part of a new democratic regime to address extreme poverty and exclusion can militate against the development of faith in the institutions of democracy on the part of ordinary citizens. Social justice can thus be seen as a crucial element of democratization.

Mamdani (1998: 9, 17) argues that the failure to address these two factors can fundamentally undermine efforts at reconciliation. In Rwanda, he argues, 'a failure to recognise that one could forge a common Rwandese political identity, without denying Bahutu and Batutsi as cultural identities', contributed to the genocide of 1994, and in South Africa, a failure to address the unequal distribution of resources that characterized apartheid may in time unleash a 'tide of revenge'. These are the dangers of 'justice without reconciliation' (as in Rwanda), and 'reconciliation without justice' (as in South Africa) (Mamdani in Hartwell, 1999: 6). These arguments will be returned to later in the chapter.

The following sections examine the roles of truth, justice and reconciliation in the democratization of both state and civil society in the aftermath of a brutal and oppressive regime.

The Role of Truth, Justice and Reconciliation in Democratization in Ethiopia and South Africa

It was argued earlier that the choice of transitional justice mechanism in a particular context will depend heavily on the nature of the transition to democracy and the resulting configuration of power relations. The Ethiopian transition was brought about by the military victory of the forces of resistance (the EPRDF) over the Derg regime, and the subsequent complete take-over of all spheres of power.[8] As a result, there is little talk of reconciliation and an emphasis instead on bringing to justice the officials of the previous regime by means of prosecution in terms of the Ethiopian Penal Code in Ethiopian courts. The South African emphasis on reconciliation and definition of justice as restorative rather than

---

[6] How exactly this is to be achieved is, of course, much debated. Solutions range from the one extreme of liberal theorists' desire to confine such identities to the non-political sphere, to group rights for ethnic communities, to the other extreme of self-determination for each such ethnic group. See, e,g, Shafir (1998) for a discussion of these debates.

[7] The concept is used here in a sociological sense, not numerical, i.e. an ethnic group may be numerically in the majority, but a minority in terms of position in the configuration of power.

[8] See Mayfield (1995) and Haile (2000).

retributive is, in contrast, the result of a transition brought about by means of negotiation against the background of a stalemate with no possibility of outright victory for either side. This means that the new regime has to contend with the reality that much power, particularly economic power, still rests in the hands of white South Africans, hence the emphasis on reconciliation between beneficiaries and victims of apartheid. This resulted in a decision to deal with the past by means of a Truth and Reconciliation Commission (TRC) which would be empowered to grant amnesty to perpetrators of gross human rights violations on condition of full disclosure and clear political motivation for such violations.[9]

The two new regimes have thus adopted very different approaches to democratization. In Ethiopia, the approach was characterized by an emphasis on justice (formulated as prosecution and punishment) as the basis for the creation of a democratic state and society characterized by accountability and a respect for human rights, and a virtual absence of a notion of reconciliation.[10] In South Africa, a project of national reconciliation was pursued which encouraged forgiveness for past wrongs in the name of a national sense of *ubuntu*, which is an African notion of community 'based on reciprocity, respect for human dignity, community cohesion and solidarity' (Wilson, 2001: 9).

The question of ethnicity was also approached very differently by the two regimes. In Ethiopia, ethnic identity and mobilization are officially and constitutionally recognized and encouraged, while in South Africa, the language of ethnicity has little official legitimacy, having been discredited by its manipulation and exploitation by the apartheid regime. Instead, the creation of a 'constitutional patriotism' (Habermas, 1996), or a sense of belonging on the basis of a shared commitment to constitutionalism and human rights and not on the basis of ethnic identity, is pursued.[11] Filatova (1994: 53, 58)[12] argues that these different approaches can be seen as responses to the approach of the previous regimes, which had devastating results: in South Africa, the 'primordialist and ethnically divisive approaches' of the apartheid regime, and in Ethiopia, the denial and repression of ethnic identities and aspirations by the Derg regime. Finally, democratization in both societies faces the formidable challenge of extreme poverty. Ethiopia is one of the poorest countries in the world, primarily reliant on agriculture affected by drought, famine,

---

[9] See, e.g. Krog (1998), Simpson (1999) and Wilson (2001) for a detailed account of these events.

[10] Where it is used, mainly by opposition politicians, it refers to attempts to bring about reconciliation between political parties and resultant power-sharing. Thank you to Tafesse Olika for pointing this out to me. Also see Haile (2000: 60).

[11] This does not mean, however, that ethnic identities have been successfully sidelined; on the contrary, there are countless examples of the assertion and mobilization of ethnic identities, and President Mbeki's reign has been characterized by a much greater emphasis on race in official discourse than that of former President Mandela.

[12] Her comparison is between South Africa and the Soviet Union, but the argument holds for the present comparison.

war, government repression and forced resettlement. South Africa, in turn, enjoys the advantage of a much greater extent of development, but the majority of South Africans live in poverty, and in addition, South Africa is one of the most unequal societies in the world.

These different approaches to democratization are clearly manifested in the transitional justice processes pursued. The mandate of the Ethiopian Office of the Special Prosecutor (SPO) is 'to establish for public knowledge and for posterity a historical record of the abuses of the Mengistu regime' and 'to bring those criminally responsible for human rights violations and/or corruption to justice'. This mandate is 'also a policy choice regarding how a society can productively deal with past abuses to create a more democratic future' (SPO report in Kritz, 1995: 559). In other words, an exclusive emphasis on truth, but only in relation to the abuses of the Derg, and justice. In contrast, the Promotion of National Unity and Reconciliation Act[13] which established the South African TRC defines its objectives as the promotion of:

> national unity and reconciliation in a spirit of understanding which transcends the conflicts and divisions of the past by [...] establishing as complete a picture as possible of the causes, nature and extent of the gross violations of human rights which were committed [...] including the antecedents, circumstances, factors and context of such violations, as well as the perspectives of the victims and the motives and perspectives of the persons responsible for the commission of the violations, by conducting investigations and holding hearings; [...] facilitating the granting of amnesty to persons who make full disclosure of all the relevant facts relating to acts associated with a political objective [...]; establishing and making known the fate or whereabouts of victims and by restoring the human and civil dignity of such victims by granting them an opportunity to relate their own accounts of the violations of which they are the victims, and by recommending reparation measures in respect of them; [...] [and] compiling a report providing as comprehensive an account as possible of the activities and findings of the Commission [...] and which contains recommendations of measures to prevent the future violations of human rights.'[14]

These two mandates indicate very different approaches to truth, justice and reconciliation and therefore to the democratization of the state and the formation of civil society.

Truth
The Ethiopian route to truth through prosecutions of officials of the Derg regime is aimed at creating an official record only of the abuses of the

---

[13] Act no. 34 of 1995.
[14] In sections 3 (1)(a)-(d).

Mengistu regime. In keeping with the Ethiopian penchant for record keeping, the Derg regime kept meticulous records of its atrocities which meant that the SPO had, in many cases, what amounts to a written confession. Executions were broadcast on the radio, and relatives often had to pay for the bullet which had killed their family member before they could claim the body. The terror was thus brazen and public. As Cohen (2001: 225) argues, however, knowledge is not the same as acknowledgement, and the trials can thus fulfil an important function of bringing public acknowledgement of private knowledge and experience of horror, and in that way validate the experiences and restore the dignity and authority of victims.[15] For example, although everyone had known that Emperor Haile Selassie had been murdered by the Derg, evidence revealed during the trial was the first time the particulars of his death and burial were publically announced. Other stories emerged revealing the importance to relatives of victims of the official naming of the victim in court. In addition, as one Ethiopian scholar commented in an interview,[16] 'sometimes you're shocked to hear the stories, things you didn't know.'[17] The trials therefore both constructed a more complete picture of the abuses of the regime and turned private knowledge into official history (see Vaughan in this volume).

An important objection to a process of truth through prosecution is that it limits the number of people who can participate in the process. The SPO decided, however, to lead thousands of witnesses in the trials, including more than 800 witnesses in the main trial against the top officials of the Derg, a strategy which has seen hundreds of victims come to court to tell their story. In this way, the trial process retains the advantages for victims of telling their story, namely empowerment and restoration of dignity through validation of experiences. However, due to the protracted pace of testimony and court proceedings, one defence attorney estimated that it was extremely unlikely that the version of the accused would ever be heard, and this could mean that the picture which emerges will be less than complete. In addition, the defendants had no incentive to cooperate and provide a full account of their actions. According to Ryle (1995: 57), 'in court, the defendants were clearly unrepentant.' The defence's argument was that the actions taken by the Derg had been justified to maintain civil order and that the court was not independent. Mengistu himself has insisted that it was 'a war that had been fought to preserve the unity of the country' (ibid.: 51), that 'millions of people came to Addis and said "defend us or arm us"' and that he

[15] The office of the SPO also conducted extensive investigations and compiled vast amounts of documentary (including audio-visual) evidence.

[16] All interviews mentioned here were conducted in Addis Ababa during May 2000 by the author and Louise Hagemeier (2001) with Ethiopian scholars, lawyers, judges, journalists, human rights activists and members of the public. In order to protect the identity of interviewees, interviews will be identified by date only.

[17] Interview, 4 May 2000.

himself 'never killed anybody' (AFP, 1999). Of course, Mengistu is living in Zimbabwe, where President Mugabe has steadfastly refused to extradite him, which means that his version of events may never be officially recorded. A further consequence of the prosecution process in Ethiopia will be a limited account of those years, as the focus is exclusively on the actions of the Derg regime, while many Ethiopians point to atrocities committed by the resistance to the regime as well (Haile 2000). It is clear that while the pursuit of truth by trial in Ethiopia has a number of advantages, particularly the empowerment of victims of the previous regime, it has shortcomings which may undermine democratization. As not all participants in the conflict are held to account for their actions, it may be difficult to entrench a culture of accountability. The adversarial process may limit the account of the past which emerges, and may also lead to the development of what Adam (2000: 88) calls 'retrogressive' memory which remains locked on past conflicts.

The South African approach of establishing the truth by means of a truth commission which includes extensive investigations and statement-taking as well as public hearings for both victims and perpetrators of human rights violations, and special hearings where the role of, among other sectors, business and labour, the judiciary, the health profession, universities and the media in apartheid was investigated, has the potential of creating a more complete picture of the past. The Commission also explicitly included the violations committed by all participants in the conflict. The outcome of the process is a massive report which details almost all aspects of the apartheid regime. The Commission's approach to 'the truth' has been much criticized: 'Truth shrank from a single emancipatory Truth to smaller, multiple truths and in the final Report, there were only four fragmented types of truth remaining.' These were factual or forensic truth, personal or narrative truth, social truth, and healing and restorative truth (Wilson, 2001: 36–7).

The consequences of this approach to truth for democratization are not easy to determine. Although one could argue that the Commission's work was characterized by an even-handedness in that it identified violations committed by all sides in the conflict, the implication that the violations committed by both the apartheid regime and resistance to it are comparable (although the Commission explicitly rejects a moral equalization of the two) has incensed members of the liberation movement, and strengthened views that the process pandered to the interests of the old guard. The ANC went as far as to attempt, in court, to prevent the publication of the final report, objecting specifically to the 'scurrilous attempts to criminalise the liberation struggle by characterising the heroic struggles of the people of South Africa [...] as gross human rights violations' (Ronnie Mamoepa from the ANC quoted in *The Star*, 1 November 1998). In fact, the report was condemned by a range of parties across the political spectrum (*The Star*, 30 October 1998).

The Commission is also criticized for not paying enough attention to the everyday violations of human rights that characterized the apartheid state, as its brief was to focus on gross human rights violations, and in this way a full picture of the horror of apartheid was not created, allowing ordinary beneficiaries of apartheid to ascribe all responsibility to a small number of brutal perpetrators. This may undermine the process of democratizing civil society as it facilitates extensive denial on the part of ordinary white South Africans. Doubts have been raised as to whether the TRC process really succeeded in obtaining a full picture even of gross human rights violations. Some have argued, for example, that the TRC failed in persuading perpetrators to apply for amnesty in KwaZulu Natal, the site of extensive political violence, as the Inkatha Freedom Party, which battled with the ANC in that region for years, adopted a policy of non-cooperation with the TRC. In addition, the TRC is criticized for not focusing on the socio-economic oppression of apartheid, which has arguably had the most enduring effect, and thus not addressing the need for economic redistribution which is crucial to the consolidation of democracy (Barchiesi, 1999).

The public truth-telling process that the work of the Commission created as well as its transparent mode of operation has been commended for the extent to which it empowered victims, treating them with great respect and dignity and validating their experiences of the brutality of the regime. However, in four ways exigencies of the task weakened the truth telling process. First, the process of collecting the stories of the victims shifted gradually from an attitude characterized as 'we let people tell their story' to a short structured interview directed by a questionnaire which 'distorted the whole story altogether' and 'destroyed the meaning' of the account. Second, it transpired that the much-vaunted opportunities for victims to tell stories in public at the Human Rights Violations Hearings did not translate into inclusion of the information in the database. Third, there was a shift from a narrative framed victim-oriented process to an approach that focused in a quasi-legal manner on perpetrators. Finally, the TRC attempt to impose a forgiving or reconciling tone on the stories told and the ways in which this was resisted both by the narrators and the audience, who often cheered on accounts of human rights violations or jeered narrators whose political affiliation they disagreed with. Victims who wanted to tell of their desire for revenge were marginalized and silenced (Wilson, 2001: 41–5; Du Toit 1999: 2). Even more controversial have been the strategies of dealing with the perpetrators in both cases.

Justice vs reconciliation
As indicated earlier, the Ethiopian process has prioritized retributive justice in its approach to perpetrators of past human rights violations. There was not much talk of reconciliation, except as something which would encourage the charging of perpetrators. The official reason for choosing this route was that it would establish a culture of accountability

and respect for the rule of law in both state and society. As Prime Minister Meles Zenawi said, 'It is very important to prove to Ethiopians that those who mess around with the law, human rights law, those who consider themselves above the law, are not really above the law, that there will be some way of reckoning' (Lycett, 1994: 34), and 'we are not motivated by a desire for vengeance. The absence of a rule of law was the reason we had these tragic events. We had to come to terms with the events of those years. The only legitimate way was a trial' (Ryle, 1995: 52).

The extent to which this has contributed to the democratization of state and civil society is, however, doubtful (see Tronvoll in this volume). Many Ethiopians see the trials not as an attempt to build accountability, but as victor's justice designed as an agenda for revenge. Ordinary people, according to one interviewee, are said to see the trials as 'the usual political machinations of the political elite, like the election process, it is a window-dressing exercise, people know the outcome.' If there is to be a trial, 'it should be conducted by an independent tribunal. How can the winner try the defeated? It is just revenge on the defeated through the legal process.'[18] In addition, the trial process itself is now seen as compounding the culture of human rights violations by disregarding the rights of the accused, by detaining them without charge or trial for unacceptably long periods and by not ensuring a speedy trial (see Elgesem and G. Aneme in this volume). Many Ethiopians believe that the trial process perpetuates vindictiveness and revenge and that what was necessary to close the chapter is to forgive. If the establishment of a human rights culture was the goal, an interviewee elaborated, 'We went the wrong route. Many of us called for reconciliation and a peace process, as we have this culture of reconciliation, forgiveness, arbitration, in all the ethnic groups'[19] (see Schaefer in this volume). In addition, 'the trials will not bring out the needed information, especially the causes', the legal process 'is difficult for people to understand, nobody talks about it, even on the university campus', and therefore 'telling the stories of what happened would be a better way, that would teach a lesson to the new generation .'[20]

There are, however, indications that the trials did satisfy the need of some victims and their relatives for justice, and this may contribute to the democratization of civil society as it enables such people to put the past behind them: 'relatives and friends of the victims [as opposed to others] want to have a trial and a verdict, and see an outcome'.[21] Woubishet (1996: 15) points out that in a nation which assumes that 'as the sky can not be ploughed, the ruler can not be prosecuted', putting former rulers on trial was 'a momentous occasion in the nation's history'. Acknowledging the faults of the Red Terror trials, these observations, nevertheless, indicate

[18] Interview 4 May 2000.
[19] Interview 3 May 2000.
[20] Interview 4 May 2000.
[21] Interview 4 May 2000.

that a trial process can indeed serve justice and make an important contribution to reconciliation as a step towards democratization.

The South African approach to dealing with perpetrators has been very different. Perpetrators of gross human rights violations could apply for and be awarded amnesty which indemnifies them from both criminal prosecution and civil action. This has been widely and fiercely contested in South Africa, to the extent that it is clear that this approach can contribute to democratization only in the most limited sense, as limited perhaps as the Red Terror trials, albeit for radically different reasons. Hendricks (1999: 11) argues that 'amnesty sends a message to future state criminals that there is the chance that they may be exonerated especially if they remain in power long enough to ensure that they are not easily dislodged, or that some compromise may be necessary to remove them from power.' Indeed, the agreement on amnesty for perpetrators of human rights violations formed an important part of the negotiation of the transition. Dugard (1997: 260) notes that the 'opaque origins' of the legislation that established the Truth and Reconciliation Commission and provides for amnesty to the perpetrators of apartheid's gross human rights violations, together with 'the understandable desire for retribution that persists in many quarters, have made it the most controversial legislation of post-apartheid South Africa'. Wilson contends, based on extensive ethnographic research, that South Africans generally have a clearly retributive notion of justice and therefore struggle to relate to the restorative meaning given to the notion of justice by the TRC and other political elites, and that this may undermine the development of a rights culture. 'It is misguided to delegitimize human rights at the national level by detaching them from a retributive understanding of justice and attaching them to a religious notion of reconciliation-forgiveness, a regrettable amnesty law and an elite project of nation-building' (Wilson 2001: 230).

The most high-profile attack on the legitimacy of amnesty came from AZAPO[22] and the families of some of the most celebrated victims of apartheid brutality, Steve Biko, Griffiths and Victoria Mxenge and Dr and Mrs Fabian Ribeiro,[23] who challenged the constitutionality of the provision for amnesty in the Constitutional Court.[24] The Court relied on the postcript to the Interim Constitution[25] to reject the challenge.[26] The

---

[22] Azanian People's Organization.

[23] Apartheid agents were either known or suspected to have murdered these four individuals.

[24] They applied for an order declaring section 20(7) of the legislation unconstitutional. 'Section 20(7), read with other sections of the Act, permits the Committee on Amnesty established by the Act to grant amnesty to a perpetrator of an unlawful act associated with a political objective and committed prior to 6 December 1993. As a result of the grant of amnesty, the perpetrator cannot be criminally or civilly liable in respect of that act. Equally, the state or any other body, organisation or person that would ordinarily have been vicariously liable for such act, cannot be liable in law' (Wits Law School 1996).

[25] Act 200 of 1993.

[26] *AZAPO and others vs the President of the Republic of South Africa and others*, CCT 17/96, available at www.concourt.gov.za.

postscript is a dramatic statement of the hegemonic approach to democratization in the new South Africa. Entitled 'National Unity and Reconciliation', it declares:

> This Constitution provides a historic bridge between the past of a deeply divided society characterised by strife, conflict, untold suffering and injustice, and a future founded on the recognition of human rights, democracy and peaceful co-existence and development opportunities for all South Africans, irrespective of colour, race, class, belief or sex. The pursuit of national unity, the well-being of all South African citizens and peace require reconciliation between the people of South Africa and the reconstruction of society. The adoption of this Constitution lays the secure foundation for the people of South Africa to transcend the divisions and strife of the past, which generated gross violations of human rights, the transgression of humanitarian principles in violent conflicts and a legacy of hatred, fear, guilt and revenge. These can now be addressed on the basis that there is a need for understanding but not for vengeance, a need for reparation but not for retaliation, a need for ubuntu but not for victimisation. In order to advance such reconciliation and reconstruction, amnesty shall be granted in respect of acts, omissions and offences associated with political objectives and committed in the course of the conflicts of the past [...] With this Constitution and these commitments we, the people of South Africa, open a new chapter in the history of our country.

The Court acknowledged that amnesty limited the applicants' right in terms of section 22 of the Interim Constitution to 'have justifiable disputes settled by a court of law, or [...] other independent or impartial forum'. However, this limitation was deemed to be sanctioned by the Interim Constitution. There are two major themes in the Court's reasoning in this case. The first was that without the agreement on amnesty for perpetrators, the transition might not have been possible at all, and the 'historic bridge' referred to in the epilogue would not have been erected. The second theme was that, without the promise of amnesty for criminal and civil liability, it was unlikely that perpetrators of human rights violations would tell the truth about their actions. This, too, would threaten the aim of national reconciliation and unity. The Court further elaborated this theme of the importance of amnesty for building the new South Africa by arguing that the granting of amnesty to the state for civil liability protected the new state from the huge financial burden that would likely result from claims against it by apartheid victims. An important consequence of the elite-pact nature of the transition was the silencing of many voices to the left of the political spectrum. This case represents an intensifying struggle over the consequences of the nature of the transition for the distribution of power. AZAPO represents a voice which was rapidly marginalized during the transition, as transition theorists[27] predicted: the

---

[27] See Adler and Webster (1995) for a discussion.

radicals in the pro-democracy forces must be sidelined in order to make compromises with the reformers in the current regime possible. The TRC attempted to promote a notion of reconciliation premised on forgiveness of perpetrators, which is of course essential if amnesty for such perpetrators is to be at all accepted. The judgement clearly indicates the Court's support for a version of the transition that emphasises the importance of compromise and reconciliation, and for a new South African discourse of reconstruction and reconciliation which marginalizes and delegitimates discourses that employ notions of justice and retribution, and, at a deeper level, redistribution of power.

It is clear that the impact of amnesty as a means of dealing with the perpetrators of human rights violations on democratization can be very negative indeed. On the one hand, there may be good reasons for elite compromises in a situation where that seems to be the only way in which to end violence and achieve a transition to democracy. But as Angell (quoted in Jung and Shapiro, 1995: 300) notes of Chile, 'what was originally a tactical agreement [...] soon became a strategy, but now has become a dominant ideology'. A good example of that process in South Africa is the shift from an approach that promised the prosecution of perpetrators who were refused amnesty or did not apply, to the real possibility of a blanket amnesty for prisoners who claim political motivation for their crimes. In May 2002, President Mbeki granted a pardon to 33 prisoners on the grounds that their crimes were politically motivated, a move which was followed by high-level negotiations between political parties aimed at including prisoners from the entire political spectrum (*Beeld*, 20 May 2002). These events followed the acquittal by the High Court of Wouter Basson, dubbed 'Dr Death' by the media for his alleged role, as medical doctor, in what amounted to a form of chemical warfare against opponents of apartheid. The Court's decision was widely condemned, and presents dramatic evidence of the difficulties of prosecuting such acts in ordinary courts: the judge was accused of being 'old guard', and indeed he was appointed during the apartheid era, but he held that the state had not produced sufficient evidence for a conviction. Finally, a crucial element of the TRC process was reparations. The final report recommended that an amount of US$21,000 should be paid to each victim over six years. In 1998, 'urgent interim relief' payments to the amount of US$330 were made to about 20,000 victims. In January 2000, the government announced that it would pay 'only token compensation of several hundred US dollars' to victims (Wilson, 2001: 22). This has incensed victims, one of whom declared, 'We have been betrayed. The previous government gave the killers golden handshakes and the present government gave them amnesty. [But] the victims have been left empty-handed' (quoted in Wilson, 2001: 23). Although reparations present a range of difficulties,[28] there is no doubt

---

[28] See Simpson (1999) for a discussion.

that the massive failure of this component of the approach fundamentally undermines the role that the TRC process can play in facilitating reconciliation.

Conclusions: A Tentative Evaluation

Analysed broadly, the transitional justice processes in both Ethiopia and South Africa have been under way for a substantial period and have in many ways been marginalized from the public agendas. Correspondingly, both societies have experienced significant difficulties in consolidating their democracies. Ethiopia continues to struggle with extreme poverty, ethnic tensions and violence, and the current government has been accused of human rights violations, including political imprisonment.[29] South Africa is experiencing deepening inequality and expanding poverty, fuelled by wide-spread lack of delivery of social services coupled with increasing commoditization of such services. Lack of access to clean water and sanitation results in regular cholera outbreaks and other diseases, and scores of people have had their electricity and water supply cut off or have been evicted from their homes for lack of payment, while many others live in informal settlements where housing and services are non-existent.[30] In addition, South Africa is ravaged by extreme rates of violent crime and by an HIV/Aids epidemic, while government policy on the issue is singularly inadequate, and has been challenged in court by activists.[31]

It is extremely difficult, under such circumstances, to tell the extent to which transitional justice processes contributed to or undermined democratization of both state and civil society in the two countries. However, the experiences do hold a number of lessons. It is clear that both approaches have major shortcomings as well as benefits. In the Ethiopian case the shortcomings included very delayed and fragmented trials and lack of emphasis on reparations or compensation for victims. Together they appear to have contributed to cynicism and lack of interest by the Ethiopian public as well as lending confidence in democratic practices. In the South African case, the provision of amnesty to perpetrators, coupled with a failed programme of reparations, has produced public outrage and disillusionment, and undermined the project of national reconciliation.[32] Turning to the benefits, the construction of the history of the Derg era by means of a legal process of collecting evidence

---

[29] See annual reports by Amnesty International, Human Rights Watch and the US State Department.

[30] See *Debate*, March 2001, for discussion of a range of these issues.

[31] Also see *BBC Focus on Africa*, July-September 2001, for discussions of problems in contemporary Ethiopia and South Africa.

[32] See *Siyaya* Spring 1998 for a discussion.

is certainly positive; moreover, the Ethiopian prosecutions initially had the effect of enhancing the international standing of the new government and the trial process itself certainly brought satisfaction to a number of victims and their relatives. Likewise, the South African TRC process initially captured the public imagination and created a vivid and detailed (if flawed) account of the atrocities of the apartheid era. In addition, the process sparked extensive and continuing scholarly work which also contributes to ongoing debates about the past and its legacy.

Against this background, it is possible to identify elements of both strategies which can contribute to the democratization of state and civil society.[33] Firstly, it appears crucial to create a comprehensive account of what had happened, including the actions of all parties to the conflict. Such a project will, of course, generate resentment in many sectors, but it is central to the creation of 'progressive memory' to avoid the appearance of a witch-hunt of certain vested parties. This has been one of the strengths of the South African TRC process. The vehicle for this process does not necessarily have to be a truth commission. Some Ethiopian scholars suggest the creation of a research centre that focuses on retrieving and analysing the Red Terror record would go a long way towards developing a non-partisan account of the past.[34] It is also crucial to ensure that the process is a focus of free and critical public debate and media attention, as only in this way can knowledge of the past be disseminated widely enough to create 'politically literate citizens' who can guard against future repression (Adam, 2000: 88).[35] This open debate is instrumental in encouraging democratic values and practices in civil society, as well as on the part of the state, by also holding the new political elite to account for their actions and facilitating public scrutiny of their past and present actions and policies.

Second, it is critical that the perpetrators of the most grievous human rights violations be prosecuted. This has been one of the strengths of the Ethiopian process. Failure to prosecute such perpetrators creates public outrage and facilitates future violations by demonstrating the unlikelihood of any serious consequences. It is, however, imperative that such prosecutions are effective, and scrupulously adhere to international standards for the rights of the accused and a fair trial. A central benefit of prosecution for the democratization of both state and civil society is that it can contribute to the development of respect for the rule of law, an object which would be defeated by unfair or ineffective prosecutions. A further benefit of such prosecutions is the sense of justice provided to the victims and their families.

This is, however, not enough. There must finally be meaningful compensation or reparations for the victims. In societies where there are

[33] Also see Haile (2000: 59–63).
[34] Interview, 4 May 2000.
[35] Also see Zalaquett in Haile (2000: 61), who argues that the truth must be 'officially proclaimed and publicly exposed.'

significant constraints on resources, it may be impossible to provide significant material compensation. However, there are creative alternatives to cash payments. There is the possibility of reparation in the form of symbolic gestures. In South Africa, this has included the honouring of the victims' memory by naming schools and hospitals for them, local memorials, and other gestures. Haile (2000: 24) notes the Chilean example of granting medical and education benefits to victims, and suggests the provision of a 'national network of medical and psychological services for victims'. Hugo van der Merwe notes, for example, the failure of the TRC to take up offers of counselling from networks of therapists in South Africa.[36] Kritz (in Haile, 2000: 24) argues that reparation can address the material dimension of the victims' loss (which could include, for example, a family's loss of a breadwinner, or a victim's disability), that it represents official acknowledgement of victims' suffering, and that it can facilitate the social reintegration of victims. This can contribute to the democratization of the state by demonstrating the financial cost of human rights violations, and can contribute to the democratization of civil society by means of dignifying and integrating the victims of brutality.

The key objective of transitional justice processes should be the creation of active democratic citizenship. Fraser and Gordon (1998: 113) note that 'citizen and citizenship are powerful words. They speak of respect, of rights, of dignity.' The meaningful practice of citizenship, as opposed to the possession of a nominal legal status, demands the provision of the minimum requirements for a dignified life for all citizens, the effective exercise of rights, the extension of respect to all citizens, the development of solidarity and a sense of shared responsibility, and meaningful participation in public life. Transitional justice processes should be designed in such a way that they facilitate, rather than undermine, these aims.

[36] Personal communication with the author.

References

Adler, G. and E. Webster. 1995. 'Challenging Transition Theory: The Labor Movement, Radical Reform and Transition to Democracy in South Africa,' in *Politics and Society*, 23, 1: 75–106.

Adam, H. 2000. 'Divided Memories', *Telos*, vol. 118, Winter: 87–108.

AFP (Agence France Presse), 1999. 'Ethiopia's Red Terror genocide was defence: Mengistu'. 28 December .

Amnesty International. 1995. *Ethiopia. Accountability past and present: Human rights in transition.* London: Amnesty International.

Asmal, K., Asmal, L. and Roberts, R.S. 1996. *Reconciliation Through Truth.* Cape Town: David Philip Publishers.

Barchiesi, F. 1999. 'Socio-Economic Exploitation, Meaning Contestation and the TRC'. Paper presented to the conference on 'The TRC: Commissioning the Past' held at University of the Witwatersrand, Johannesburg, 11–14 June.

BBC Focus on Africa. July–September 2001, 12, 3. London: BBC Africa.

Chabal, P. and J-P. Daloz, 1999. *Africa Works.* Oxford: James Currey Publishers.

Cohen, S. 2001. *States of Denial: Knowing about atrocities and suffering.* Cambridge: Polity Press.

Constitutional Court of South Africa. *AZAPO and others vs the President of the Republic of South Africa and others*, CCT 17/96. At www.concourt.gov.za

Debate: Voices from the South Africa left. March, 2001. Johannesburg: Witwatersrand University.

Dugard, J. 1997. 'Is the Truth and Reconciliation Process compatible with international law?', *South African Journal on Human Rights*, 13, 2.

Dugard, J. 1999. 'Dealing with crimes of a past regime: Is amnesty still an option?' Paper presented to the conference on 'The TRC: Commissioning the Past' held at University of the Witwatersrand, Johannesburg, 11–14 June 1999.

Du Toit, A. 1999. 'The Product and the Process: On the impact of the TRC report'. Paper presented to the conference on 'The TRC: Commissioning the Past' held at University of the Witwatersrand, Johannesburg, 11–14 June.

Elgesem, Frode 1998. *The Derg Trials in Context: A study of some aspects on the Ethiopian Judiciary*, Human Rights Report No.1, Norwegian Institute of Human Rights, University of Oslo.

Filatova, I. 1994. 'The awkward issue: Some comments on the South African debate on nation-building and ethnicity', in *Democratic Nation-Building in South Africa.* Pretoria: HSRC.

Fraser, N. and L. Gordon 1998. 'Contract versus Charity: Why is there no social citizenship in the United States?' in Shafir, G. (ed.), *The Citizenship Debates.* Minneapolis: University of Minnesota Press.

Habermas, J. 1992. 'Citizenship and national identity', *Praxis International*, vol. 12, no. 2: 1–19.

Habermas, J. 1996. *Between Facts and Norms.* Cambridge, MA: MIT Press.

Hagemeier, L. 2001. 'The Derg Trials'. Unpublished research report. University of the Witwatersrand, Johannesburg.

Haile, D. 2000. *Accountability for crimes of the past and the challenges of criminal prosecution: The case of Ethiopia.* Leuven: Leuven University Press.

Hartwell, M.B. 1999. 'The role of forgiveness in reconstructing society after conflict'. *Journal of Humanitarian Assistance*, 3 May. At www-jha.sps.cam.ac.uk.

Havel, V. 1991. *Open Letters.* London: Faber and Faber.

Held, D. 1987. *Models of Democracy.* Cambridge: Polity Press.

Held, D. (ed.) 1993. *Prospects for Democracy: North, south, east, west.* Cambridge: Polity Press.

Hendricks, F. 1998. 'Prosecute or Pardon?' Paper presented to the World Congress of Sociology, Montreal.

——. 1999. 'Amnesty and Justice in Post-Apartheid South Africa'. Paper presented to the conference on 'The TRC: Commissioning the Past' held at University of the Witwatersrand, Johannesburg, 11–14 June.

Huyse, L. 1998. *Jonge democratieen en de keuze tussen amnestie, waarheidscommissie en vervolging.* Instituut Recht en Samenleving, KU Leuven.

Jung, C. and Shapiro, I. 1995. 'South Africa's Negotiated Transition: Democracy, Opposition, and the New Constitutional Order,' *Politics and Society*, vol. 23, no. 3: 269–308.

Kritz, N. (ed.) 1995. *Transitional Justice: How emerging democracies reckon with former regimes.* Washington, DC: United States Institute of Peace Press.

Krog, A. 1998. *Country of my Skull.* Johannesburg: Random House.

Kundera, M. 1980. *The Book of Laughter and Forgetting.* Harmondsworth: Penguin Books.

Lycett, A. 1994. 'Mengistu's henchmen face trial,' *New African*, September.

Mamdani, M. 1998. *When does reconciliation turn into a denial of justice?* Sam Nolutshungu Memorial Lecture. Pretoria: HSRC.

Marais, H. 1998. *South Africa: Limits to Change.* Cape Town: University of Cape Town Press.

Mayfield, J. 1995. 'The Prosecution of War Crimes and Respect for Human Rights: Ethiopia's Balancing Act,' *Emory International Law Review*, Fall.

Nash, K. 2000. *Contemporary political sociology.* Oxford: Blackwell.

Parlevliet, M. 1998. 'Considering Truth: Dealing with a legacy of gross human rights violations,' *Netherlands Quarterly of Human Rights* vol. 16, no. 2.

Parlevliet, M. 2000. 'Truth Commissions in Africa,' *International Law Forum*, 2, 98–111.

Republic of South Africa. *Constitution of the Republic of South Africa*, Act 200 of 1993.

—— *Promotion of National Unity and Reconciliation* Act 34 of 1995.

Roederer, C. 1999. '"Living well is the best revenge" – If one can,' *South African Journal on Human Rights*, vol. 15, no. 1: 75–97.

Ryle, J. 1995. 'An African Nuremberg.' *New Yorker*, October 2.

Saul, J. 2000. 'Lubango and After: "Forgotten history" as politics in contemporary Namibia'. Unpublished paper.

Shafir, G. (ed.) 1998. *The Citizenship Debates.* Minneapolis: Minnesota University Press.

Simpson, G. 1999. 'A brief evaluation of South Africa's Truth and Reconciliation Commission'. Paper presented to the conference on 'The TRC: Commissioning the Past' held at University of the Witwatersrand, Johannesburg, 11–14 June.

Siyiaya, Spring 1998. Cape Town: Idasa.

The Star, 30 October 1998.

The Star, 1 November 1998.

Trend, D. (ed.) 1996. *Radical Democracy.* New York: Routledge.

Waag Communications News Digest Service. *Ethiopia: Seven days update.* Ethiopia: Waag Communications Enterprize Pvt. Ltd.

Wilson, R. 2001. *The Politics of Truth and Reconciliation in South Africa: Legitimizing the Post-apartheid State.* Cambridge: Cambridge University Press.

Wits Law School. 1996. Summary of judgement in *AZAPO and others vs the President of the Republic of South Africa and others*, CCT 17/96. At www.law.wits.ac.za.

Woubishet, D. 1996. 'International Criminal Prosecution,' *Human Rights Tribune*, vol. 3, no. 4: 15–17.

8
Beyond the Red Terror Trials | Analysing Guarantees of Non-Repetition

GIRMACHEW ALEMU ANEME

Introduction

While states have a duty under international law to provide an effective remedy for past human rights violations, the content of this duty is far from being definite. Nevertheless, the UN-sanctioned 'van Boven principles' provide that the right to effective remedy should contain the following minimum components: investigation and prosecution, compensation, restitution, rehabilitation, satisfaction and guarantees of non-repetition.[1] Investigation and prosecution are aimed at punishing human right violators and documenting the violations. In undertaking the tasks of investigating the past violations and prosecuting those responsible, while providing due process of law, states are dispensing justice to victims as well as reaffirming the importance of the rule of law and sending a deterrent message to potential violators. Compensation, on the other hand, not only alleviates the economic burdens caused by human rights violations, but is also a symbolic gesture of acknowledging responsibility for what happened to the victims and an appeal for forgiveness and reconciliation.

Although retributive justice might be dispensed after prosecution and compensation, this can not ensure by itself the reintegration of the victims into a stabilized and secured life in society. There is thus a need for restitution and rehabilitation, which should consist of an overarching course of action to empower the victims to regain their hold on life as individuals and members of the society. Publicizing and acknowledging what happened through different mechanisms is the idea behind another component of the right to effective remedy: the duty of satisfaction. Thomas Nagel (in Orentlicher 1995: 492) rightly pointed out the importance of public acknowledgement when he stated that 'it is the difference between knowledge and acknowledgement. It's what happens

---

[1] General Assembly resolution, A/Res/60/147.

116

and only happens to knowledge when it becomes officially sanctioned, when it is made part of the public cognitive scene.'

Arguably, among the minimum components of the right to effective remedy provided under the van Boven principles, the most important part is the duty of states to provide guarantees of non-repetition. Guarantees of non-repetition provide the minimum institutional and legal guarantees that should be observed by the state in order to prevent the reoccurrence of human rights violations. This chapter is based on the premise that the Red Terror trials are only a partial remedy to the massive human rights violations during the Derg regime in Ethiopia.

By using the major standards of guarantees of non-repetition provided under the van Boven principles, this chapter will critically assess the performance of the Ethiopian institutional and legal structures that are crucial for the prevention of a repetition of the massive human rights violations experienced by the country in the past.

The four major institutional and normative guarantees that are discussed below are the independence of the judiciary; the protection of legal, media professionals and human rights defenders; human rights education; and conflict prevention and resolution mechanisms.[2]

Strengthening the Independence of the Judiciary

Judicial independence is a fundamental obligation placed on states by the Universal Declaration of Human Rights (UDHR),[3] International Covenant on Civil and Political Rights (ICCPR)[4] and the African Charter,[5] to which Ethiopia is a party (see Elgesem and G. Aneme in this volume). Judicial independence is a major precondition for the rule of law and the protection of human rights. The rule of law is a classic principle that requires, *inter alia*, the supremacy of law, equality before the law and the protection of individual rights (Elwyn-Jones 1991:44). The relationship between the rule of law and the protection of human rights was reaffirmed in the Declaration of Delhi as follows:

> The Rule of Law is a dynamic concept for the expansion and fulfilment of which jurists are primarily responsible and which should be employed not only to safeguard and advance the civil and political rights of the individual in a free society, but also to establish social, economic, educational and cultural conditions under which his legitimate aspirations and dignity may be realised.[6]

[2] All these standards are provided under the van Boven principles found in General Assembly resolution, A/Res/60/147.

[3] General Assembly resolution 217A (III) Article 10, Article 11.

[4] General Assembly resolution 2200(XXI) Article 14.

[5] African Charter on Human and Peoples' Rights – Article 7.

[6] Centre for the Independence of Judges and Lawyers, April–October 1990, p.5.

The independence of the judiciary is not an end in itself. It is rather a major precondition for the existence of the rule of law in a country. The UDHR stated the absolute necessity of the rule of law in the following terms: 'It is essential, if man is not to be compelled to have recourse, as a last resort, to rebellion against tyranny and oppression, that human rights should be protected by the Rule of Law.'[7]

The general principle of the independence of the judiciary requires that 'the judiciary shall decide matters before it impartially, on the basis of facts and in accordance with the law, without any restrictions, improper influences, inducements, pressures, threats or interference, direct or indirect, from any quarter or for any reason.'[8] The principle of the independence of the judiciary can be expressed, *inter alia,* in terms of the following three major standards against which the judiciary in Ethiopia will be analysed.[9] These are the existence of laws declaring the independence of the judiciary, conditions of service and tenure of judges, and qualifications, selection and training of judges.

The existence of laws declaring the independence of the judiciary
The Federal Democratic Republic of Ethiopia (FDRE) Constitution declares that the judiciary is independent and that judges shall exercise their functions in full independence directed only by the law.[10] Furthermore, the FDRE Constitution declares that all judicial powers in the country are vested in courts.[11] Against these declarations, however, the power to interpret the Constitution is given to the House of Federation,[12] a non-judicial and political body composed of representatives of the nations, nationalities and peoples in the country.[13] When any Federal or State Law is contested as being unconstitutional, the courts are supposed to submit such a dispute to a body called the Council of Constitutional Inquiry.[14] The Council of Constitutional Inquiry is supposed to give its advisory opinion to the House of Federation, which then makes the final decision regarding the constitutional interpretation.[15] Such relinquishment of power to interpret the Constitution to

---

[7] General Assembly resolution 217A (III), Preamble.
[8] Centre for the Independence of Judges and Lawyers, April–October 1990, p. 18.
[9] See General Assembly resolution 40/32 for the standards.
[10] Proclamation 1/1995 Articles 78 and 79.
[11] Proclamation 1/1995 Article 79.
[12] Proclamation 251/2001 Articles 46 and 47, the House of Federation is a majoritarian body where each nation, nationality and people is represented by at least one member and by one additional member for each one million of each nation, nationality and people. Article 2(5) of the same proclamation provided that Nation, Nationality and People are a group of people who share a large measure of a common culture or similar customs, mutual intelligibility of language, common or related belief of identities, a common psychological make-up, and who inhabit an identifiable, predominantly contiguous territory.
[13] Proclamation 1/1995 Article 62; Proclamation 251/2001 Article 3.
[14] Proclamation 1/1995 Article 82 and Article 84.The Council is an advisory body to the House of Federation on constitutional disputes.
[15] Proclamation 1/1995 Article 84.

a political body reflects and responds to a populist or sceptical conception of the rule of law and the role of the judiciary. The function and power of the judiciary in checking the actions of the legislative and executive organs of the government vis-à-vis constitutional rights is seen under this view as the 'antithesis' of the sovereignty of the people (Beatty 1994:4). Assefa Fiseha (2005:16) noted that 'Often top executive officials spoke about the importance of *Hizbawi Dagna*, 'popular judge', implying one who is ideologically affiliated with the ruling party or perhaps an elected one.' The view is based on the opinion that handing over the power to define the limits of legitimate government and popular rule to an elite group trained in law violates people's sovereignty. The members of the judiciary are not popularly elected and therefore are the least accountable to the people.

This opinion poses conceptual and practical difficulties. First and foremost, the terms of the FDRE Constitution that give the power to interpret the Constitution to the House of Federation contradict the very declarations of the Constitution that proclaim that all judicial power is vested in courts. Second, the provision of the FDRE Constitution that gives the power to interpret the Constitution to the House of Federation takes away the most important function of courts of law: the inter-pretation of the supreme law of the land. The constitutional declaration that gives all judicial powers to courts is meaningless as long as the most crucial judicial power of interpretation is given away to a political body with quasi-legislative functions. If courts do not possess the power of judicial review, they will not be able to check the acts of the legislative and executive branches of the government against the Constitution.

Third, the power of constitutional interpretation given to the House of Federation implies that courts are expected to send each and every case that may involve constitutional interpretation to the House of Federation. Such requirement not only makes the genuine application of the Constitution doubtful, but is also unrealistic. In the words of Clyde Willis (1997:19) 'requiring them[the courts] to decide each and every mundane case that comes down the pike in which constitutional principle is implicated is irrational – it can not, it will not be done – in Ethiopia or elsewhere, for that matter.'

The rule of law presupposes that all rights, including and primarily the rights contained in the Constitution, are to be defined and enforced by courts of law proper. The doctrine of judicial review is a basic principle of the Rule of Law aimed at curbing legislative and executive encroachment, in order to protect constitutionally protected rights and freedoms. Judicial review integrates 'two great principles of the liberal democratic form of government – the rule of law and the sovereignty of the popular will in a way which maximises the opportunity of the people to define the kind of community and social order within which they want to live' (Beatty 1994: 50). The provision of the FDRE Constitution that gives constitutional interpretation to a political body is contrary to the independence of the judiciary and the rule of law. If constitutionally guaranteed rights and freedoms are to be protected, the power of giving them meaning and checking whether the government is actually respecting the rights should be given to courts proper.

Conditions of service and tenure of judges
Another major standard that reflects upon the independence of the judiciary is the terms and conditions of the service and tenure of judges. Two major aspects of the judicial system are implicated. One is the conditions of service of judges, including the remuneration and access to legal materials; and the second is the tenure of judges, which is the term of the occupation of office and removal of judges.

Currently, judgeship is not attractive work in Ethiopia. The working conditions for judges in Ethiopia suffer a serious setback in relation to income and access to legal materials. The remuneration for judges is not commensurate with the load of work. Moreover, most judges, especially those working outside the capital city, face a serious shortage of legal materials crucial for their work. There is no system of consolidating laws and distributing them to judges in the country. While the economy of the country is one crucial factor in the power of the government to pay remuneration to any public servant, there are many other ways that can be used to make the judges' working conditions better apart from direct monetary increment in their salaries. Unlike the provision made for the holders of many public offices, there is for instance no transportation service for judges. The offices of judges, in most cases, are in poor condition in terms of relevant working equipment and infrastructure. Improvements in their working conditions can be made by helping judges get access to better service like access to updated legal materials and better living and working places. These and other similar improvements might contribute to the efficiency of the courts and reduce the significant outflow of skilled and experienced judges from the courts to other competitive institutions.

The terms of tenure and removal of judges are proclaimed by the FDRE Constitution. Judges are not to be removed before their retirement age except for violation of disciplinary rules, gross incompetence or inefficiency and illness and in accordance with the decision of the concerned Judicial Administration Council at the federal or the state level as approved by the majority vote of the House of People's Representatives or the concerned state council.[16] It is a required standard that any charge or complaint against a judge based on the above grounds must follow an established procedure and the judge's right to fair hearing must be recognized.[17] The Delhi Congress on the Judiciary and the Legal Profession under the Rule of Law reiterated that 'the reconciliation of the principle of irrevocability of the judiciary with the possibility of removal

---

[16] Proclamation 1/1995 Article 79.
[17] General Assembly resolutions 40/32, Article 17.

in exceptional circumstances necessitates that the grounds of removal should be before a body of judicial character assuring at least the same safeguards to the judge as would be accorded to an accused person in a criminal trial.'[18] The composition of the Judicial Administration Council should also be free from the executive and legislative members of the government.[19] The composition of the Federal Judicial Administration Council fails to meet this criterion since it includes three members of parliament.[20] It is the organ primarily responsible, *inter alia*, for the promotion, suspension and removal of federal judges.[21] In light of the power of the Council, the fact that three of its seven members are parliamentarians may lead to the constant control of the judiciary by political representatives from the ruling party, thereby seriously threatening its independence. This fact may also incapacitate the judiciary from playing its role of checking possible legislative and executive encroachments on individual rights.

Qualifications, selection and training of judges
The basic principles concerning the independence of the judiciary provide that 'persons selected for judicial office shall be individuals of integrity and ability with appropriate training or qualifications in law'.[22] In the Ethiopian case, the acute shortage of qualified lawyers is a major problem. The attempt to produce more lawyers to serve as judges and prosecutors in a very short time has also created problems connected with the ability to understand and interpret the law. Judges who are appointed after only a short-term legal training need to have continuous and persistent training at certain intervals of time. The lasting solution lies in the opening of new schools of law to produce lawyers of good quality and quantity in the long run. However, the mass production of 'lawyers' through short-term training courses with little or no understanding of law and justice is much more disastrous than having very few competent lawyers. Therefore, the quality of programs should be closely examined in both public and private schools of law.

The level and quality of training has a great impact not only on the understanding and application of the law but also on the degree of independence of judges. As one study on the Ethiopian judiciary shows, judges with short-term legal education tend to be less independent judges due to the fear of not being able to find another job in cases of dismissal by the government (Elgesem 1998: 17). Furthermore, the selection of judges should be free from any discrimination based on race, colour, sex, religion or political or other opinion, national or social origin, property, birth or status.[23]

---

[18] Centre for the Independence of Judges and Lawyers, April–October 1990, p. 85.
[19] Centre for the Independence of Judges and Lawyers, April–October 1990, p. 121.
[20] Proclamation No. 24/1996 Article 4.
[21] Proclamation No. 1/1995 Article 79 and Proclamation No.24/1996 Article 5.
[22] General Assembly resolution 40/32, Article 10.
[23] Ibid.

The FDRE Constitution proclaims that the House of Representatives at the federal level and the state councils in each state appoint judges.[24] In practice, however, the criteria for the selection of judges are not clear. Close reading of the criteria established for selection of judges at the federal level shows that some of the requirements are overly vague.[25] For instance, the criterion of 'loyalty to the Constitution' is a very abstract criterion with no clear standard to differentiate between candidates who are 'loyal' and who are not. The criteria of 'good sense of justice' and 'good conduct' are also overly vague.

The training of judges at both federal and state levels can be approached in two ways: pre-office training and on-the-job training. As far as the pre-office training is concerned, a serious consideration must be given to the idea of establishing a judicial training centre so that appointees to judgeships can become acquainted with crucial ethical, legal and social principles of the judiciary and of judging. On-the-job training for judges in federal and state courts is also crucial to update their knowledge of law. Consistent training and education are especially crucial for judges with a very limited period of legal education. Judges at all levels also need to be trained and educated in different legal fields. For instance, with the new jurisprudential and substantive developments in both national and international law, the judiciary will need judges with specialized knowledge in specific areas of the law. At the time of writing, the establishment of a Judicial Training Institute under the Federal Supreme Court to train judges, prosecutors and registrars both on a pre-office basis and on-the-job-training is being finalized.

It is obvious that the process of the creation of an independent judicial body will take sustained efforts for many years. Apart from factors connected to the above-mentioned issues, the long years of regressive political culture in Ethiopia have resulted in a dependent judiciary and in judges with 'self-imposed restraints' in cases involving governmental interests (Elgesem 1998:87). The rule of law presupposes a judiciary that is independent of governmental or self-imposed restraints. If the government attempts to resolve the practical problems that curb the independence of the judiciary, which is proclaimed by the Constitution, the self-imposed restraint will eventually die out. Equal responsibility of working for the independence of the judiciary and respect for the rule of law lies on the shoulders of the judges and all members of the legal profession.

Protecting the Legal Profession, Media and Human Rights Defenders

There are a number of groups in a community which have a special and wider mandate and duty to work for the maintenance of the rule of law

[24] Proclamation No. 1/1995 Article 81.
[25] See Proclamation No. 24/1996 Article 8.

and the protection of constitutionally guaranteed rights and freedoms. The most notable of these groups are lawyers, journalists and human rights defenders. The following sub-sections explain the responsibility of these groups in Ethiopia.

Legal profession

Legal professionals are one of the prominent groups with a unique responsibility towards the public. In effect, the duty of lawyers as professionals goes beyond their immediate clients to the promotion of justice. In particular, lawyers in developing societies are expected to take the leading role in establishing legal as well as institutional guarantees of individual freedom and protection of human rights which are pre-requisites for meaningful economic development. It is as a result of a commitment to a strong and independent public service that lawyers need to organize themselves as professionals. An organized legal profession free to manage its own affairs is mandatory to the maintenance of the rule of law.[26] The freedom of the association is expressed in terms of, *inter alia*, controlling admission to the profession and the discipline of its members. In the absence of an association, the power to discipline lawyers should be exercised by the judiciary and never by the executive branch of a government. This is because the judiciary is assumed to be more impartial and committed to the rule of law. The independence of the association of lawyers is needed to nurture lawyers who will defend constitutional rights. The ideal bar association exists to 'vindicate and to advocate the rights of the citizen, not merely to protect the interest of its own members' (O'Flaherty 1992: 176).

The Ethiopian Lawyers Association was established in accordance with Article 404 of the Ethiopian Civil Code of 1960. Article 4 of its 1993 Revised Articles of Association shows that membership is limited to licensed lawyers. Article 3 of the same provides the protection of human rights as one of the goals of the association. The power of admission and control of practising lawyers at the Federal level, however, is under the full control of the executive through the federal Ministry of Justice.[27] Similarly, the power of admission and control of practising lawyers at state level is under the full control of the respective justice bureau of each federal state.[28] The power of the Federal Ministry of Justice and the State Justice Bureau in the admission, discipline, suspension and removal of practising lawyers has a direct negative effect on the free execution of the duties of lawyers in the country. The legal profession comes under direct pressure from the executive and is thereby likely to become much less efficient in contributing to the maintenance of the rule of law. What is worse, however, the Federal Ministry of Justice and the State Justice

---

[26] Centre for the Independence of Judges and Lawyers, April–October 1990, p. 87.

[27] Proclamation No. 4/1995 Article 23 (12); Proclamation No. 199/2000 Article 19.

[28] See, for instance, Megleta Oromia, Proclamation No. 7/1995 Article 24 (i).

Bureaus are not only chief legal advisors to the respective executive organs but are also parties to proceedings that involve the rights and interests of the executive organs.[29] The effect of the power of the Federal Ministry of Justice and State Justice Bureaus over practising lawyers is not only unjust in cases involving the government (as one litigant in the proceeding is controlling the other) but will have a negative impact on the independence of practising lawyers in the country. As a result, practising lawyers may not contribute as much as they could and should to the maintenance of justice and protection of human rights in the country.

Notwithstanding any reason that may be forwarded, giving the power of controlling the practice of law to the executive branch is an ill-conceived action. The first step towards the establishment of a strong and meaningful legal profession will be realized if, among other measures, the power to control the profession is given to another body, such as the judiciary, until such time as a strong bar association is established and is able to administer its own affairs.

Media

The protection and maintenance of strong media is another guarantee that helps to prevent human rights violations and enhance governmental accountability. The protection of the media is the obligation of the country under the UDHR,[30] ICCPR[31] and the African Charter.[32] Explaining the connection between strong media and the protection of human rights, journalist and political analyst Anna Husarska (2000: 339) explained that the media often indicate the action that needs to be taken when describing and presenting facts about human rights violations. She further described the power of the media in investigating human rights violations as 'far more than descriptions to advance human rights' and with far greater impact than the most powerful human rights organisations' (ibid.: 340).

Strong media can be one major tool in fighting human rights violations. The maintenance of strong and responsible media presupposes the protection of the freedom of expression. The freedom of expression encompasses the right to communicate ideas and information through any media.[33] John Stuart Mill (in Korrtteinen et al. 1999: 395) has luminously provided the justifications for the protection of freedom of expression and the plurality of opinions:

> A suppressed opinion may be true. Even if the suppressed opinion would be false, it might still contain elements of truth. The prevailing

[29] Proclamation No. 4/95 Article 23, see, for instance, Megeleta Oromia-Proclamation No. 7/1995 Article 24.
[30] General Assembly resolution 217A (III) Article 19.
[31] General Assembly resolution 2200(XXI) Article 19.
[32] The African Charter on Human and Peoples' Rights Article 9.
[33] General Assembly resolution 217 A (III) Article 19.

public opinion is not usually the whole truth. It is only through the combination of contradictory opinions whereby one may achieve a more comprehensive understanding of truth. Established opinions transform into stereotypes if their strenuous critique is not allowed. It is not possible to have a reasoned personal conviction, if the free formation of opinions is prevented.

Freedom of expression has been severely restricted in all the past governments in Ethiopia. After the coming to power of the Ethiopian People's Revolutionary Democratic Front (EPRDF), the FDRE Constitution recognized the right to freedom of expression.[34] A press law was issued to implement the right to freedom of expression recognized by the Constitution.[35] Article 4(1) of the press law proclaims that the 'press stands for the pursuit of fundamental freedom, peace, democracy, justice, equality and for the acceleration of social and economic development.' The press law defines the word 'Press' as follows:

> Any establishment of mass medium activity such as newspapers, magazines, periodicals, journals, pamphlets, news agencies, radio, television, motion pictures, pictures, films, cartoons, books, music, electronics publishing, plays and includes all media of mass communication.[36]

Among the mass media covered by the definition, television is not yet open for private investors. The FDRE Constitution, as well as the press law, prohibits any kind of censorship or any similar restriction on the press.[37] The step of abolishing censorship is a step forward in the history of the Ethiopian media. For the first time in Ethiopia, there were over 200 private newspapers registered by the Ministry of Information even though the distribution of most of the newspapers is limited to the capital city, Addis Ababa.

However, despite the promising broadening of the freedom of expression, there are controversial elements of the press law and its interpretation.[38] One of the controversial issues in the press law concerns the authorities endowed with the power to issue licences to carry out press activity. The application for licence is to be made to the Ministry of Information at the federal level and to the regional Information Bureaus at the state level.[39] The fact that such authorities are part of the executive may work against the freedom of expression. This is because, in contrast to an independent licensing body directly responsible to the legislature, the chance of misinterpreting the law and

---

[34] Proclamation No. 1/1995 Article 29.
[35] Proclamation No. 34/1992.
[36] Proclamation No. 34/1992 Article 2.
[37] Ibid, Article 3(2), Proclamation No.1/1995 Article 29(3).
[38] See Article 19, *The Legal Framework for Freedom of Expression in Ethiopia – Global Campaign for Free Expression*, for detailed analysis of the 1992 Press Law.
[39] Proclamation No.34/1992 Article 7(1).

abusing it is far greater in the case of the executive in relation to the private press.

The power of the Ministry of Information is further made controversial because of the vague limitations set on the freedom of the press in the press law. Article 10 of the press law enumerates highly vague limitations, that are open to many kinds of interpretations and manipulations.[40] Such vague limitations may cause unjustified prosecutions against members of the private media. Even if the press law has taken an important step forward in abolishing direct censorship, the unjustified post-publication liability as a result of the highly vague limitations may be used as indirect censorship. Licence requirements may also be used as a means of indirect censorship. Article 7 of the Ethiopian press law enumerates the particulars to be entered in the application for a licence to carry out any press activity, but it is not clear if these enumerated requirements are exhaustive. The Federal Ministry of Information or the state Information Bureaus are expected to issue the required licence within 30 days from the date of submission of the application.[41] If the authorities fail to issue the licence within the 30 days time limit, it is deemed granted.[42] The requirement of application for licence seems to serve publicity purposes only since, if the authorities fail to issue the licence within the given time limit, the applicant can assume that he or she is free to engage in press activity.

In January 2003 the federal Ministry of Information unveiled a new draft press law that was meant to improve the 1992 press law. However, the 2003 draft press law was criticized as highly draconian, since, *inter alia,* it retains harsh criminal penalties for journalists, gives vague powers to the Ministry of Information to decide on who could practise journalism, forbids financial aid to newspapers and reporters from foreign organizations or states and limits the public right to receive information.[43]

It is evident under the international obligation of the country that the right to freedom of expression has limitations that are aimed at protecting the rights or reputations of others, national security, public order, public health and morals.[44] The limitations on the freedom of the press under the press law need to be proclaimed and interpreted in conformity with the limitations set out under the international obligation of the country with regard to the freedom of expression. According to John Rawls (in Korrtteinen et al. 1999: 395), the criteria for delimiting freedom of expression should be restricted only to allow the protection of freedom itself or 'of other basic liberties such as the fair value of political liberties'

[40] The limitations under the article include 'criminal offence against the safety of the state', 'incitement of conflict between people' and 'any agitation of war'.

[41] Proclamation No.34/1992 Article 7(2).

[42] Proclamation No.34/1992.

[43] See, for instance, analysis of interview given by Amare Aregawi, Editor-in-Chief of private newspaper *The Reporter* found on www.RAP21.org. The new draft press law is still not implemented at the time of writing.

[44] General Assembly resolution 2200(XXI) Article 19.

as a last choice for the protection of the competing values. In contrast to this, it should also be stressed that members of the private press also share equal responsibility in presenting reports and articles from dependable bias-free sources. Currently most of the private press cannot be characterized as responsible and free from bias. The lack of rational and informative writing on the side of the private press can be attributed to the low level of training of the editors and writers as well as the firm control by political and other groups over the publications. Training in journalism can in the long run help in ensuring the quality and independence of the press.

Human rights defenders

Human rights activists connected to national human rights organizations or acting independently may be victims of attack because of the very nature of their activities, which include publicizing human rights violations that are committed by governmental as well as non-governmental bodies. The Ethiopian Human Rights Council (EHRCO) and the Ethiopian Women Lawyers Association (EWLA) are the two most prominent organizations involved in monitoring, protecting and promoting human rights in the country.

EHRCO is an independent, non-partisan organization which was established on 10 October 1991. Its broad objectives include working for the establishment of a democratic system through respect for the rule of law and the protection of human rights.[45] Since its establishment, EHRCO has been involved in raising public awareness of human rights and the rule of law by organizing seminars, workshops and panel discussions and by disseminating periodicals. It has also issued a series of reports on human rights violations of governmental and non-governmental bodies in the country. It is evident that the government can make use of the series of reports to prevent similar human rights violations from happening and to bring those responsible for the violations to justice. However, the government has accused EHRCO of having its own political agenda against it and has consistently rejected its reports and recommendations. It is also reported that members of the organization face constant harassment from security forces when trying to monitor violations in the regional states.[46]

The other prominent non-governmental organization involved in the protection and promotion of human rights in Ethiopia is EWLA. EWLA is a private, non-profit organization established by Ethiopian women lawyers. EWLA has been performing a respectable task of defending women's rights all over the country since it was legally established on 7 June 1995.[47] EWLA aims to eliminate all forms of discrimination against women, establish the equal treatment of women and men in education, employment, and access to public services and benefits and promote

---

[45] Statutes of the Ethiopian Human Rights Council 1995.
[46] Human Rights Watch, Ethiopia: *Human Rights Watch Report*, 2/5/98.
[47] Ethiopian Women Lawyers Association, *Activity Report 2001*, p. 1.

remedial and affirmative measures for women. Beyond providing legal aid services for many thousands of its clients, EWLA functions as a centre where research is conducted to identify discriminatory laws and bring them to the attention of the government for revision.[48] EWLA has also proved to be an effective association in mobilizing a pressure group in the reformulation and amendment of laws that are against the rights of women.[49]

Beyond formal recognition of human rights, the state needs EHRCO, EWLA and similar associations in order to realize constitutionally protected rights and freedoms. Human rights defenders are spokespersons for the actual and potential victims of violation of human rights. If the protection of human rights is to be strengthened, the government should extend its protection to human rights defenders against attacks by governmental and non-governmental violators of human rights. The establishment of national governmental organizations, which are indispensable partners in the protection and promotion of human rights and the rule of law in the country, needs to be encouraged. In the present age and in the Ethiopian context, the protection and promotion of human rights and the rule of law can not be achieved without the free and full involvement of civil society. An organized and free civil society is vital in the creation of a vigilant community which is active in the protection of its rights.

Conducting and Strengthening Human Rights Training

Education is the best means of bringing about dynamic transformation on both the individual and community levels. Education is also the best means of ensuring the protection of human rights. The United Nations Committee on Economic, Social and Cultural Rights reiterated the importance of education in the following terms:

> Education is both a human right in itself and an indispensable means of realising other human rights. As an empowerment right, education is the primary vehicle by which economically and socially marginalized adults and children can lift themselves out of poverty and obtain the means to participate fully in their communities [...]. Increasingly, education is recognised as one of the best financial investments states can make. But the importance of education is not just practical: a well-educated, enlightened and active mind, able to wander freely and widely, is one of the joys and rewards of human existence.[50]

[48] Ethiopian Women Lawyers Association (2002).

[49] *Dimtsachen* June-July 2000, p. 2, *Reflections* No.4, December 2000 p. 54, In particular EWLA had successfully mobilized large numbers of women and influenced the revision of the 1960 family law which had discriminatory provisions against women and which was revised and enacted on July 4, 2000. It has also forwarded its comments and concerns on the current revision of the 1957 Penal Code.

[50] UN doc. E/C. 12/1999/10, p. 1.

The international obligation of Ethiopia with regard to the right to education is provided under the UDHR,[51] the ICESCR[52] and the African Charter.[53] The obligation to ensure the right to education includes the objective of ensuring respect for human rights and fundamental freedoms.[54] The preamble of the UDHR also proclaims that education should be used to promote respect for the rights and freedoms found in the declaration.[55] Ethiopia is bound by the terms of the above international obligations to realize the right to education as one means of establishing a long-lasting respect for and continuous promotion of human rights. Human rights education is a crucial instrument in developing a community culture favourable to the respect and protection of human rights. Indeed, many of the violations of and disrespect for human rights that occur in a country can be attributed to a lack of social culture that takes up freedom and protection of rights as one of its fundamental values.

The FDRE Constitution provides an extensive human rights framework. However, human rights will hardly be respected and protected if, *inter alia*, the social culture is not developed to meet institutional and normative developments. Education is the best tool to meet these goals. Most public officials, especially at the lower levels of administration, lack awareness of the human rights guarantees provided under the Constitution. This is also true of law enforcement, military and security officials as well as members of the media. Most of the public are also not aware of the meaning and means of enforcement of their rights. Human rights education is not included in the curriculum of primary or secondary schools or in most institutions of higher education.

In order to ensure sustainable protection of rights and freedoms provided under the Constitution, the country's education policy must make human rights education an integral part of the curriculum in primary, secondary as well as tertiary levels of schools. People who are able to go to school should be taught about the existence and content of the human rights under the FDRE Constitution at the earliest grade possible. The curriculum at all levels of schooling should be developed so as to ensure continuous education in human rights for people going through formal education. Human rights education should also be included in detail in the curriculum of schools and training centres for the police, the army and security personnel.

For many who are not able to go through formal education, non-formal ways of empowerment in human rights are indispensable, as these are the very people whose rights may be most frequently violated. Public officials also need consistent, non-formal training on their duties in respecting and protecting human rights guaranteed by the Constitution. Human

---

[51] General Assembly resolution 217A (III) Article 26.
[52] General Assembly resolution 2200 A (XXI) Articles 13 and 14.
[53] African Charter on Human and Peoples' Rights Article 17.
[54] General Assembly resolution 2200 A (XXI) Article 13.
[55] General Assembly resolution 217A (III) Preamble.

rights education at all levels needs to focus on the following minimum
goals set out by UNESCO:[56]

   i)   fostering the attitudes of tolerance, respect and solidarity inherent
in human rights;

   ii) providing knowledge about human rights, in both their national
and international dimensions, and the institutions established for
their implementation;

   iii) developing the individual's awareness of the ways and means by
which human rights can be translated into social and political
reality at both the national and international levels.

The involvement of governmental and non-governmental bodies in
non-formal education should be highly encouraged by the government. A
society with a positive climate towards the promotion of human rights
and awareness of its rights through formal and non-formal education will
be a fertile ground for the protection of human rights and maintenance of
peace.

Creating Mechanisms for Monitoring Conflict Resolution and Preventive Intervention

Conflicts are likely to occur in any society. The failure to address and
prevent human rights violations is one major reason for the escalation of
conflicts. One key mechanism for addressing and preventing human rights
violations provided by the FDRE Constitution is the establishment of the
Human Rights Commission and the institution of the Ombudsman.[57] An
international conference aimed at developing awareness of the mechanisms of establishing Human Rights Commissions and the institution of the
Ombudsman was convened in Addis Ababa from 18 to 22 May 1998, and
views and experiences of different countries and scholars were exchanged.

The establishment of the institution of the Ombudsman is aimed at
providing a forum for complaints for anyone who may be a victim of
administrative abuse and misinterpretation of the Constitution and other
laws of the land. Moreover, the institution of Ombudsman provides a
relatively cheap and fast response to administrative abuses compared
with the more formal and time-consuming process in the courts. The
relevance of the institution of the Ombudsman to Ethiopia is evident from
the fact that the courts are overloaded with cases and many people do not
have the knowledge or means to utilize courts of law against frequent
administrative abuses. The preamble of the Proclamation establishing the
institution of the Ombudsman reflects upon the purpose for establishing
the institution;[58]

[56] UNESCO and Human Rights (1999: 344).
[57] Proclamation 1/1995 Article 55.
[58] Proclamation No.211/2000 Preamble.

Whereas, the inter linkage of the activities, and of the decision-making power of the executive organs of the government with the daily lives and the rights of citizens is an ever-increasing and widening circumstance;

Whereas, it is necessary to duly rectify or prevent the unjust decisions and orders of executive organs and officials thereof, given under said circumstance;

Whereas, in order that citizens, having suffered from maladministration, are not left without redress, their want of an institution before which they may complain and seek remedies with easy access needs to be fulfilled [...].

The institution of the Ombudsman is accountable to the House of Peoples' Representatives having such powers and duties, *inter alia*, of supervising administrative directives and executive organs against the constitutional rights of citizens, preventing maladministration and making recommendations for the revision of existing laws and practices with a view to bringing about better governance.[59] The organization of the institution shows a Council of Ombudsmen at the top, to be followed by a Chief Ombudsman, a Deputy Ombudsman, an Ombudsman heading the Children and Women Affairs division, Ombudsmen heading branch offices (the Head Office is in Addis Ababa) and the necessary staff.[60]

The Human Rights Commission is another key institution that may be used as a safeguard against human rights violations. The basic tasks of the Human Rights Commission include handling complaints, conflict resolution, submitting reports, recommendations and proposals on any issues relating to human rights to the government, parliament or any other competent body, promoting conformity of national laws and practice with international human rights standards, contributing to the reporting procedure under international instruments and formulating and assisting in human rights education.[61]

A series of issues need to be dealt with in connection with the establishment of the Human Right Commission and the institution of the Ombudsman. Among the issues that need serious consideration are increasing the awareness of the public at large (especially people in the countryside who constitute more than 80 per cent of the population), public officials and civic organizations on the basic purpose of the institutions as well as the mechanisms they employ. Another key point that needs to be clarified is the issue of jurisdiction between the two institutions and their relation with the courts. The training of skilled manpower well versed in the purposes and mechanisms of the institutions should also be an immediate concern. The involvement of the

---

[59] Proclamation No.211/2000 Articles 6 and 13.
[60] Proclamation No.211/2000 Articles 8 and 9.
[61] Proclamation No. 210/2000 Article 6.

Ombudsman and the Human Rights Commission in education should also be given prominence to publicize their own purposes and, in the long run, to develop a human rights culture.

The establishment of the institution of the Ombudsman and the Human Rights Commission may be a step forward in the protection of human rights in Ethiopia. However, it must be emphasized that the mere establishment and existence of the Ombudsman and Human Rights Commission do not serve as a guarantee against human rights violations. In some instances Human Rights Commissions end up being the tools of repressive regimes to deflect international criticism and to silence local institutions that are engaged in human rights protection.[62] The Ethiopian Human Rights Commission is expected to conform to international standards, especially in its mandate and composition, the facilities, powers and investigative methodology involved and in its reporting and follow-up action.[63] The Commission is expected to 'combine the advantages of state support through funding and status, with the independent character of a non-governmental institution, and serve its specific and general purposes' (Lindsnaes et al. 2000: 1). Moreover, neither the Human Rights Commission nor the institution of the Ombudsman should be seen as a replacement of the courts of law and the judicial system as a whole, nor of other civil institutions established to safeguard human rights. An independent and well functioning judiciary is indispensable for the protection of human rights in the country. The Human Rights Commission and the institution of the Ombudsman are institutions meant to enhance the work of the judiciary, not replace it.

Conclusion

Have Ethiopia, its people and government, learned any lessons from the Red Terror and other atrocious human rights violations committed all over the country during the Derg era? The analysis of the guarantees of non-repetition discussed above may help us to partially answer this question. Many of the guarantees of non-repetition of human rights violations discussed in this chapter are fragile. An independent judiciary and a well functioning legal system capable of protecting constitutionally guaranteed rights and freedoms are still far from being just that, independent. The protection and quality of professionals of law and the private media have not yet reached the required level. A strong and

---

[62] See www.amnesty.org, Reports, Ethiopia, May 1998 ' Open Letter from the Secretary General of Amnesty International to Participants at a Conference in Addis Ababa, 18–22 May 1998, on the Establishment of a Human Rights Commission'.

[63] For detailed analysis of the recommendations for the Ethiopian Human Rights Commission visit www.amnesty.org, Reports, Ethiopia, May 1998 'Open Letter from the Secretary General of Amnesty International to Participants at a Conference in Addis Ababa, 18–22 May 1998, on the establishment of a Human Rights Commission'.

vibrant civil society is not a reality yet. Human rights education is far from reaching the majority of the population. The Human Rights Commission and the institution of the Ombudsman are still in their early years of establishment. The protection of rights and freedoms under the FDRE Constitution and the acceptance and ratification of international human rights treaties by the country are one step forward. However, the mere proclamation and ratification of international human rights treaties can not guarantee the protection and promotion of human rights. Among the major guarantees are the maintenance of the legal and institutional independence of the judiciary and the strong organization and independence of professionals engaged in one another way in the maintenance of the rule of law. The development of a strong and free civil society involved in public awareness-building and influencing policy-makers needs to be seen as a major and indispensable task in the implementation of constitutionally guaranteed rights and freedoms. The issue of human rights education at all levels of the society needs to get serious and genuine attention from governmental as well as non-governmental bodies.

The non-repetition of the past unspeakable violations cannot be assured unless all the above legal and institutional guarantees are reinforced. The only way to prevent the reoccurrence and spread of human right violations is strict observance of the institutional and legal guarantees of non-repetition. It is only then that we can be sure that the future is changed for the better in Ethiopia. If the fragile institutional and legal safeguards are not improved, human rights violations will be rampant. As such, the Red Terror trials and the past human rights violations will remain mere political and historical events from which no lessons were drawn.

References

International instruments

General Assembly resolution, A/Res/60/147, Basic Principles and Guidelines on the Right to a Remedy and Reparation for Victims of Gross Violations of International Human Rights Law and Serious Violations of International Humanitarian Law, December 16, 2005.

UN doc. E/CN: 4/2000/62, Civil and Political Rights, including the questions of Independence of the Judiciary, Administration of Justice, Impunity.

UN doc. E/C. 12/1999/10, CESCR, Implementation of the International Convention on Economic, Social and Cultural Rights, General Comment No.13.

General Assembly resolution 40/34 of 29 November 1985, Declaration of Basic Principles of Justice for Victims of Crime and Abuse of Power.

African Charter on Human and Peoples' Rights. Adopted by the Organization of African Unity, Nairobi, Kenya, June 26, 1981.

General Assembly resolutions 40/32 of November 1985 and 40/146 of 13 December 1985, Basic Principles on the Independence of the Judiciary, Article 17.

General Assembly resolution 2200 (XXI) of 16 December 1966, International Covenant on Civil and Political Rights.

General Assembly resolution 217A (III) of 10 December 1948, *Universal Declaration of Human Rights*.

National laws

Proclamation No. 4/1995, Definition of Power and Duties of the Executive Organs of the Federal Democratic Republic of Ethiopia, *Negarit Gazeta*, Addis Ababa.

Proclamation No. 1/1995, Proclamation of the Constitution of the Federal Democratic Republic of Ethiopia, August 21,1995, *Negarit Gazeta*, Addis Ababa.

Megleta Oromia, Proclamation No. 7/1995, a Proclamation from the Federal State of Oromia on the Structure of the Federal State, *Negarit Gazeta*, Addis Ababa.

Proclamation No. 24/1996, A Proclamation to Provide for the Establishment of the Federal Judicial Administration Commission, *Negarit Gazeta*, Addis Ababa.

Proclamation No. 34/1992, A Proclamation to Provide for the Freedom of the Press, *Negarit Gazeta*, Addis Ababa.

Proclamation No. 199/2000, Federal Courts Advocates Licensing and Registration Proclamation, *Negarit Gazeta*, Addis Ababa.

Proclamation No. 210/2000, Ethiopian Human Rights Commission Establishment Proclamation, *Negarit Gazeta*, Addis Ababa.

Proclamation No. 211/2000, Institution of the Ombudsman Establishment Proclamation, *Negarit Gazeta*, Addis Ababa.

Proclamation No. 251/2001, Consolidation of the House of Federation and the Definition of its Powers and Responsibilities Proclamation, *Negarit Gazeta*, Addis Ababa.

C. Books and articles

Assefa Fiseha. 2005. 'Federalism and the Adjudication of Constitutional Issues: The Ethiopian Experience,' *Netherlands International Law Review*, vol. 52, No. 1.

Beatty, David. 1994. 'Human Rights and the Rules of Law' in *Human Rights and Judicial Review – A Comparative Perspective*. David M. Beatty, ed. The Hague: Martinus Nijhoff Publishers.

Elgesem, Frode 1998. *The Derg Trials in Context – A study of some aspects on the Ethiopian Judiciary*, Human Rights Report No. 1, Norwegian Institute of Human Rights, University of Oslo.

Elwyn-Jones, Lord. 1991. 'Judicial Independence and Human Rights' in *Human Rights for the 1990s*. Robert Blackburn and John Taylor, eds. London: Mansel Publishing Limited.

Husarska, Anna. 2000. '"Conscience Trigger": The Press and Human Rights' in *Realizing Human Rights – Moving from Inspiration to Impact*. Samantha Power and Graham Allison, eds. New York: St. Martin's Press.

Korrtteinen, Juhani et al. 1999. 'Article 19 of the Universal Declaration of Human Rights', in *The Universal Declaration of Human Rights – A Common Standard of Achievement*. Gudmundur Alfredsson and Asbjørn Eide, eds. The Hague: Martinus Nijhoff Publishers.

Orentlicher, Diane F. 1995 *Settling Accounts: The Duty to Prosecute Human Rights Violations of a Prior Regime*, in *Transitional Justice – General Considerations*. Volume 1. Neil J. Kritz, ed. Washington, DC: United States Institute of Peace Press .

O'Flaherty, Hugh. 1992. 'The Independent Bar and the Defense of Human Rights', in *Human Rights and Constitutional Law*. James O'Reilly, ed. Dublin: The Round Hall Press.

Willis, Clyde E. 1997. *Essays on Modern Ethiopian Constitutionalism*, Addis Ababa: Faculty of Law, Addis Ababa University.

D. Other documents

Article 19. 2003. *The Legal Framework for Freedom of Expression in Ethiopia*. London: Article 19.

Centre for the Independence of Judges and Lawyers, April–October 1990, The Independence of Judges and Lawyers-A Compilation of International Standards, (Special Issue), No. 25–26.

Centre for the Independence of Judges and Lawyers. 2000. 'Strengthening Judicial Independence – Eliminating Judicial Corruption,' *Yearbook*, Volume IX De Becker v. Belgium, EHRC, HUDOC REF00000018, 1962.

Dimtsachen, Bilingual magazine of Ethiopian Women Lawyers Association (EWLA), June-July 2000.

Dimtsachen, Bilingual magazine of Ethiopian Women Lawyers Association (EWLA), Special Issue (date unspecified).

Ethiopian Human Right Council (EHRCO), *A Bilingual Manual*, Addis Ababa (date unspecified).

Ethiopian Women Lawyers Association, 2002. *Activity Report, January – December 2001.*

Lindsnaes, Birgit et al. (eds). 2000. *National Human Rights Institutions – Articles and Working Papers.* The Danish Center for Human Rights.

Reflections, Number 4, December 2000, Documentation of the Forum on Gender, Published by Panos Ethiopia, Addis Ababa.

Statutes of the Ethiopian Human Rights Council, October 15,1995.

UNESCO and Human Rights. 1999, *Standard Setting Instruments*, Paris: United Nations Educational, Scientific and Cultural Organisations (second edition).

9

Concluding the Main Red Terror Trial ▓ *Special Prosecutor v. Colonel Mengistu Hailemariam et al.*

KJETIL TRONVOLL
CHARLES SCHAEFER &
GIRMACHEW ALEMU ANEME

Introduction

The Federal High Court issued its final verdict in the main Red Terror trial in the case *Special Prosecutor v. Colonel Mengistu Hailemariam et al.* on 12 December 2006.[1] A total of fifty-five top officials of the Derg-WPE government were convicted and sentenced. Twenty-two of the top officials – including Colonel Mengistu Hailemariam, the military leader of the Derg and former Ethiopian head of state 1977–91 – were convicted in *absentia*. To an extent the verdict and sentencing test the efficacy of the judicial process in Ethiopia and offer a unique contribution to the discourse on transitional justice. The main Red Terror trial was tried in Ethiopia, based on the 1957 Ethiopian Penal Code, argued in court by Ethiopian prosecutors and defence lawyers, and judged by three Ethiopian judges. As outlined in Chapter 4, beyond some initial legal advice and technical assistance – related mainly to developing a computer data base for all the atrocities committed in the 1970s – there was minimal foreign influence on the legal proceedings. The contribution of the Ethiopian Red Terror trials to transitional justice is predicated precisely on their autochthonous nature.

Transitional justice, a term coined to depict societal attempts to account for atrocities committed against people or social groups in the past, basically divides into two camps: retributive justice and restorative justice. Retributive justice emphasizes a punitive element; however, since the Nuremberg trial most trials have been conducted by non-nationals in international courts, by lawyers and judges unfamiliar with the cultural and historical situation, in court rooms far removed from the country in question. The International Criminal Tribunal for Rwanda in

[1] *Special Prosecutor v. Colonel Mengistu Hailemariam et al.*, First Division Criminal Bench, Verdict, Judges Medhin Kiros, Nuru Saiid and Solomon Emeru, File No. 1/87, 12 December 2006.

Arusha, Tanzania is a case in point. Conversely, restorative justice aims to reconcile offender with victim to ensure societal healing through, for instance, truth commissions. South Africa's Truth and Reconciliation Commission is perhaps the most famous of over 30 in existence. Both transitional justice options have generated large followings and spawned voluminous criticisms. Ethiopia's Red Terror trials are examples of ret-ributive justice done in-country; hitherto a little tried option over which advocates of retributive justice have theorized.

The verdict, sentence and appeal of the main Red Terror trial – *Special Prosecutor v. Colonel Mengistu Hailemariam et al.* – reveal much about the internal integrity and continuity of the trial from commencement to conclusion. Several chapters in this book have analyzed various deficien-cies in the trial process, including the rights of the accused and problems associated with the twofold mandate of the SPO. But the SPO's twofold mandate also led to some successes, including the collection and cata-loguing of documentation pertaining to the abuses of the Derg and efforts to allow victims their say in court in far greater numbers than the prose-cutorial process warranted. In one sense it had shades of South Africa's Truth and Reconciliation Commission but without emphasizing the for-giveness and reconciliation component. In this concluding chapter, to a large extent, those issues will be skirted to go straight to the heart of what the Ethiopian judges believed were the central arguments of the main Red Terror trial. The Conclusion also assesses the arguments in the dissenting opinions of two different judges on the verdict and sentencing respective-ly, for they reveal much about the domestic context of the trial.

The Charges and Verdict

The judgement document over Col. Mengistu Hailemariam and his accomplices totals over seven hundred and ninety-one pages in the Amharic version which is the only one issued by the Federal High Court to date. The judgment contains a synopsis of the charges brought by the SPO, analysis of the evidence and arguments of the defendants, the court's verdict and the sentence. The charges have been outlined in detail in Chapter 3; thus they will only be restated here in general form. The defendants were collectively and independently charged with 209 counts of genocide, aggravated homicide, grave and wilful injury, abuse of power and unlawful detention in violation of the 1957 Ethiopian Penal Code.

After examining the arguments and evidence presented by the SPO and defendants, the Federal High Court, First Division Criminal Bench, passed the verdict on 12 December 2006.[2] First, the Court found all

[2] *Special Prosecutor v. Colonel Mengistu Hailemariam et al.,* First Division Criminal Bench, Verdict, Judges Medhin Kiros, Nuru Saiid and Solomon Emeru, File No. 1/87, 12 December 2006, pp.742–4.

except one defendant guilty of genocide.[3] Second, the Court found all but nine defendants guilty of aggravated homicide.[4] Third, the Court found all but one defendant guilty of public incitement to commit genocide.[5] Fourth, the Court found all but twelve defendants guilty of abuse of power.[6] Fifth, the Court found all but one defendant guilty of unlawful arrest and detention.[7] One defendant, however, was set free by the Court as he was found to have defended his case against all charges. The verdict of the Court was passed by a majority vote of two to one; the dissenting opinion is thus worth exploring in order to illustrate the contentious legal issues inherent in the trial.

Dissenting Opinion on the Verdict
A dissenting opinion in the verdict of such an extremely important case as the charges against Colonel Mengustu Hailemariam and his top officials, may be seen as a critical blow to the arguments presented by the SPO. The dissenting judge, Judge Nuru Saiid, provided the following reasoning behind his stand on the verdict; the defendants should not have been convicted of genocide, since part of Article 281(a) of the 1957 Penal Code, which was used by the majority to convict the defendants of the crime of genocide, was repealed by Proclamations No. 1/74,[8] 110/77[9] and No.129/77[10] issued by the Derg. Part of Judge Nuru Saiid's dissenting opinion reads:

> It is to be recalled that the defendants presented preliminary objection arguing that their actions were authorized by law. The Court has rejected the preliminary objection ruling that the 1957 Penal Code has never been repealed during the Derg. However, the ruling of the Court did not consider if the specific provisions on which the charges are based were repealed. It is clear that the 1957 Penal Code had never been repealed in its totality until it was replaced by the 2004 Criminal Code. However, it is imperative to investigate if particular provisions of the 1957 Penal Code were repealed. If a specific provision under the 1957 Penal Code is repealed, it does not cause the repeal of the whole Penal Code. Conversely, the fact that the whole Penal Code was not repealed does not mean that some provisions could not have been repealed. Therefore when the defendants claimed that their actions were authorized by law, it is imperative to examine if the laws cited by

[3] In violation of Articles 32(1) (b) and 281(a) of the Penal Code.
[4] In violation of Articles 32(1) (b) and 522(1) (a) of the Penal Code.
[5] In violation Articles 32(1) (a) and 286(a) of the Penal Code.
[6] In violation of Articles 32(1) (b) and 414(1) (a) of the Penal Code.
[7] In violation of Articles 32(1) (b) and 416 of the Penal Code.
[8] Proclamation No. 1/74, A Proclamation to provide for the establishment of the Provisional Military Government of Ethiopia (PMAC).
[9] Proclamation No.110/77, A Proclamation to redefine the powers and responsibilities of the Provisional Military Administrative Council and the Council of Ministers.
[10] Proclamation No. 129/77, A Proclamation to provide for the establishment of a National Revolutionary Operations Command.

the defendants have repealed specific provisions of the 1957 Penal Code.[11]

Judge Nuru's argument rested on whether Proclamations No. 110/76 and 129/76 had repealed Article 281(a) of the 1957 Penal Code. His analysis reached the conclusion that Proclamation No.110/76 gave the Chairman of the Derg the power to eliminate 'anti-revolutionary' and 'reactionary groups' as directed by the General Assembly and Central Committee of the Derg. Moreover, Judge Nuru found that the Derg had the legal power[12] to lead a nation-wide security operation under the then National Revolutionary Operations Command to destroy 'anti-unity' and 'reactionary' elements. The dissenting judge noted further that the Derg had the power to incite, organize and coordinate people to participate in the efforts to take action against 'anti-unity' and 'anti-revolutionary' elements.[13] The judge reasoned that the law[14] allowed for the elimination of political groups that were opposed to the Derg. Accordingly, it was therefore clear that the legal protection for political groups (under Article 281(a) of the 1957 Penal Code) was in conflict with the legal permission to eliminate the same groups (under the above-mentioned provisions of Proclamations No.110/77 and No.129/77). Judge Nuru pointed out that in such instances of conflict of laws, Article 10 of Proclamation No.1/74[15] provided the solution: the provisions of the Proclamations No.110/77 and No.129/77 would prevail over all past laws including Article 281(a) of the 1957 Penal Code.

Consequently, Judge Nuru concluded that the actual protection by law[16] for political groups against genocide was effectively repealed. Such general and tacit repeal of laws is the prerogative of Ethiopian legislations, according to Judge Nuru. Moreover, he reasoned that the fact that the 1948 Convention on Genocide does not protect 'political' groups means that the Derg did not violate international law by repealing the protection of political groups from genocide.[17] However, Judge Nuru stressed that it cannot be assumed that the whole of Article 281(a) of the 1957 Penal Code was repealed. In this regard, he pointed out that the Derg was not entitled to repeal the totality of protection against genocide (with the exception of the protection of political groups) and crimes against humanity including homicide, bodily injury and torture as recognized under international law.

---

[11] *Special Prosecutor v. Colonel Mengistu Hailemariam et al.*, First Division Criminal Bench, Verdict, Judges Medhin Kiros, Nuru Saiid and Solomon Emeru, File No. 1/87, 12 December 2006, pp.745–6.

[12] Ref. Articles 8(3), 14(7) and 16(6) of Proclamation No.129/77.

[13] Ref. Articles 14(8), 16(5), and 18(7) of Proclamation No.129/77.

[14] Proclamations No.110/77 and No.129/77.

[15] Proclamation No. 1/74, A Proclamation to provide for the establishment of the Provisional Military Government of Ethiopia (PMAC), Article 10 states: 'Unless they are contrary to this proclamation and to laws, decrees and policies to be promulgated in the future, all existing laws shall remain in effect.'

[16] Provided under Article 281(a) of the 1957 Penal Code.

[17] Under Article 281(a) of the 1957 Penal Code.

According to the dissenting opinion, since Article 281(a) of the Penal Code was partly repealed in relation to the protection of political groups, the Court should not have convicted the defendants for the commission of genocide[18] and for incitement to commit genocide.[19]

The Sentence

When assessing the sentence to be imposed on the defendants, the Federal High Court resorted to the 2004 Ethiopian Criminal Code. The Court did not provide any justification for using the 2004 Criminal Code rather than the 1957 Penal Code, which was used hitherto in the trial. The 2004 Criminal Code proclaims that the Court may apply the provisions of the Code if the new law is favourable to the defendants.[20] However, the Court did not state whether the 2004 Criminal Code was more favourable to the defendants or not. The 2004 Criminal Code provides the maximum and minimum punishment for each provision that was violated by the defendants. Accordingly, the crime of genocide is punishable with rigorous imprisonment from five years to life imprisonment and in cases of exceptional gravity, with death.[21] The crime of aggravated homicide is punishable with rigorous life imprisonment or death.[22] Public incitement to commit genocide is punishable with rigorous imprisonment of not more than five years, while abuse of power, unlawful arrest and detention are each punishable with rigorous imprisonment of up to five years and a fine.[23]

Once the verdict was passed, the Court instructed the SPO and the defendants to present their pleadings on the sentence. Accordingly, the SPO argued that there were aggravating circumstances of punishment and requested the Court to impose the death penalty on 30 of the defendants and to sentence the rest to rigorous life imprisonment for the following major reasons.[24] First, the SPO argued that it had proved to the satisfaction of the Court that the defendants committed the crimes with meticulous planning and resolve after establishing the necessary institutions by using public resources. Second, the SPO pointed out that the commission of the crimes continued for many years under the leadership and coordination of the defendants. Third, the SPO also

[18] In violation of Articles 32(1) (b) and 281(a) of the Penal Code.

[19] In violation of Articles 32(1) (a) and 86(a) of the Penal Code.

[20] Article 6 of the 2004 Penal Code of Ethiopia provides that 'where the criminal is tried for an earlier crime after the coming into force of this Code, its provisions shall apply if they are more favourable to him than those in force at the time of the commission of the crime. The Court shall decide in each case whether, having regard to all the relevant provisions, the new law is in fact more favourable.'

[21] Article 281(c) of the 1957 Ethiopian Penal Code.

[22] Article 522 (1) (a) of the 1957 Ethiopian Penal Code.

[23] Articles 286, 414 and 416 of the 1957 Ethiopian Penal Code.

[24] See Article 84 of the 2004 Ethiopian Criminal Code on aggravating circumstances of penalty.

pointed out that the defendants committed multiple crimes on persons who were under their protection and custody. Fourth, the SPO submitted evidence showing that a number of the defendants had already been sentenced to death and life imprisonment in similar trials in other federal and regional courts.

Conversely, the defendants pleaded for a reduced penalty because of the following extenuating circumstances.[25] First, the defendants argued that they were relatively unaware, somewhat naïve and possessed only basic education when the revolution broke out in the mid-1970s. Second, the defendants argued part of the responsibility for what happened should also be shared by the militant opposition groups targeted by the Derg, since they killed people and destroyed public property. Third, the defendants pointed out that they had no previous criminal records and served their country with dedication and honesty prior to taking over political power. Fourth, the defendants begged the Court to consider their old age and the much delayed detention without conviction. Fifth, the defendants pointed out to the Court that they had asked the government to give them the chance to apologize to the Ethiopian people in the course of the trial (see G.A. Aneme 2006 for elaboration on this point). This, the defendants argued, demonstrated their remorse and reformation.

The Court began its reasoning on the sentence by analyzing Article 117 of the 2004 Criminal Code. Accordingly, the Court reasoned that Article 117 (1) of the 2004 Criminal Code provides the following four conditions that need to be fulfilled for the Court to impose the death penalty: 1) the existence of grave crimes and exceptionally dangerous criminals; 2) the existence of specific provisions of the law that impose the death penalty; 3) crimes that are completed; and 4) the absence of any extenuating circumstances. According to the Court all but the last one were fulfilled in *Special Prosecutor v. Colonel Mengistu Hailemariam et al.*. In this regard, the Court stated that some of the extenuating circumstances presented by the defendants were admissible.[26] Moreover in an interesting addendum, the Court pointed out that it was entitled to make its own assessment of extenuating circumstances other than situations specifically provided under the law.[27]

With these provisions in mind, the Court found the following points as extenuating circumstances of the penalty. First, the Court noted that it was proven that the defendants served their country well in different capacities before they took power. According to the Court, some of the defendants participated in international peacekeeping efforts, while some sustained injury while defending their country. Second, the Court took notice of the undue delay in the trial of the case. Third, the Court noted that many of the defendants were now quite feeble senior citizens.

---

[25] See Article 82 of the 2004 Ethiopian Criminal Code on extenuating circumstances of penalty.
[26] Under Article 82(1) (a) of the 2004 Penal Code.
[27] This is provided under Article 86 of the 2004 Ethiopian Criminal Code.

Fourth, the Court looked positively upon the attempt of the defendants to apologize to victims and the wider population even while acknowledging that it came very late. Fifth, the Court also took note of the evidence presented by many of the defendants showing that they had been training themselves in various fields while in detention. The Court concluded that because of all these extenuating circumstances, and because the aim of punishment is reform rather than revenge, it rejected the SPO's request for the imposition of the death penalty on some of the defendants.[28]

After rejecting the death penalty, the Court imposed rigorous life imprisonment on 48 defendants, 25 years of rigorous imprisonment on two defendants and 23 years of rigorous imprisonment on five defendants by a majority vote of two to one. The Court ruled that the sentence was not applicable for those defendants who were already sentenced to death in other federal or regional courts for other crimes.[29] The Court also ruled that the defendants imprisoned for life may not participate in elections and are permanently barred from holding any public office, while the defendants sentenced to 25 and 23 years of rigorous imprisonment are barred from participation in elections and from holding public office for five years from their date of release.[30]

Dissenting opinion on the sentence

The presiding judge of the trial, Judge Medhin Kiros, dissented on the sentencing and argued that the situations presented by the defendants and accepted by the Court as extenuating circumstances of penalty were not covered under the law.[31] Judge Medhin Kiros pointed out that, even if there were extenuating circumstances, they should not be applicable to defendants tried in *absentia*. Furthermore, he reasoned that the reality that the defendants were trying to justify their acts all through the trial rather than show remorse, that the defendants were the top leaders of the Derg, that they had meticulous plans and took time to commit concurrent and serious crimes such as genocide and aggravated homicide, and the fact that some of them were sentenced to death and imprisonment in other courts, were all aggravating circumstances that should lead to the imposition of the maximum death penalty on nine of the defendants. Judge Medhin Kiros also pointed to the paradox of imposing lesser punishment on the defendants who were the top leaders of the Derg, while some lower-ranking officials of the defunct regime were sentenced to death in other similar trials.[32]

---

[28] Firew K. Tiba (2007) contended that an additional reason for the Court to reject the death penalty could be to facilitate the extradition of Mengistu and many others who were being tried *in absentia*.

[29] Six of the defendants in the case *Special Prosecutor v. Colonel Mengistu Hailemariam et al.* face the death penalty in other federal and regional courts.

[30] See Articles 123 (a), 124(1) (2), 125(1) (2) of the 2004 Criminal Code of Ethiopia.

[31] Article 82(1) of the 2004 Criminal Code.

[32] See Elgesem and G.A.Aneme in this volume on capital punishment.

The Appeal (2008)

After the conviction in December 2006 and the sentencing in January 2007 of the defendants by the Federal High Court, the SPO and some defendants filed their appeals at the Federal Supreme Court in January 2007. The major grounds of appeal of the parties and the decision of the Federal Supreme Court are explained below.

The SPO's appeal

The SPO appealed against the sentence passed by the Federal High Court on some of the defendants. Specifically it appealed against the sentence passed on 21 of the defendants. The SPO's appeal against one of the defendants was suspended by the Court because of his death.[33] Among the 20 defendants, 18 were sentenced to life imprisonment and two were sentenced to 25 years rigorous imprisonment by the Federal High Court. The SPO pleaded the appellate Court for the imposition of the death penalty (the maximum penalty) on all 20 respondents. The SPO's arguments in support of its appeal include the following:[34]

1. The extenuating circumstances pointed out by the Federal High Court did not have any basis under the law.
2. The respondents were convicted of serious concurrent crimes. This fact is considered to be an aggravating circumstance of penalty under the law. The respondents who were members of the Permanent Committee of the Derg were convicted of violations of Articles 281, 286(a) and 522 on all counts where it was shown that thousands of individuals had lost their lives. The Federal High Court sentence did not consider all these circumstances during sentencing.
3. The respondents were members of the Permanent Committee of the Derg and senior officials who made the plans and passed the decisions to carry out the crimes. As such they should not have been sentenced to a lesser penalty than the Revolutionary Guards and other lower officials who carried out their orders.

The defendants' appeal

Thirteen of the respondents in the SPO's appeal and ten other defendants (a total of twenty-three defendants) lodged their own appeal to the Federal Supreme Court against both the verdict and the sentence passed by the Federal High Court. The arguments of the twenty-three appellants include the following:

---

[33] The 7th respondent Colonel Tesfaye GebereKidan.

[34] Appellant- *Special Prosecutor v. Respondents- Colonel Mengistu Hailemariam et al.,* Federal Supreme Court, Judgement, Judges Dagne Melaku, Amare Amogne and Kedir Aley, File No. 30181, 26 May, 2008, p.9.

1. The appellants argued that the SPO's evidence did not establish that they committed the crimes. The appellants explained that even though the SPO was able to call on several witnesses, none of these witnesses testified that he/she had seen or knew that any of the appellants committed or caused the commission of the crimes they were charged with. Moreover, the appellants argued that none of the documentary evidence presented by the SPO mentioned their names.

2. The appellants further contended that their conviction by the Federal High Court was collective punishment solely based on their membership of the Derg. The appellants argued that they should not be convicted merely because they were members of the Derg.

3. The appellants argued that for several reasons their conviction for the commission of the crime of genocide was wrong. In this regard, the appellants raised the contentious issue of the protection of political groups under Article 281 of the 1957 Penal Code and presented two alternative arguments: A) They argued that Article 281 of the 1957 Penal Code did not provide protection against the killing or elimination of members of political groups. B) The appellants also contended that the notion of the protection of political groups from genocide under Article 281 of the 1957 Penal Code is generally unacceptable as it contradicts the definition of the crime of genocide under international law.[35]

The decision of the Federal Supreme Court
The Federal Supreme Court passed its decision on the appeals of both parties on 26 May, 2008.

The decision on the defendants' appeal
The Federal Supreme Court first examined and passed its decision on the appeal by the defendants. In this regard the Court found that the SPO had presented enough evidence at the Federal High Court to establish that the appellants planned and executed the murder, bodily harm, serious injury to the physical or mental health and disappearance of members of various political groups. As indicated above, the defendants provided multiple grounds to oppose their conviction for the commission of genocide by the Federal High Court. The defendants argued that Article 281 of the 1957 Penal Code did not provide protection to members of political groups. According to the defendants, the protection of political groups from genocide was also against the Genocide Convention.[36] However, the Supreme Court declared that the defendants did not challenge that Article 281 of the 1957 Penal Code provides the protection of members of political groups. According to the Court, the defendants were rather

---

[35] Ibid., pp. 10-11.
[36] General Assembly resolution 260 A (III) of 9 December 1948, Convention on the Prevention and Punishment of the Crime of Genocide.

contesting that such protection should not have been provided under Article 281 of the 1957 Penal Code.[37] The Court then went on to explain that members of political groups were actually protected from genocide under Article 281 of the 1957 Penal Code. In its explanation, the Supreme Court pointed out that the protection of members of political groups under Article 281 of the 1957 Penal Code could also be gathered from the much clearer wording under the corresponding Article 269 of the 2004 Criminal Code.[38] Conversely, the Supreme Court noted that even though the majority of the killings, injury and disappearance under the 209 counts in the case were proved to be the commission of genocide in violation of Article 281 of the 1957, the SPO did not show the connection between the plan to eliminate members of political groups and some of the killings. The Court noted in this regard that it could have been better to characterize some of the killings as aggravated homicide in violation of Article 522 of the 1957 Penal Code rather than the commission of genocide in violation of Article 281 of the 1957 Penal Code. Nevertheless, the Court concluded that it was better to leave the conviction of the Federal High Court unchanged, as the commission of aggravated homicide in violation of Article 522 of the 1957 Penal Code carries a stronger penalty for the appellants. Based on the above and other similar reasons, the Federal Supreme Court rejected the defendants' appeal against the verdict of the Federal High Court. The Federal Supreme Court also rejected the defendants' appeal for a lower penalty than that imposed by the Federal High Court. In this regard, the Court explained that all the defendants were convicted of serious and concurrent crimes which made them responsible for the loss of thousands of lives. Moreover, the Court explained that some of the defendants were also charged and sentenced with serious crimes in similar other trials. According to the Court, these reasons were aggravating rather than extenuating circumstances of the penalty.

The decision on the SPO's appeal
The Federal Supreme Court began its examination of the SPO's appeal by stating that in considering the sentence on the respondents it should first examine the principle on the determination of the sentence under Article 86 of the 1957 Penal Code and the corresponding Article 88 of the 2004 Criminal Code and, second, consider aggravating and extenuating circumstances specified under the law.

[37] See Appellant- *Special Prosecutor v. Respondents- Colonel Mengistu Hailemariam et al.,* Federal Supreme Court, Judgement, Judges- Dagne Melaku, Amare Amogne and Kedir Aley, File No. 30181,26 May, 2008, p. 67.

[38] Article 269 of the 2004 Criminal Code, first paragraph reads 'Whoever, in time of war or in time of peace, with intent to destroy, in whole in part, a nation, nationality, ethnical, racial, national, colour, religious or political group, organises, orders or engages in:'. The Court did not explain the relevance and value of Article 269 of the 2004 Criminal Code for the acts committed before the entry into force of the 2004 Criminal Code.

Accordingly, the Court first considered the preconditions for the imposition of the death penalty under Ethiopian law. According to the Court, Article 15 of the Ethiopian Federal Constitution provides the possibility of the death penalty when a person commits a serious crime determined by law.[39] Moreover, the Court noted that Article 117(1) of the 2004 Criminal Code provides that '[s]entence of death shall be passed only in cases of grave crimes and on exceptionally dangerous criminals, in the cases specifically laid down by law as punishment for completed crimes and in the absence of any extenuating circumstances. A sentence shall be passed only on a criminal who, at the time of the commission of the crime, has attained the age of eighteen years.'[40]

The Court explained that the above conditions provided by the law should be fulfilled to impose the death penalty on the respondents as requested by the SPO.[41] The first condition for the imposition of the death penalty indicated under the above-quoted provision is the existence of grave crimes and exceptionally dangerous criminals. In this regard, the Court found that it was proved that the first ten respondents[42] were responsible for the death of more than one thousand people under the second charge.[43] The Court further explained that the number of people killed and the manner of the killings show the seriousness of the crime. Moreover, the Court pointed out that all respondents were convicted of the commission of genocide in violation of Article 281 of the 1957 Penal Code, which provides for the death penalty. The Court noted that the first, second, third, sixth, seventh, ninth, and eleventh respondents were also convicted of aggravated homicide in violation of Article 522(1) (a) of the 1957 Penal Code, which provides for the possibility of the death penalty.[44] It also noted the multiple conviction and sentence on the following respondents in other similar cases of the Red Terror trials. According to the Court, the twelfth respondent was already convicted of genocide and aggravated homicide and sentenced to life imprisonment in two cases of the Red Terror trials before his conviction under the present case. The thirteenth respondent was also convicted of genocide in another case for the killings of 306 individuals and was

---

[39] Article 15 of the Constitution of the Federal Democratic Republic of Ethiopia reads 'Every person has the right to life. No person may be deprived of his life except as a punishment for a serious criminal offence determined by law.'

[40] In similar parlance to that of the Federal High Court, the Supreme Court did not provide any justification for the use of various provisions of the 2004 Criminal Procedure in its decision on the appeal.

[41] See Annex I for the respondents in the SPO's appeal.

[42] See the first twelve respondents in Annex I with the exception of Colonel Tesfaye Gebrekidan and Colonel Kassahien Tefese who died before the lodging of the appeal.

[43] See the charges in Chapter 3.

[44] See first, second, third, sixth, seventh, ninth, and eleventh respondents under Annex I. These respondents were convicted of aggravated homicide for the killings under Count 6. The Court also noted that the second defendant was additionally convicted with aggravated homicide for the killings of seven people.

sentenced to life imprisonment. Similarly, the fifteenth respondent was already convicted of genocide and aggravated homicide in another case and was sentenced to life imprisonment. The eighteenth respondent was convicted of genocide and was sentenced to 18 years of rigorous imprisonment before his conviction in the current case. The Court calculated that in all cases the twelfth and thirteenth respondents were responsible for the killing of more than 500 individuals each, while the fifteenth and eighteenth respondents were responsible for the killing of more than 200 people each. The Court explained that the sentence on the above four respondents in the present case should take into consideration the penalty imposed in prior cases based on 'Article 186 of the 2004 Criminal Code'.[45] According to the Court, the assessment of the penalty should consider the total penalty that would have been imposed on the respondents if they were sentenced simultaneously for the concurrent crimes they were convicted of. The appellate Court found that the Federal High Court failed to do this.

The Court also found that the sentence on some of the other respondents who were convicted in other similar cases of the Red Terror trials was suspended awaiting the conclusion of the present case. In this connection the Court noted that the sixteenth and the seventeenth respondents[46] were already convicted of the commission of the crime of genocide (in violation of Article 281 of the 1957 Penal Code) and unlawful detention (in violation of Article 416 of the 1957 Penal Code). Similarly, the Court noted that the fourteenth and twentieth respondents[47] were convicted of aggravated homicide (in violation of Article 522 of the1957 Penal Code) in other cases of the Red Terror trials. The last respondent[48] was also found guilty of the commission of the crime of genocide in violation of Article 281 of the 1957 Penal Code in other similar cases. The Court calculated that all the above five respondents were responsible for the death of more than 200 people each in all the crimes they were convicted of. The Court lamented that the Federal High Court failed to take these convictions into consideration when calculating the sentence on the respondents in the present case.

After explaining the concurrent convictions and sentences on the respondents, the Federal Supreme Court found that the abuse of the position of leadership and public administration the respondents held while committing the crimes, the seriousness of the crimes of which the respondents were convicted, and the systematic, repetitive and continuous commission of the crimes by the respondents for many years proved

---

[45] Appellant- *Special Prosecutor v. Respondents- Colonel Mengistu Hailemariam et al.,* Federal Supreme Court, Judgement, Judges Dagne Melaku, Amare Amogne and Kedir Aley, File No. 30181, 26 May, 2008, p.89. The Court did not explain the relevance of Article 186 of the 2004 Criminal Code in calculating the sentence in the case under discussion.

[46] See Annex I for the respondents.

[47] See Annex I for the respondents.

[48] See Annex I for the respondents.

that the respondents were dangerous criminals. Thus, the Court concluded that the first condition for the imposition of the death penalty under the law was satisfied.[49]

The Court then considered the second condition for the imposition of the death penalty, i.e. whether there were any extenuating circumstances of the penalty. In this connection, the appellate Court indicated that Article 79 of the 1957 Penal Code and Article 82 of the 2004 Criminal Code provide extenuating circumstances. Moreover, the Court noted that both Article 83 of the 1957 Penal Code and Article 86 of the 2004 Criminal Code allow it to consider other extenuating circumstances than those already specified under the law. The Court then proceeded to examine the extenuating circumstances specified by the Federal High Court. With regard to the first extenuating circumstance, the appellate Court explained that the respondents were responsible for systematic murder and injury of mainly peaceful people under their detention. Therefore, the Supreme Court rejected the Federal High Court's assertion that the respondents committed the crimes as a result of trepidation. Similarly, the Court pointed that many of the respondents were not illiterate but rather well trained individuals who were elected to represent their colleagues in the Derg. Thus, the appellate Court also rejected the Federal High Court's reasoning that the respondents had low awareness when they committed the crimes.

The Supreme Court also indicated that none of the defendants had admitted the commission of the crimes in the course of the trial. Therefore, the Court concluded that the respondents could not be considered to be remorseful about the crimes they committed. According to the Court, the fact that they wrote a letter to the government asking for a forum to apologize did not tally with the meaning of remorse under the law. In this regard, the Supreme Court explained that Article 82 (1) (e) of the 2004 Criminal Code provides that a criminal should extend help to the victim or compensate the victim to show his/her remorse. The Court noted that the respondents did not do anything as provided under the law to show their remorse. The Supreme Court also rejected the lack of prior conviction of the respondents as an extenuating circumstance by stating that this condition could not be seen separately from all other conditions under Article 82(1) of the 2004 Criminal Code. Finally, the Supreme Court rejected the Federal High Court's consideration of the age and ailments of the defendants, the long years of trial of the present case and the long years that had passed since the commission of the crimes, having previously lamented that none of these conditions could be taken as extenuating circumstances under Article 86 of the 2004 Criminal Code. Consequently, the Federal Supreme Court concluded that all conditions for the imposition of the death penalty on the respondents were satisfied.

---

[49] As indicated earlier, the first condition provided under Article 117(1) of the 2004 Criminal Code is the existence of grave crimes and exceptionally dangerous criminals.

In this connection, the Supreme Court stated that the Federal High Court was wrong in reasoning that the conditions for the imposition of the death penalty on the respondents were not fulfilled. The Supreme Court also emphasized that the imposition of the death penalty on the respondents should not have been considered as revenge but as appropriate punishment for the very serious and systematic crimes they committed.

By way of summary, the Federal Supreme Court noted that it was proved that the respondents committed the crime of genocide and homicide in massive violations of the Criminal Code and the human rights conventions ratified by the country. The Court also pointed out that the respondents developed and executed the policies of extra-judicial killings and Red Terror as a result of which countless young students, intellectuals and workers were murdered. The Court further noted that it was also proved that the respondents were responsible for torturing and injuring countless individuals. The Court specifically pointed out that the murder of the former Emperor Haile Selassie by the first respondent and the building of his office on the grave of the Emperor in the palace was an extremely shameful act.

The Federal Supreme Court finally concluded that the imposition of the maximum penalty on the respondents as requested by the SPO was justified and reasoned that the imposition of a strong penalty on the former government officials would also provide lessons for others in similar positions. Accordingly, the Federal Supreme Court increased the sentence passed by the Federal High Court and imposed the death penalty on 18 respondents.[50] The Federal Supreme Court closed the case by stating that the death penalty on the 18 respondents would be carried out when it was approved by the Head of State as per Article 117(2) of the 2004 Criminal Code.[51]

Concluding Remarks: The Legacy of the Red Terror

The Red Terror trials have been under way for 15 years and are still running. As this is being written, the outcome of the appeals for the top-level officials of the former Derg regime is uncertain. If the appeal of the defence on the merits of the case is accepted, a new full trial process needs to be undertaken, which will prolong the Red Terror trials for years. Regardless of the outcome of the appeals of Col. Mengistu Hailemariam and the main group of defendants, however, the trials against defendants of lesser stature are still being heard in various federal and regional

---

[50] See Annex II for the list of respondents sentenced to death by the Federal Supreme Court.
[51] See also Article 28(2) of the Constitution of the Federal Democratic Republic of Ethiopia on the possibility of commutation of death penalty with life imprisonment by the Head of State. Five of the respondents sentenced to death have reportedly appealed to the Cassation Bench of the Federal Supreme Court.

courts. Furthermore, death penalties are still being handed down as this is being written,[52] once again validating the inconsistency that Judge Medhin Kiros pointed out in his dissent to the sentencing. It is uncertain when the various trials under Red Terror charges will be finalized, since thus far it has been impossible to obtain an overview of the progress of the cases being heard in the regional courts.

An inventory of the main Red Terror trial's successes and failures provides Ethiopia and the international community with lessons to be incorporated into the growing scholarship on transitional justice. *Special Prosecutor v. Colonel Mengistu Hailemariam et al.* is a domestically conducted trial in contradistinction to various hybrid and international judicial formats. As such, the trial, verdict, sentencing and appeals processes indicate that histories of genocide and mass violence can be adjudicated in national courts, under domestic law. Yet the Red Terror trials fall short on many counts: the rights of the accused did not conform with national and international laws in their incarceration without charge for an illegal period of time before the SPO could formally charge them; impediments to documentary evidence; problems in representation; continuance of the trial for over fifteen years during which time the accused were imprisoned; and other issues outlined in Chapters 3 and 4. The twofold mandate of the SPO to prosecute while collecting and cataloguing all evidence pertaining to the abuses of the Red Terror led to needless delays. The fact that the team of three presiding judges revolved on and off the bench affronts, moreover, basic norms of jurisprudence.

The main Red Terror trial also illuminates an issue that is central to transitional justice: namely, the prerogative of the state to defend itself. From the very beginning and culminating in a dissent to the verdict, the issue most perplexing to the bench was determining whether or not actions by state officials against 'anti-revolutionary' political elements constitutes 'genocide'. While there is no doubt that Col. Mengistu Hailemariam and the military leader of the Derg committed untold abuses and mass violence, was it necessary to add genocide to the counts of aggravated homicide, grave and wilful injury, abuse of power and unlawful detention, all of which violated the 1957 Ethiopian Penal Code and would have been sufficient for prosecution? To an extent the Red Terror trials illustrate how the term genocide has become politicized.

Perhaps the most significant shortcoming of the Red Terror trial is its attempt to account for an abusive past to the satisfaction of the Ethiopian people and bring about national reconciliation. Many factors contributed to the population ignoring the trial, verdict and sentencing. For one, its elongated timetable could not maintain public interest. Second, restriction on access to the trials meant that they were conducted in something comparable to a vacuum. Third, while the media initially followed the

---

[52] Reuters: 'Ethiopia sentences five Mengistu officers to death', 5 April 2008.

trial, both the media and the general public quickly got tired of it. Finally, because of the long delay and lack of publicity, the trial ended up being perceived by the public as no more than victor's justice.

But there are also positive aspects to the Red Terror trial. The trial does uplift the Ethiopian government's attempt to account for past atrocities in national courts under domestic law. Looking beyond the retributive justice offered by the verdict and sentencing in the trials, a facet of the SPO's mandate seems to be partly unfulfilled, this has to do with the documentation of the abuses of the Red Terror in the 1970s. Hopefully, the SPO – or Ethiopian authorities at large – will give priority to establishing a commemorative 'centre' or library open to the general public where people can read about Ethiopia's violent past in order for the Ethiopian people and their leaders to draw lessons from their endeavour to establish accountable frameworks and institutions of governance.[53]

Transitional justice mechanisms are established in order to cater for exactly a *transition* away from unaccountable politics and human rights abuses, in order to establish new institutions of accountability and to foster a new political culture where tolerance and human rights are internalized into the body politics of the nation. To accomplish these overarching goals of transitional justice takes considerable time and enduring efforts to establish the institutional and normative guarantees of non-repetition indicated in this volume. The Red Terror trials, no matter their shortcomings described in this volume, will mark a juncture in history where ideally law trumps violence and will be understood as the starting point in the transition towards societal justice in Ethiopia.

[53] See Firew K. Tiba (2007) who observed that 'Given that in Ethiopia there are no official gazettes where court judgements are published, it is unlikely that the public will be able to read the judgement and thus become aware of what had happened.'

Annex I List of the respondents in the SPO's appeal against the sentence passed by the Federal High Court

1.   Colonel Mengistu H/Mariam   (in *absentia*)
2.   Captain Fikreselassie W/Deres
3.   Lt. Colonel Fiseha Desta
4.   Colonel Kassahun Tafese   (deceased)
5.   Major Birehanu Bayih   (in *absentia*)
6.   Capt. Legesse Asfaw
7.   Colonel Tesfaye G/Kidan   (deceased)
8.   Major Hadis Tedla   (in *absentia*)
9.   Lt. Colonel Endale Tessema
10. Capt. Gessesse W/Kidan
11. Major General Wubshet Desse

12. Major Kasaye Aragaw
13. Lt. Colonel Debela Dinsa
14. Capt. Begashaw Atalayi
15. Lt. Sileshi Mengesha
16. Lt. Colonel Nadew Zekarias
17. Sub/Lt. Petros Gebre
18. Sub/Lt. Aragaw Yimer
19. Lt. Aklilu Belayneh
20. Major Dejene Wondimageghu
21. Sub/Lt. Desalegn Belay

Annex II List of the respondents who were sentenced to death by the Federal Supreme Court

1. Colonel Mengistu H/Mariam   (in *absentia*)
2. Captain Fikreselassie W/Deres
3. L/Colonel Fiseha Desta
4. Major Birehanu Bayih (in *absentia*)
5. Capt. Legesse Asfaw
6. Major Hadis Tedla (in *absentia*)
7. L/Colonel Endale Tessema
8. Capt. Gessesse W/Kidan
9. Major General Wubshet Desse
10. Major Kasaye Aragaw
11. Lt. Colonel Debela Dinsa
12. Capt. Begashaw Atalayi
13. Lt. Sileshi Mengesha
14. Lt. Colonel Nadew Zekarias
15. Sub/Lt. Petros Gebre
16. Sub/Lt. Aragaw Yimer
17. Major Dejene Wondimageghu
18. Sub/Lt. Desalegn Belay

References

Firew Kebede Tiba. 2007. 'The Mengistu Genocide Trial in Ethiopia,' *Journal of International Criminal Justice*, vol. 5: 513–28.

Girmachew Alemu Aneme. 2006. 'Apology and trials: The case of the Red Terror trials in Ethiopia,' *African Human Rights Law Journal*, vol. 6: 64–84.

Proclamation No. 414/2004, The Criminal Code of the Federal Democratic Republic of Ethiopia, *Negarit Gazeta*, Addis Ababa.

Proclamation 22/92, Proclamation for the Establishment of the Special Prosecutor's Office, 1992, *Negarit Gazeta*, Addis Ababa.

Transitional Period Charter of Ethiopia, Transitional Conference of Ethiopia, *Negarit Gazeta*, July 22, 1991.

Penal Code of the Empire of Ethiopia, *Negarit Gazeta*-Extraordinary issue, No.1, 1957.

INDEX

153